Sexism and Church Law

SEXISM AND CHURCH LAW
Equal Rights
and
Affirmative Action

edited by

JAMES A. CORIDEN

PAULIST PRESS
New York/Ramsey, N.J./Toronto

Library of Congress
Catalog Card Number: 77-70638

ISBN: 0-8091-2010-0

Published by Paulist Press
Editorial Office: 1865 Broadway, N.Y., N.Y. 10023
Business Office: 545 Island Rd., Ramsey, N.J. 07446

Printed and bound in the
United States of America.

Contents

Introduction

Women's struggle for equal rights is one of the most significant social movements of the 20th Century. The eventual extent of its success is hard to predict and its impact on our society has yet to be measured. However, anyone committed to the cause of human freedom and dignity cannot but rejoice at the progress achieved thus far.

Inevitably the demand of women for equal and equitable treatment in the areas of political life, employment opportunities, family, social structures, and sports had to be raised in the community of faith as well. The Church has been challenged to reflect and respond. Much has been written recently about women in biblical literature, in the history of the Christian churches, and in theology, especially the ordination question. A wealth of serious scholarship is now available; this study adds to it and carries the issue into the life and structures of today's Church.

The chapters in this book are concerned with the practical equality of women in the Roman Catholic Church. That is, they treat of what the law allows and how women are actually regarded as members and ministers. Where did Church laws which discriminate against women come from, and why are they still with us? Precisely which laws need to be changed, and how can that be accomplished? Although the authors approach the question of women's situation in the Church from a variety of scientific backgrounds, personal experiences, and points of view, they are focused on the Church's discipline and life. They recommend specific changes in law and practice.

Francis Morrisey provides an overview of the present law of the Church and woman's place in it. He adds those changes which have been proposed for the revision of canon law, and suggests some elements necessary for women's genuine equality before the law.

Katherine Meagher examines the specific underlying issue of women in relationship to the twin "powers" of Orders and jurisdiction. After an historical exploration she reviews the reasons for the exclusion of women from priesthood, and then presents new perspectives and modifications since the Second Vatican Council.

The changes in forms of ministry which took place in the critical and pivotal fourth century are presented in the chapter by Hamilton Hess. The structure, styles, and theories of ministry which exclude women from equal roles which were developed then remain with us to a large extent.

The theological senses of "tradition" and its mutability are explored by Francine Cardman. She discusses the restoration of meaning which might be accomplished in the faith community by the ordination of women.

Nadine Foley scrutinizes the major statements which have emanated from the Holy See in recent years and analyzes them for the notion of "woman" which they contain. She compares that vision with other contemporary insights and raises both serious questions and hopeful signs for the Church of the future.

Edward Kilmartin studies the participation of women in the life of the Church, and the ecumenical implications of changes in the legal status of women. He also reviews the theological arguments for excluding women from sacramental ministry and speculates on the possibilities for change.

John Finnegan writes of the spectrum of present positions—from the staunchest feminist to the entrenched clericalist—and suggests some strategies for realistic progress.

The chapters of this book were originally composed for a symposium on "Women and Church Law" sponsored by the Canon Law Society of America and Rosemont College, and held on the campus of the college on October 9-11, 1976. After reflecting on the authors' presentations, the symposium participants entered into animated discussions. They then formulated a set of observations, conclusions, and recommendations which form the "Consensus Statement" in this book. The suggestions directed to the Canon Law Society were adopted by the Society's members who met in their annual convention in Philadelphia, October 11-14, 1976. After the symposium the authors of the chapters then made some modifications of their own work for this publication.

This book and the interdisciplinary meeting from which it emanated take their place as the most recent in a series of scholarly investigations of issues vital to the renewal of Church law sponsored by the Canon Law Society of America.* This one was initiated by the Society's Committee on the Status of Women (Lucy Vasquez, O.P., Judy Barnhiser, O.S.U., Elizabeth Carroll, R.S.M., Doris Gottemoeller, R.S.M., Harmon Skillin) which reported to the national convention of the Society in October, 1975. At that meeting the membership authorized the proposed symposium. Bertram Griffin, the President of the Society in 1975-76 and Donald Heintschel, the Executive Coordinator, fostered and encouraged the project. It was my privilege to make arrangements for and to chair the symposium.

Ann Durst, S.H.C.J., President of Rosemont College, graciously provided the hospitality and fine facilities of that beautiful College for the symposium as well as co-sponsorship of the event. Mary Popit, S.H.C.J. and her co-workers in campus ministry at Rosemont coordinated the practical and liturgical arrangements and helped to make the encounter a pleasure as well as an enrichment for the participants.

Two recent documents of exceptional importance and relevance to the subject of this book have recently appeared and are appended to this volume: (1) a report from the Pontifical Biblical Commission on the New Testament evidence for women's place in the ministry of the Church, and (2) a Declaration on the Question of the Admission of Women to the Ministerial Priesthood (October 15, 1976) from the Congregation for the Doctrine of the Faith. Even though this latter declaration was released after our symposium, it is reprinted here for the reader's convenience. L. Mason Knox of Sacred Heart Seminary in Hales Corners, Wisconsin, an Episcopal priest and canonical scholar, is responsible for the index of this book.

It is my strong hope that this study of women's status in the Church will contribute to the ongoing reform of canon law. Women must be permitted full equality as members of the Church, and they should be welcomed as full partners in every level of the Church's ministry. In terms of their rights, such equal treatment is only just; in terms of pastoral effectiveness, it is a critical need.

To eliminate sexist discrimination in the Church's law and life will not be easy or uncomplicated; it will require enthusiastic and persistent affirmative action. But the "signs of the times" in the world around us seem to indicate that it is the will and work of the Lord. And the benefits for the community of faith and its ministry—for Christian mission and witness—will be simply incalculable. If women enter fully into the leadership of the Church, and if they bring a fresh view and a creative vigor, it will cause a major and much-needed renewal. May the Spirit of God lead and guide us in this reform.

James A. Coriden

---

*The previous studies have been published as follows: *Law for Liberty: The Role of Law in the Church Today*, ed. James Biechler (Baltimore: Helicon, 1967); *We, The People of God . . . : A Study of Constitutional Government for the Church*, ed. James Coriden (Huntington: Our Sunday Visitor, 1968); *The Bond of Marriage: An Ecumenical and Interdisciplinary Study*, ed. William Bassett (Notre Dame: University of Notre Dame Press, 1968); *The Case for Freedom: Human Rights in the Church*, ed. James Coriden (Washington: Corpus, 1969); *The Once and Future Church: A Communion of Freedom*, ed. James Coriden (New York: Alba House, 1971); *Who Decides for the Church? Studies in Co-Responsibility*, ed. James Coriden (Hartford: Canon Law Society, 1971).

The Juridical Status of Women in Contemporary Ecclesial Law

FRANCIS MORRISEY, O.M.I.

The second Vatican Council was indeed prophetic when, on numerous occasions, it recommended that we be attentive to the signs of the times.[1] Some of the signs that seem to characterize the second half of the twentieth century, to date, are a recognition of the dignity of the human person, an earnest quest for justice, a desire to promote the well-being of the under-privileged, a search for true and lasting spiritual values—as opposed to temporal considerations—to mention but a few. There is, however, another sign that is creating considerable interest, and difficulty, today: the awareness of the necessity of recognizing women's rights in society, and, more especially, in the Church. Our civil governments have approved legislation granting equal status to women before the law, or at least recognizing their right to equal opportunity; likewise, a number of disabilities have been removed from the statutes. The Church, as a whole, has not been as quick to recognize some of the inadequacies of its legislation relating to women, although much has, in fact, been done in the past fifty years. The very universality of the Church makes any quick or rapid change in this area unlikely, if not impossible.

It would be helpful, I believe, to give an overview of the canonical legislation regarding women, as it now stands. It would no longer be of great importance or value to belabour the fact that the Code legislation of 1917 is inadequate for today's needs.[2] We have all recognized this and attempts have been made, successfully in part, to overcome some of the deficiencies. But, when we compare the progress made in other areas of legislation—and I am thinking particularly of matrimonial law—we can easily see that much remains to be done.

In our study of the present legislation, we shall consider three principal topics, of very unequal length, which will enable us (I) to determine the juridical status of women in Church law, (II) to examine the changes in legislation already announced or foreseen, and (III) to consider some elements which are necessary for a greater juridical recognition of the basic equality of all members of the People of God.

We are only too well aware of the fact that, in addition to the legislation that applies to the universal Church, there are numerous social and cultural factors to be considered. It would be unrealistic, I believe, to propose modifications that must necessarily be applied everywhere. A number of points are fundamental; others are more particularly related to a specific cultural context. We will keep the North American context in mind, without any pretense of speaking for or about the universal Church.

I. THE JURIDICAL STATUS OF WOMEN IN CHURCH LAW[3]

The Code legislation, as it stood in 1917, certainly ascribed a subordinate status for women, who were considered almost as dependent, passive, or inferior members in the Church. Laws regarding the status of persons were defined in terms of the male, as can be verified in such juridical areas as domicile, rite, accessibility to Tribunals, position in regard to the sacraments, and identification of what was considered to be sexually wrong.[4] But this was greatly due to an "accepted" way of thinking and, at the time, was probably not considered repressive. This goes to show that in specific matters of legislation, the social and cultural context exerts great influence. Likewise, the theological perspectives were not as developed as they are now. In fact, it was Pius XII who, in the encyclical letter *Mystici Corporis*, fostered a renewed appreciation of the Church as the Mystical Body of Christ. This encyclical, as W.J. Egan writes, "revitalized the Pauline and patristic concept of the Church as a supernatural organism composed of all the baptized united to Christ the head of the Body, and to each other"; in which Body every Christian, lay and cleric alike, "has a dynamic function to fulfill as a participant in the total mission of the Church perceived as the spatio-temporal extension of Christ the mediator."[5] At the same time, the Popes were also promoting the active participation of the laity in the liturgical renewal and in the apostolate known as "Catholic Action". These notions progressed rapidly and a newer, comprehensive theology of the Church as People of God was elaborated in the Council. One of the principal aspects of this renewed theological understanding was a better comprehension of the notion and consequences of membership of all in the Church.

1. THE PEOPLE OF GOD

a. *A Universal Call to Holiness*

The concept of the Church as Mystery and as People, that is, as a group composed of men and women, and not identified primarily in terms of structures, has led to what may be called a "revolution" in particular areas of religious thought and practice that have their eventual repercussions on the status of women. Pope Paul VI himself stated that the Council told us so much about the Church that "we are experiencing a certain sense of conceptual dizziness";[6] or, as H.V. Heffernan stated,

> The Church is presented as a People who are guided by the Spirit in the way of truth, unified in communion and ministry, given gifts necessary for its purpose, and thus shines forth as a People made one with the unity of the Father, Son, and Holy Spirit.[7]

Among the things the Council reminded us of in respect to the status of women, we could mention the universal call to holiness in the Church. Holiness is no longer considered as the special prerogative of any sex, of any person, of any state of life, but it becomes "the very goal of the Church both in this life and in the next"[8] (cf. *L.G.*, 39).

Likewise, the Church is presented as a new creation, calling all, without discrimination, to "share a common dignity from their rebirth in Christ" (*L.G.*, 32).

> Hence, there is in Christ and in the Church no inequality on the basis of race or nationality, social condition or sex, because "there is neither Jew nor Greek; there is neither slave nor freeman; there is neither male nor female. For you are all one in Christ Jesus" (*L.G.*, 32).

The teaching of *Lumen Gentium* is also quite clear on the fact that in spite of its ideals, the Church has not yet reached the fullness of its potential: it "is at the same time holy and always in need of being purified" (*L.G.*, 8).

Thus, while the basic qualities are understood to exist, yet in another sense they are not yet realized. This will only come in the fullness of the Kingdom of God (*L.G.*, 5). It is no wonder, then, that the Council frequently refers to the need for growth and reform within the Church (cf. *G.S.*, 43). In this realm, one of the points that perhaps needs closer examination is precisely the topic we are considering. But before seeing how this teaching can be applied, let us take note of what the Council said on the subject of the dignity of the human person.

b. *The Dignity of the Human Person*

Through the ages, there has continually been division over the primacy of community or of person. A person was often considered in terms of a solitary, self-fulfilling individual; community was the restrictive bonding of individuals. We assert readily today that institutions are for persons, and not persons for institutions. It is argued that the Church is not simply an institution, but is first of all a community of believers existing in radical dependence upon a divine revelation.[9] But is it not also asked whether in the Church, as we know it, it is the revelation that is primary, and that believing persons are submitted to it? This is a significant question for women, who are assigned status because of sex, and the rationale for doing so is often simply the accord with God's plan.[10]

While communal experience defines the person, a non-manipulative community must remain the ideal. Indeed, can the community define the person? The answer may be found in such documents as *Gaudium et Spes*[11] where the conciliar Fathers affirm a "dynamic-evolutionary" perspective on man: men and women find self-actualization in community; while God makes possible their future, He also makes men and women responsible for that future. In this perspective, the Council's teaching on the dignity of the person embraces many aspects, which could simply be alluded to as follows.

● *The unity of the human person.* Firstly, Vatican II clearly affirms that "man is one" (*G.S.*, 14). The body must be regarded as good; but the mind must find its good in God (cf. *G.S.*, 13).

● *Dignity of mind.* All men and women are called to a search for truth, and to go beyond truth itself (*G.S.*, 15). To exclude any particular perception of truth, or any particular possession of wisdom, would be a disservice in the discernment of truth itself.

● *Liberty and independence.* The excellence of liberty as a concomitant for human dignity is affirmed by the Council, for only in freedom can man direct himself toward goodness: "authentic freedom is an exceptional sign of the divine image within man" (*G.S.*, 17). The obligation to seek truth can only be discharged in men and women who enjoy "immunity from external coercion as well as psychological freedom" (*D.H.*, 2).

● *A new creation.* The conciliar notion of the dignity of the human person sees it both in the male and in the female, in a new creation where "all the members ought to be moulded into Christ's image until he is formed in them" (Gal. 4, 19).

Thus, we see that the Council has presented two important trends of thought to be kept in mind in evaluating the juridical status of women: we are all members of one people, without distinctions based on sex or race; the dignity of each person is to be fostered in terms of unity and liberty, in the perspective of a new creation to be brought to fulfillment in Christ.

2. THE STATUS OF WOMEN ACCORDING TO THE CONCILIAR DOCUMENTS

The study of the juridical status of women as recognized in the Conciliar documents could be carried out in many ways. For our purposes, it will be sufficient to study the question under separate headings. It could be mentioned that the word *"mulieres"* is not used too often alone in the documents, but is often found in the expression *"viri et mulieres"*, or is understood from the context of the passages.

a. *The Conciliar Thinking on Non-Discrimination*

Of the dozen or so references to non-discrimination in the Church, most of these are specific about sex discrimination. In *Lumen Gentium* it is understood, apparently, that any distinction that might appear as discriminatory, must have as reason the manifest will of Christ (*L.G.*, 32). This seems to imply that any restriction on the dignity and/or the activity of the faithful directed toward the building up of the Body of Christ, must be of divine ordinance. But the point should not be belaboured.

Gaudium et Spes affirms the essential equality of all persons since they have the same nature and origin, have been redeemed by Christ, and enjoy the same divine calling and destiny (*G.S.*, 29). While the texts of these two Constitutions indicate an awareness of the equivalence of the male/female manifestation of the human species, with the inference of the basic rights of each to full self-determination, they recognize a diversity that is seen as rooted in the "divine ordinance", resulting also from diversity of intellectual and moral resources.

Nevertheless, in spite of the universality of such declarations, when speaking of the process of reproduction, a rather male-centered outlook is still evident. For instance, *Gaudium et Spes* states that mothers and the female sex are to receive "due consideration" (*G.S.*, 67). This could be taken as a subtle type of protective discrimination; indeed, might it not have been possible to speak of "due consideration" for fathers and mothers of families?

One idea that recurs in the Council texts, is reference to the activities of women "in accord with their nature". Women, in other words, would have a "proper" role, and it is not a woman's self-determining consciousness of her "right" to culture that determines her liberation from ignorance, etc., but her nature and proper role (*G.S.*, 6).

Dignitatis Humanae (*D.H.*, 6) is quite open to the question of non-discrimination; likewise, *Nostra Aetate* (*N.A.*, 5). But, the declaration *Gravissimum Educationis* (*G.E.*, 1; 8) reminds us that teachers are asked to "pay due regard in every educational activity to sexual differences and to the special role which divine Providence allots to each sex in family life and in society".

It goes without saying that differentiation based upon sex is most evident in the statements relating to ordination and reception of ministries (*L.G.*, 55, 56; *O.T.*, 2; *A.G.*, 16; etc.). Regrettably, but understandably so at the time, no recognition was given to the new ministries being carried out by women (religious and lay), nor is it acknowledged, as is the case for men, that works performed by women are also in need of effective sacramental grace.

b. *Women and Symbols*

At least five passages in *Lumen Gentium* reflect not only the symbol, but also an underlying attitude towards women through the use of symbolic language (*L.G.*, 7, 8, 9, 56, 64). One symbol is the Eve/Mary sign used in the traditional meaning of death and life. Other symbols used are: mother and bride (to depict the Church), subject-bride, and one body. While they are traditional and an integral part of our heritage, it may be asked whether they are truly compatible today with the Conciliar doctrine of male and female equivalence in human and Christian dignity: woman is presented in terms that do little to depict the mutuality and equality of both men and women.

c. *Women and the New Creation (New Order)*

In equality and mutuality, men and women were blessed and told to "be fruitful, multiply, fill the earth and conquer it" (Gen., 1, 28). We are all aware of what eventually happened, and how a new creation in Christ was necessary. In the new creation, the mutuality of man and woman is expressed clearly, as the renewal brought by Christ manifests itself in a human interdependence which grows more tightly drawn and spreads by degrees over the whole earth, and "involves rights and duties with respect to the whole human race" (*G.S.*, 26). A series of such rights is then enumerated and no element of discrimination is found therein.

The new creation notion is indeed the fullest expression of a dimorphic outlook; for to the balanced awareness of the mutuality of man and woman in all spheres of life and mission, is added the concept of incorporation into Christ which raises such mutuality into the manifestation of Christ Himself in the prolongation of His work in history.

d. *Women and New Relationships in the Church*

Gaudium et Spes, while not suggesting that the basic unity of mankind is something new, does call attention to mankind's growing awareness of common bonds forming a new world community (*G.S.*, 33; see also *U.R.*, 4).

In the passages of the Conciliar documents that refer to the establishment of new relationships in society and in the Church, sometimes described as the new order, the man/woman collaboration is mentioned specifically in at least five passages: through the local Church (*A.G.*, 21), in service of the truth (*G.S.*, 3), through earthly progress (*G.S.*, 39), by unity of faith and daily life (*G.S.*, 39), and in government through justice and holiness (*G.S.*, 34).

Women are expected, along with men, to effect the new order so that the Church will not only mirror the changing social patterns, but will display leadership and directive example, as the Holy Spirit contrives to inspire the new order in Christ.

e. *Women and Marriage*

In the area of marriage, we find very positive statements concerning the status of women. Both Christian husbands and wives are cooperators in grace and witness of faith on behalf of each other, their children, and all others in their household (cf. *G.S.*, 5; *A.A.*, 11).

In a passage now well enshrined in canonical jurisprudence, *Gaudium et Spes* (*G.S.*, 48) refers to the intimate partnership of married life and love, established by the Creator and qualified by His laws. The text happily stresses the mutuality of help and service rendered to husband and wife through the marital unity of their individual persons and actions.

The structure of marriage is simply stated as flowing "from the equal personal dignity" of wife and husband, a dignity that is implemented in mutuality and love (*G.S.*, 49).

The same passage also shows an awareness of the active and equally contributive part played by women and men in the procreation of children, and perhaps even suggests a more shared domestic responsibility on the part of father and mother (*G.S.*, 48). Nevertheless, the Council does not declare mutuality of responsibility for child care:

> The active presence of the father is highly beneficial to their formation. The children, especially the younger among them, need the care of their mother at home. This domestic role of hers must be safely preserved, though the legitimate social progress of women should not be underrated on that account (*G.S.*, 52).

Though seemingly aware of a need for concern in the area of child care, the above passage falls back (albeit somewhat apologetically) on the assumption that woman has either a "natural" or "assigned" domestic role; whereas the father's presence is "highly beneficial", certainly not essential.

In spite of this possible weakness, the great change from looking on the familial structure as male-centered, observable in the *Codex Iuris Canonici*, to one that is mutually participatory and responsible for both spouses, is one of the great advances presented in the second Vatican

Council that will continue to have liberating influences on women.

f. *Women and Religious Life*

When referring to religious life, the mutuality of man and woman is clearly indicated. From the start, it should be mentioned that a clear distinction is made between the clerical-religious life (reserved to men), and the lay-religious life (open to men and women) (*P.C.*, 9). After the Council, it became customary to speak of three states of life: lay, religious, and clerical. But the lay-clerical distinction is still quite common in the thinking of many people.

The decree on the appropriate renewal of religious life rightfully calls for the continual formation and preparation of both male and female religious (*P.C.*, 18), but the institution of the papal cloister is maintained only for women. Several passages are found which place men and women together in such a way as to depict a mutuality of mission and participation in the extension of the Kingdom (cf. *A.G.* 6; *A.A.*, 25).

Any significant differences in the Conciliar pronouncements regarding male and female religious are based more on the clerical-lay distinction, than on the masculine-feminine one. In spite of this, however, a question that underlies the entire Conciliar teaching is whether ordination is a divisive juridical fact in itself, establishing a different norm for rights and duties in the person, and not in the mission of that person. The question does not yet seem to have been resolved satisfactorily.

g. *Women and the Closing Messages of the Council*

At the end of the Council, a number of closing messages were read, one of which was addressed to women; there was no corresponding message to men. The message is written in terms that generally refer to dependency relationships that may occur in a woman's life: it speaks to daughters, wives, mothers, widows! Again, these relationships might not have been considered in this dependent perspective. The attitude of men tending to think of women in terms of the relationships, rather than in terms of their existent realities as human beings, is quite evident here. Women are spoken to in terms of their sexual-relational roles, not in terms of their personhood or their accomplishment (cf. the messages addressed to intellectuals, scientists, artists, etc.).

In spite of this inherent weakness, the message does show an awareness of change in woman's position, though the outcome seems to be envisaged in terms of increased influence and perhaps not so much in terms of independent self-actualization. But we must remember that the text was universal in scope, covering numerous situations.

Apparently, the message shows little or no evidence of any real awareness of woman's equality with man, her right to be considered as a mature, responsible person, capable of self-determination in the area of her roles, her activities, her mutuality with man in the establishment of the Kingdom.

This brief overview of some of the Council's teachings on women shows a marked renewal of understanding; but there are still to be found numerous references presenting women in their traditional "roles" and not in terms of their independent self-realization.

The juridical status assigned is one of equality, with any reservations being dependent upon what was considered to be the will of God. While the texts still speak of proper "nature" of women, the fundamental juridical principle is well defined and enshrined in law.

3. CANONICAL IMPLICATIONS OF THE CONCILIAR TEACHING

a. *Principles To Be Observed*

The first question we should ask ourselves in regard to the Council documentation on women, is its canonical significance. Not everything written in the documents may, or even should be, interpreted as juridical ordinances. After promulgating the documents, Pope Paul explained that all the Conciliar laws must be respected, but that on many occasions, the Council

> formulated principles, criteria, desires which must be given concrete expression in new laws and instructions, in new organisms and offices, in spiritual, cultural and moral movements, and in organizations.[12]

In other words, the parts of the Conciliar documents that will be expressed in ecclesiastical laws, will be forthcoming in post-conciliar legislation. Did the principles put forward by the Council referring to women find their expression in canonical legislation?

There is no doubt that the principles of *Lumen Gentium* on the mystery of the Church are firmly established in doctrine and must be respected. Likewise, the doctrine of the dignity of the human person is part of our faith and must be manifested in legislative norms. But, when we come to specific details, the question is not as simple. What are some of the things we should be looking for in the new legislation? To help answer this question, the following criteria could be of assistance.

Looking more closely at the pronouncements, we must remember that men have enjoyed the juridical situation of being without status before the law by reason of their sex, so it may be somewhat difficult for them to realize that this is the basic right that women are claiming; status had been assigned for state of life, offices, merit and qualifications, not for sex.

As a consequence, in the law we should be looking for equality of juridic personality. All members of the People of God should have the same rights, responsibilities, and the same protection and penalties in all laws that relate to them. Then, all laymen and laywomen should also have the same rights and responsibilities, the same protection and penalties, in accord with lay status. This would mean that all protective norms for women would either be removed or extended to men.

In questions of temporal ecclesiastical affairs, restrictions had been placed on women whenever certain canons restricted lay functions to men. These restrictions would have to be removed by law.

In matters referring to the apostolate, women should no longer be excluded from anything that pertains to the life and mission of the Church solely on account of their female sex.

It would be quite illogical to proclaim the equality of the juridic personality of men and women at both the levels of human nature and of the People of God, and then assume that at the level of the social and/or interpersonal relationships, the factor of sex assumes a paramount importance. It seems, then, that no "proper" sphere for women should be indicated.

Changes will be required in regard to married women, the matter of domicile, rite, place of burial, etc. Authority patterns should not be determined in terms of the patriarchal-type family, but with principles of mutual consent, consensus, and self-determination. The authority figure over children should not be determinative of legitimacy (the father) or illegitimacy (the mother).

All structures within the Church, established on the concept of automatic male authority, whether in the family, religious life, or the Church community, may still be "hierarchical" by function, but the assignment of men to the leadership roles on account of "maleness" is no longer tenable.

The limits set by the Code on a woman's active participatory role in regard to the liturgy must be reassessed in terms of Conciliar statements of lay participation and non-discrimination. It would seem that whenever a sacramental and/or liturgical action does not relate directly to the power of orders, no distinction should be made on the basis of sex among the members of the laity.

Were these principles applied in the post-conciliar legislation?

b. *Post-Conciliar Orientations on Women*

i. *Pope Paul VI's Views concerning Women's Status*

Undoubtedly, as the first legislator in the Church, Pope Paul lost no time in fostering the good news of the Council. In his message *Africae Terrarum* of October 29, 1967, the Holy Father makes special reference to women; his thinking includes elements from natural law, conjugal love, the children's training ground, and the common good of society. At times, he both affirms and questions the emergence of women,[13] without condemning such change. He states that it is not the Church, but "Christian teaching" that speaks about woman's touch of gentleness, but, possibly in view of the particular context of the message, the Pope does not seem to speak of her as a responsible and creative agent. Thus there is, it seems, little evidence shown of mutuality, of mission for the Kingdom of God.

In the encyclical letter *Humanae Vitae*, he strongly affirms the mutuality of the marital life and mission which have full regard for the dignity and the responsibility of the wife and of the husband.[14] The teaching of this document is of the greatest importance in this regard.

Analysing some of Pope Paul's later pronouncements, we seem to find alternating views, probably depending on the particular circumstances of his addresses.

In an allocution given on March 5, 1969, he presents a beautiful development of the new orientation towards mission, with its special focus on the lay activity. His approach here is fully missional, not functional, something that is required if the apostolate of the laity is to be given its rightful recognition.[15]

As of 1970, his addresses seem to stress more the practical issues of service and new structures: a certain concern about lay inertia begins to appear.[16] When St. Theresa was proclaimed a doctor of the Church on September 27, 1970, the Pope summed up the "sublime" mission of women: the mission of prayer, the profession of faith, collaboration with grace, and cooperation with men.[17] The address has a somewhat functional approach to woman's mission and not a missional outlook, as was evident in his earlier addresses.

In 1971, he begins to show a growing concern for the alienation of the world and the lack of response on the part of the laity to do something about the situation. There is also more emphasis on the need of hierarchical direction of the laity.[18]

Later addresses on such topics as morality (e.g., against abortion), seem to define woman in terms of her vocation to be a mother.[19]

It would be only natural to expect some statements on the subject of women's status to have been given during International Women's Year. Some were given, yet, in this particular period of time, the Holy Father seems to be insisting more on human rights in general, than on woman's status in particular.[20] There also appears a questioning of the Church's own witnessing to human rights and justice.[21]

But, through all of the Pope's addresses on the subject, it would appear that he has a deep awareness of the implications of the fundamental equality of men and women, and of the need for an expression of this equality in the roles assumed by men and women in society. Above all, the responsibility of the Church to measure this development in relation to our new creation in Christ, and not totally in terms of cultural development and change, is being expressed. These, and other such insights into what the whole issue of woman's personhood in Christ really means, can only be assessed as tremendous progress for woman's position in the Church. The "problem" is beginning to be understood.

ii. Changes in Legislation

Numerous documents, of varying importance, have been issued by the Holy See since the Council. We shall limit our considerations to an examination of some of them.

While the statements emanating from the Synod of Bishops are not juridical texts, they inevitably lay the foundation for future legislative acts. It is most encouraging to note that in the synodal statements on the ministerial priesthood, justice in the world, and evangelization, there is almost nothing found therein that could be considered as relating specifically to women's "role"—their mission is well founded and great concern is expressed for equality among all persons. These texts will eventually exert their influence on Church law.

Likewise, in the reform of the Curia, new departments were of import to the laity as a whole: the Council for the Laity, and a number of Pontifical Commissions. The establishment of these organisms is a significant step in opening opportunities to the laity for leadership and direction in the Church. We could mention, in particular, the Commission on Justice and Peace, and the various new Secretariates which are departments opened onto the special role of the laity. The Pontifical Commission on the Role of Women in the Church (May 3, 1973), is a significant step forward, even though its terms of reference are couched in traditional concepts of women, and portray a somewhat functional concept of women.[22] With all of these bodies, though, it will take years before great positive influence is felt; however, they too are all important steps in the right direction.

The Commission on Human Rights issued, in October 1975, a statement reaffirming the equality of all mankind, without distinction based on sex. However, that same month, October 19, 1975, the S.C. for the Evangelization of Nations issued a report on the role of women in evangelization.[23] In spite of its opening assertions about non-discrimination, this text could be considered highly discriminatory. The diversity of roles assigned to men and to women at all levels of evangelization *because* of maleness and femaleness, is not a recognition of role diversity based on human merit and qualifications. Yet, in spite of incidences of "role specification", two sections are relatively broad in their outlook: selection and preparation of women for evangelization, and, forms and modalities of feminine involvement. We still find inserts in the text on "feminine qualities"; equivalent qualifications nowhere serve in the selective norms for evangelization; roles are assigned to women, but they are still the supportive types of work that women have been permitted to perform.

On the diocesan and pastoral levels, significant recognition has been assigned to women in the various pastoral councils established to further the mission of the Church. Norms on diocesan synods were also revised, as is seen in the Directory for the Pastoral Ministry of Bishops, February, 1973: the entire People of God is to be educated about the Kingdom; those who share in the synod, laity, clergy, and religious, have the same consultative vote. There is no wording in the documents which establish the various consultative councils in the Church that is opposed to women or to their mission.

iii. *Pertinent Legislation affecting Women*

A number of legislative documents, promulgated since the Council, refer directly to women. For purposes of clarity, we shall simply allude to them in the order of the canons of the Code.

In the faculties granted to religious superiors of the Oriental Rites (June 27, 1972), the same norms apply for confessions of male and female religious, although reference is made to possible abuses regarding the confessions of women.

Norms regarding the liturgical functions of women have always been divisive. For instance, a response of the Consilium for Liturgy, December 4, 1968, stated that women lectors, if used, were to take a position outside the sanctuary. Women are not allowed to serve the priest at the altar.[24] Many other norms are of this nature.

The powers of superiors general of lay Institutes in regard to the secularization of members under temporary vows[25] recognizes a mutuality of competence to men and women superiors.

The decennial faculties of 1971 still retain preference for husbands who wish to put away their wives, without interpellations. No mention is made of the converse situation.[26]

The new rite for the consecration of virgins (May 31, 1970) raises some questions. Do we find a possible androgenic focus on physical sexuality rather than on a Christian morality for men and women that includes chastity in every state of life?

The decree *Dum canonicarum legum*, December 8, 1970, rectified a number of situations regarding the confession of women religious. But the norms of August 15, 1969, regarding the Papal cloister are exclusively drawn up for women; no similar prescriptions exist for men.

Religious men and women have been authorized to celebrate baptism when no ordinary minister is available (October 12, 1970). Norms for lay ministers of the Eucharist preferred a man to a woman,[27] although, lately, they have been again revised to remove discrimination.[28]

We are all aware of the prescriptions of the Motu proprio *Ministeria quaedam*, excluding women from admission to the ministries of lectorate and acolyte.[29]

The norms on mixed marriages (March 31, 1970) specifically provide for recognition of respect of the liberty of the consciences of both parties in the marriage and the mutual responsibilities of husband and wife in the education of children.

The ecumenical development holds great promise for women. No distinctions seem to be made against them (or for them) in the documents of May 14, 1967, and April 16, 1970.

Regarding judicial procedures, lay men have been authorized to serve as judges, but women have been explicitly refused access to this position, as well as to other roles in a court, except those of notary and advocate. This is one area where the law must be changed—and quickly so—because there is absolutely no justification for this untimely discrimination.

In non-consummation cases, there is still reference to the physical examination of women, who are now free, nevertheless, to refuse to undergo this procedure (March 7, 1972).

Finally, penalties for violation of the cloister have been dropped (August 15, 1969).

To summarize these changes, we can state that this revised legislation has a number of interesting orientations or trends. In no place does it seem that the Conciliar doctrine of the equality of men and women as the People of God, and as members of the laity, has been clearly given juridic force, although in some documents, such as those dealing with ecumenism, migrants, tourism, and such like "social" responsibilities, both men and women are designated for service. As regards the lay ministry in the

Church, though both men and women are mutually responsible, the right to perform this ministry is frequently curtailed for women. They are still excluded from many personnel offices now open to lay men. However, in the legislation, the assumption of the subordination of women has been removed. Her participation in various aspects of the lay apostolate has been gradually broadened. In many instances, the broad general norms enunciated by the Roman Congregations were adapted to the pastoral needs of particular countries through the various Episcopal Conferences.

II. CHANGES ANNOUNCED FOR THE NEW LAW

After referring to the Conciliar teaching on the laity, and on women in particular, it is easy to see where the new law should be heading. Since the new Code has not yet been promulgated, we must necessarily limit ourselves to conjectures, using the draft *schemata* already distributed as a guide, as well as the reports in the periodical *Communicationes*. It will be sufficient simply to outline some general orientations.

The guiding principles for revision were approved by the first Synod of Bishops in 1967. There is nothing in them that is discriminatory or male-centered. Perhaps the plan of the Code, referring to the three *munera* or functions of the Church seems to be more clerically inclined, reserving the functions of teaching, sanctifying, and governing, not to the prophetic, priestly, and kingly powers of the People of God as a whole, but to those in authority, through reception of orders. We must await the final promulgation of the Code, though, to see how this will be in fact.

The draft text of the *Lex Fundamentalis*, distributed in 1971, caused considerable discussion and controversy. Pastors were presented as the *active* ingredient in the Church, working on the *passive* element, the laity. While canon 10 unambiguously stated that there was to be no discrimination between men and women, this was to take effect according "to their own state"! Most of the rights proposed in canons 10-25 had the same qualifying clauses, or something similar.

In the *Lex*, all legislative, executive and juridical powers were apportioned to the Pope, the bishops, and the clergy (c. 83), with little left for the laity. There seemed to have been no significant alterations of approach from former times in this document. What was given on the one hand, was removed on the other by a series of qualifying clauses. There was little evidence of declericalization of either orders or jurisdiction. Nor did the draft that was circulated give any clear manifestation of the principle of non-discrimination of sex in all areas. A new draft has been prepared and, hopefully, it will remove a number of these negative aspects. The time is probably not yet ripe for the formulation of concepts of dimorphic equivalence.

The proposed new law on persons, not distributed to the bishops, but published in the *National Catholic Reporter* of December 19, 1971, presents the same characteristics as the draft *Lex Fundamentalis*. The exercise of the Christian mission, received from Christ Himself, does not seem to carry with it universal rights and duties, but is regulated by each individual's "juridical status". There is no indication that this juridical status is that of the People of God and is common to all. In spite of this, canon 4 would state that lay persons are, through baptism, deputed by God to the apostolate, that is, to participate in the saving mission of the Church. This canon has no limitations by state or condition, and could be of great significance in the ministry of women. Lay persons would also be eligible, according to canon 5, to be heard as experts or consultors by the shepherds of the Church.

The canons on persons would still generally be qualified by role, condition, or law. Thus, while none of the proposed canons are specifically discriminatory against women, the legal loopholes for discrimination are written into the canons themselves. While they certainly show a more comprehensive and integrated awareness of the lay apostolate and of its significance, there is a legal possibility of continuing the discrimination against women that was sometimes evident in the past. But also, the possibility of development is written into these norms, since they insist on a "qualification" approach. The qualifications will vary according to the thinking of the time, but this should be of help in the years to come if, by chance, the canons were published as presented in 1971.

In the proposed new law for religious, all distinctions between masculine and feminine Institutes and their members would be dropped, with the exception of canons referring to cloister and to clerical Institutes.

The state of a person in law is determined according to age, mental development, physical development, origin, domicile or quasi-domicile, relationships, and rite. The norms for domicile would remain unchanged, retaining a subordination concept (i.e., the wife following the domicile of the husband). Other norms would seemingly not be discriminatory.

As far as the Sacraments are concerned, distinctions regarding women are generally dropped, with the exception of Orders, and, in many cases, norms relating to the minister of the sacraments.

In the proposed new penal legislation, there are still prescriptions against priests living in concubinage, but these are probably more related to priesthood than to the woman involved in the situation.

On the whole, the proposed new law, as distributed to date, as well as the post-conciliar documentation which will be integrated into the new Code, have little discriminatory content. There has been a progressive awareness of the seriousness of the issue of women's mission in the

Church. There is still, however, a preoccupation with her role as mother which leads to obscuring the issue of her struggle for mutuality of human rights with men. The stand against ordination seems adamant, though the reasons for it seem to change.

The presence of the laity in the Curia is growing regularly, and the membership of women on Commissions is manifest. This is an excellent sign of future happenings.

In spite of a significant number of positive elements to date, the reports in *Communicationes* indicate that most of the voluminous legislation that has been promulgated over the past decade will be codified in the revision. Thus, the orientations discerned in the legislation will be somewhat observed in the *schemata*. If those orientations which limited rights in accord with condition, state and particular law are maintained, there might be some occasions when the very principle of basic equality and non-discrimination is implied. We will have to watch this closely in commenting on the *schemata*.

If the new Code is delayed for more time, women stand to gain much. Ten years is too short a period of time to overcome twenty centuries of assumed subordination. The women of the Church will have to become aware of their own need to define themselves in juridical terms.

III. NECESSARY ELEMENTS FOR RECOGNITION OF EQUALITY

After this overview, a number of points stand out clearly. They are not all of the same juridical significance.

1. STATE OF WOMEN

It will be necessary to avoid, wherever possible, anything in our law that refers to the "state" or "special role" of women. They will have to be recognized for their qualities, and for what they truly are. This does not disregard differences that exist, but these differences are to be considered juridically as complementary, not subordinate.

2. RE-EDUCATION

Before any new law is promulgated, a re-education process in the Church is almost a necessity. The longer we wait for the new law, probably the less intent will be the need for re-education, since it will have become part of our heritage and viewpoint. At the present time, this need is most evident on the level of those who are preparing documents for promulgation, either at the universal or at the national or diocesan levels. But it must not remain there. Every member of the Church must strive to see that all are aware of the need of promoting equality for women, based on qualifications, and not on sex differences.

3. RIGHT TO THE SACRAMENTS

It seems difficult to hold—although the present law states so—that half of mankind is to be excluded from one of the Sacraments, simply because of sex. However, the question is so important, and has been given much publicity lately that there is no need to repeat it here. Suffice it to mention Pope Paul's recent letters to the Archbishop of Canterbury on the subject.[30]

4. TRIBUNAL PERSONNEL

No effort should be spared to take steps to see that women may be appointed to offices in ecclesiastical tribunals, if they have the necessary qualifications. This is a change that should be relatively easy to obtain and would consecrate steps already taken to show that the power of jurisdiction is separate from the power of Orders.

5. ADMINISTRATIVE WORK

All restrictions against women carrying out administrative work that does not require the power of Orders, should be removed. Thus, women should be able to be appointed chancellors of dioceses, grant dispensations and faculties, and perform all other aspects of the apostolate for which they are qualified. I realize that this statement is more functional than missional, but it is nevertheless important.

6. PROPOSED NEW CODE

It will be very important when evaluating any drafts of the new Code to watch for elements which might be discriminatory in nature or in scope. If these points are not pointed out in the responses, they will possibly be overlooked.

7. FACT BEFORE LAW

It is probably necessary that some notions regarding the equality of women become a fact of life before they are enshrined in law. This is often the case with any ecclesial institution. Possibly, certain prophetic gestures will have to be posed by some churchmen before the facts become law. Even though some think that time is running out before the new law is promulgated, there are still a number of possibilities open to us. Let us use our imagination in this regard.

CONCLUSION

This lengthy overview has not solved any problems. It has tried to show how the post-conciliar Church is trying to live its new understanding of the teachings proposed to us. We have come a long way in some regards; in others, we are just beginning.

Many are still opposed to the whole question of equality of women. Let us hope that they will awaken soon to this new and exciting dimension of the Church as we know it, and as we would love for it to be.

NOTES

1. Cf. *Gaudium et Spes*, No. 4.

2. Among many studies on this question, see Lucy Vasquez, "The Position of Women According to the Code", in *The Jurist*, 34(1974), p. 128-142.

3. I wish to express my gratitude to Sister Katherine Meagher, S.C., for permission to use extensively the manuscript of her doctoral dissertation on this particular subject. Most of the documents quoted and many of the ideas presented are taken directly from her work, or from conversations with her.

4. See, for instance, canons 93, 98, 876, 909, 1561, etc.

5. W.J. Egan, "Theology of the Laity", in *New Catholic Encyclopedia*, 6, p. 328.

6. Paul VI, "Pope Paul Explains Spiritual Purpose of Trip to Far East", in *The Catechism of Modern Man*, Boston, St. Paul Editions, 1968, p. 407.

7. Paraphrase of H.V. Heffernan, *Outline of the 16 Documents of Vatican II*, New York, The America Press, 1965, pp. 2-5.

8. Cf. W.M. Abbott, ed., *The Documents of Vatican II*, Chapman, 1972, p. 65-66, footnote 181.

9. Cf. James B. Ashbrook, *Humanitas*, New York, Abingdon Press, 1973, p. 138.

10. Cf. A. Schaldenbrand, ed., *Primacy of the Person in Christ*, Notre Dame, Fides, 1967, p. 43.

11. Cf. *Gaudium et Spes*, Nos. 5, 9, 12, etc.

12. Cf. Pope Paul VI, August 17, 1966, in *La Documentation catholique*, 63(1966), c. 1478.

13. Cf. *The Pope Speaks*, 13(1968-1969), p. 20-21.

14. Cf. Encyclical letter *"Humanae Vitae"*, No. 17, in *A.A.S.*, 60(1968), p. 493.

15. Cf. *The Pope Speaks*, 14(1969-1970), p. 19-22.

16. Cf. *The Pope Speaks*, 15(1970-1971), p. 30-33; 252-255: March 21, 1970; July 8, 1970.

17. Cf. *The Pope Speaks*, 15(1970-1971), p. 221.

18. Cf. *The Pope Speaks*, 16(1971-1972), p. 43: March 18, 1971.

19. Cf., for instance, addresses of Pope Paul VI, December 9, 1972, "Defense of the Right to Birth"; September 25, 1972, in *The Pope Speaks*, 17(1972-1973), p. 250-252.

20. Cf. *Origins*, 5(1975-1976), p. 161, 163-170 for the report of the Pontifical Commission for Justice and Peace. For some addresses of Pope Paul VI on the subject of International Women's Year, see *Origins*, 4(1974-1975), p. 344; *The Pope Speaks*, 20(1975-1976), p. 264-267; *ibid.*, p. 37-40, 180-183, etc.

21. Cf. *Origins*, 5(1975-1976), p. 163.

22. Cf. *Origins*, 2(1972-1973), p. 741, 743.

23. Cf. *Origins*, 5(1975-1976), p. 702-707.

24. Cf. S.C. Divine Worship, September 5, 1970, Norm 7, in *Canon Law Digest*, 7, p. 48.

25. *Religionum laicalium*, May 31, 1966; enlarged November 27, 1969, in *Canon Law Digest*, 6, p. 154, No. 3; 7, p. 77.

26. Cf. *Canon Law Digest*, 7, p. 84, No. 17.

27. March 10, 1966; March 9, 1971. Cf. *Canon Law Digest*, 7, p. 651.

28. Cf. *Canon Law Digest, Supplement 1973*, c. 845, p. 1.

29. August 15, 1972, Norm 7; *C.L.D.*, 7, p. 694, No. VII.

30. Cf. *Origins*, 6(1976-1977), p. 129, 130-132.

Women in Relation to Orders and Jurisdiction

KATHERINE MEAGHER, S.C.

While the status of women in the *Codex Iuris Canonici* and the new perspectives on women that can be gleaned from the documents of Second Vatican Council and post-conciliar legislation, may give a fairly comprehensive understanding of woman's current juridic condition in the Roman Catholic Church, perhaps a more specific understanding of woman's position may be gleaned by limiting the issue to "Women in Relation to Orders and Jurisdiction." In some ways, changes in the area of orders and jurisdiction may even be considered as the "heart" of the problem of sex relations within the Church.

The main thrust of the paper will be to explore some of the changes that have occurred in regard to orders and jurisdiction over the centuries and where possible to emphasize the trends that may be of significance for women today. To this end, a few historic perspectives will be recalled,[1] the *Codex* will be examined to focus on the canonical base from which we are currently operating, and pertinent conciliar and post-conciliar documentation will be reviewed to assess the changes that may have taken place concerning orders and jurisdiction. From this, a few observations on the current issue of the ordination of women will be proposed.

Historic Perspectives

In ancient Rome, the term *ordo* was used to denote a definite social body as distinct from the people, the *plebs*; and Christians used the term to denote a special place of clergy within the people of God. The Theodosian Code made it official by speaking of the *ordo ecclesiasticus* (*Cod. Theodosianus* 16.5.26). With time, the word came to stand for the different degrees within the *ordo* itself, such as the *ordo episcoporum* and *ordo presbyterorum*. The change from the collective to the "hierarchic" sense of *ordo*, seemed to reflect a change in concepts. In the ancient collective term, the emphasis was on "reception" into the order; as the emphasis was shifted to the "receiving" of a specific order, there came a resultant distinction among the various degrees and powers of the clergy.[2]

Besides the changes in the meaning of *ordo*, changes in the rituals for ordination also occurred over the ages. In the earliest rituals, such as those of the *Apostolic Tradition* of Hippolytus of Rome (c. 215 A.D.), the neighboring bishops, clergy and people assembled; the bishops imposed hands on the bishop-elect and a consecratory prayer was read asking the Holy Spirit to grant to the elect, the power to shepherd the flock, to fulfill the office of priesthood in a blameless manner, and to offer sacrifice and forgive sins. This rite remained substantially the same in the East, but in the West changes occurred from the seventh to the fifteenth centuries, mainly denoting a change from the "ordination" to the "consecration" of bishops. This seemed in accord with a shift from the concept of a bishop entering another class (*ordo*) from the priest, to a concept of the bishop as consecrated for certain functions or jurisdiction within the priesthood. In line with this, it was also during these centuries that the symbols of office began to be used in the rites; for example, the ring and staff as symbols of the bishop's jurisdiction were used at Seville in the early seventh century, and in the twelfth century the Papal Pontifical introduced the imposition of the Gospel Book on the head of the bishop-elect with the admonition to preach to the people committed to his care.[3]

In the rituals of ordination for priests and deacons, the imposition of hands and the consecrating formulas were fairly constant. In ancient practice, the ordinations took place with the *presbyterium* and the faithful assembled with the bishop; and from the sixth to the ninth centuries a ratification for the ordinand was asked from the people. In the West, around the tenth century, the rite for the priestly ordination emphasized the handing over (*porrectio*) of the instruments (chalice and paten), with the prayers stressing the power to preside at the Eucharist. With time, the tradition of instruments came to be regarded as the essential rite in the West. However, in 1947, Pope Pius XII, in the constitution *Sacramentum Ordinis*, placed the essential rite in the ordination of bishops, priests and deacons, in the laying-on of hands.[4]

In all three rituals of bishops, priests, deacons, a change was seen from ancient times in which the community of the faithful participated in some way, to the gradual elimination of the people after the tenth century. Even more significantly for the topic of orders and jurisdiction, it would appear that on occasion, episcopal consecration was "conferred on candidates who were not yet priests, but merely deacons, readers, or even laymen," and that the practice appeared so normal in the eighth and ninth centuries that "it is officially provided for by a Roman Ordo of the eighth century."[5]

But besides the ritualistic changes already noted, the evolution of the offices of bishop, priest, deacon also indicates changing concepts. The title of bishop (*episcopos*) is found in the New Testament though the word did not have the precise meaning it afterwards came to have. The bishops seem to be the overseers of the Christian communities (1 Tim. 3:5). The title between bishop and presbyter is not clearly expressed, though it seems to be the *presbyterium*, with the power of laying-on of hands together with the apostle, that institute new ministers (1 Tim. 4:14; Acts 13:3). However, in the writings of St. Ignatius of Antioch and the *Apostolic Tradition*, the pattern begins to emerge of a single bishop surrounded by a *presbyterium* as his council to help in governing and on occasion to be delegated for the eucharistic celebration. The superiority of the bishop over the priests was expressed in other ways than jurisdiction: for a long time the word *sacerdos* signified only the bishop and the presbyter was designated as *sacerdos secundi ordinis*, a priest of the second rank.[6] While the authority of the bishop was not questioned, in the West some came to hold that at the sacramental level there was no difference between the bishop and the priest, the distinction of the two degrees of hierarchy being based only on a difference of jurisdiction. The problem of the "distinctions" of the hierarchy seemed to begin around the end of the fourth century, and included in time the three ranks of bishops, priests, deacons.

It all started in Rome during the pontificate of St. Damasus (366-384 A.D.) where the deacons acquired positions of such importance that they regarded themselves as superior to the priests. St. Jerome vigorously protested this claim, and even considers that in the primitive Church there was no distinct episcopate and that it was the presbyters who collectively governed the local churches. Such ideas gained ground, and while the traditional teaching of the bishop as possessing the fullness of the priesthood was maintained, many famous theologians considered the episcopate as only a dignity or higher jurisdiction.[7] Finally, the Council of Trent, in the twenty-third session on the "Sacrament of Orders," declared that bishops not only belong in a special degree in the hierarchy of orders, but that on this level they are superior to priests. The Council also recalled that orders as a sacrament is an outward sign conferring grace. What is the grace of the episcopate? Tradition has, on the whole, seen this as the charisma of leadership. St. Irenaeus described it as "a definite charism of truth," and St. Thomas Aquinas holds that "the episcopate is a separate order, an external sign conferring grace and special sacramental powers: it is the fullness of the priesthood."[8]

It would appear, then, that in the primitive Church the sacerdotal aspect was seen mainly in the bishop, and the presbyters (while often delegated to preside over the Eucharist in place of the bishop) had their main role in assisting the bishop in governing. With the multiplication of urban and rural churches, priests were assigned to them and in time the priest habitually offered the Eucharist in the absence of the bishop. In the first centuries, also, it was the bishop who reconciled penitents to the Church; but here, too, the help of presbyters was needed in increasing numbers. In time, theologians came to consider that the power of consecrating and absolving was given to the priest at ordination (not through delegation). But the power required "matter," that is, a Christian under his jurisdiction. The matter, apt for absolution, is given to the priest by the bishop who has his own power as head over the Mystical Body.[9]

In the early writings, it would seem that priests by their ordination became members of the priesthood, helpers of the episcopal body in its own function of feeding and guiding the people of God. With the passing of time, the theology of order concentrated more and more on the sacramental powers conferred, in particular on the powers related to the Eucharist. The priest as *sacerdos* increased in importance. By the time of *Sacramentum Ordinis*, in the ordination to the priesthood, the imposition of hands is required, and the prayer refers to "the dignity of priesthood," received in the office "of second rank," which they receive from God.[10]

The diaconate has also undergone changes over the centuries. There are clear references to deacons in the New Testament (1 Tim. 3:8-10, for example). Theologians, on the whole, have agreed that the diaconate is a degree of the sacrament of orders, and this was attested by Pius XII in *Sacramentum Ordinis*. Originally connected with the service of the table, the aspect of service has always been associated with the diaconate. Hippolytus designated deacons as not ordained to the priesthood, but for "the service of the bishop." In time, with their confidential office close to the bishop, deacons came to exercise a sort of control over public morals and were often charged with important official missions (St. Gregory sent the deacon Castorius to inquire into the conduct of bishops and priests—*Letters* 5, 28, and 32). In time, also, deacons came to be assigned to priests. As a sign of the sacrament, the deacons were ordained to represent Christ in his serving mission and as Mass could not be celebrated by the priest without a deacon "to serve," deacons were needed in every parish. These deacons were often married. While they could not celebrate the Eucharist, they could distribute communion, preside over prayers, preach, baptize, settle questions, assist the poor, prepare catechumens. Why, then, did the order of deacons begin to die out in the Western Church in the fifth century?[11]

Joseph Lecuyer, on the topic of "The Diaconate," proposes several reasons: With the introduction of private masses in the West, with the stress on the Eucharistic celebration by the priest, some felt that the diaconate as a permanent office lost its justifications; the prohibition against marriage (or its use) was extended to deacons in the fourth century, and recruitment became more difficult; as theology concentrated more and more on the sacramental powers conferred, and the diaconate did not confer the sacral power for the administration of the main sacraments, the importance of the diaconate diminished. The diaconate became a temporary office leading to the priesthood and diaconal tasks were performed by priests and laity.[12]

The three orders considered so far (bishops, priests, deacons), have shown certain developments in the history of the ministry of men in the Church. What developments occurred in the history of the ministry of women?

In the primitive Church, women had at least two offices: they functioned as an order of widows and as deaconesses (1 Tim. 5:9; Rm. 16:1), and as prophets they were accorded recognition in public worship (1 Cor. 11:5). There seemed to be a controversy that centered on women as official teachers and preachers of the Word to the congregation (1 Cor. 14:34-35; 1 Tim. 2:11-12). At all events, these passages were interpreted as meaning that women could not teach authoritatively; they were thus denied the privileges of presiding in the congregation and of offering the Eucharist. By the third century, the order of widows had become an institution. Clement of Alexandria (*Paed.* 3:14, 97), lists widows after the three male orders, as do many other early writers. The establishment of widows up to the end of the fourth century is attested by St. John Chrysostom (*Hom. 66 on Matthew*), but it is on the wane. As it disappears, another institution, that of the deaconess, came to take its place.[13]

The *Apostolic Canons* show deaconesses with an important role to play. They are mentioned immediately after the deacons, are numbered among the clergy, and receive an ordination by the laying-on of hands. The importance of deaconesses in the East in the fourth and fifth centuries is confirmed by extant literature. In the West, the institution of deaconesses did not appear before the end of the fourth century, and then it seemed to be an honorary distinction.

In his research on deaconesses in "The Ministry of Women in the Early Church," Jean Daniélou concludes, "I would say then that I see none of the duties of the minor orders which, so far as the female aspect of them is concerned, cannot be, and in fact, have not been undertaken by women." He also remarks that in the West, the Church has always opposed conferring a definite status of ministry on women, that it was the "nuns" who inherited the chief works of the deaconesses and widows, and in later centuries it was the religious women who "provided the answer to the needs." This leads Daniélou to affirm: "We have thus three possible ways of ordering the ministry of women: lay, clerical, religious. It can be said that all three are equally tradition."[14]

The main historic perspectives in regard to jurisdiction in the Church may be seen to center around the papal formula of *"plenitudo potestatis,"* the fullness of power vested in the pope. Jurisdiction, as distinct from the power of orders, or the administrative duties of temporal matters in the Church, is hard to verify before the thirteenth century. In a letter to his vicar, Anastasius of Thessalonica, Leo I (440-461 A.D.) insisted that the vicar was called merely *in partem sollicitudinis, non in plenitudinem potestatis*; that is, had not received the full powers which Leo could have granted him. Around 1076, Bernold of Constance interpreted the texts of Leo I, as authority for the assertion that the Roman Pontiff is the universal ordinary, holding universal and primary power over the subjects of bishops as well as over all bishops. From Gregory IV to the time of Gratian, the term *plenitudo potestatis* was found in several canonical collections. To some, it meant a limitation of the powers of papal legates; to others, that metropolitans were called only *in partem sollicitudinis*, not to the fullness of power enjoyed by the pope. The "scientific" understanding of the distinction of ecclesiastical powers was to be found in Gratian and his commentators, though Gratian himself was concerned with the office of primate which pertains to government and not to orders.[15] It is still Gratian, however, who is credited with providing the substance and the technical language which provided the decretists and others with the later doctrine of *plenitudo potestatis*, and the power of jurisdiction.[16]

In his article on the "Power of Jurisdiction," S. E. Donlon argues from the need of jurisdiction, to the presence of the power within the Church. As the service of God and the cult of worship require the cooperation of others, "inevitably these concrete, divinely established relationships will entail the presence and the intervention of a recognized agency with social power to assign tasks and adjudicate differences."[17] It might seem, then, that the power of jurisdiction does not have the same substantial backing in tradition that is manifest in the historic perspectives on the power of order.

Rationale for Women's Exclusion from the Priesthood

Assuming that these historic perspectives present some of the facts, it would seem that while there is a tradition for women in the diaconal order, minor orders and ministries, yet the evidence points to the fact that women were excluded from the sacramental-priesthood strictly so-called; that is, the order of priests and bishops. To try to give justification for this exclusion is another research in itself. Here, only a few possibilities are offered.

1. *The Sacral-Sacramental Argument*—In the words of René van Eyden, in his study on "The Place of Women in Liturgical Functions,"

after pointing to the shift from ministry as service and charism, and the emphasis from the proclamation of the good news as the main function of bishop or priest to that of a sacral priesthood with distinctive powers, "From the beginning of the third century onwards, the person of the minister and his liturgical actions came to be regarded as sacral." Since sexuality was thought to be unclean and improper in this sacral sphere, "the priest had to be unmarried and women were exluded from sacral functions because of their periodic cultic uncleanness."[18]

2. *The Philosophic Argument*—An example of the philosophic argument may be found in the writings of St. Augustine. He describes "man" as created to the image of God (that is, with the powers of reason and understanding) on account of which he was set over all irrational creatures, and "as in his soul there is one power which rules by directing, another made subject that it may obey, so also for the man a woman was corporeally made, who, in the mind of her rational understanding should also have a like nature; in the sex, however, of her body should be in like manner subject to the sex of her husband, as the appetite of action is subjected by reason of the mind to conceive the skill of acting rightly."[19] The spiritual equality of women and men is thus proclaimed, but Augustine and his followers, also asserted the "inferiority" of the female sex to the male sex. The rationalizing for the exclusion of women in the official ministry of the Church is closely linked to woman's "natural" incapacity.

3. *The Subordination Argument*—St. Thomas Aquinas seemed to assume the biological inferiority of women. Under the heading of impediments to orders (q. 39, a. 1), the first article deals with the impediment of "female" sex. Aquinas argues that a woman cannot be a priest because she has a subordinate status, that she is incapable of receiving the tonsure required "as the first step to ordination (1 Cor. 11:6)." The supporting scripture passage reads: "In fact, a woman who will not wear a veil ought to have her hair cut off." Saint Paul had just said that it would be a disgrace for a woman to have her hair cut off. Does Aquinas see in this, a command from scripture that women could not receive the tonsure? In reality, his argument is not built on this point of tonsure. Aquinas seemed to assume (and firmly accept) the Aristotelean concept of women as the passive element in generation, the male as the sole possessor of "seed," and the active and directive force. Aquinas thus seems to reason that a subordinate status, of its nature, is incapable of rising through the various "orders" of the hierarchy.

4. *The Sociological Argument*—The exclusion of women from the priesthood is linked by some to the beginnings of the Christian Church when the general status of women in society was inferior. Some degree of anti-feminism, very obvious in a Tertullian, which one often finds in the

Fathers of the Church and authors of the Middle Ages, may have been derived from a somewhat contemptuous attitude towards women, sociologically and culturally speaking. Such attitudes certainly had the effect, at certain periods, of putting restrictions upon even the legitimate ministries of women.

5. *The "tradition" Argument*—This argument is often given by Code commentators. The words of Stanislaus Woywod are typical: "St. Paul's teaching in 1 Cor. 14:34, and 1 Tim. 2:11, is absolutely opposed to the ministry of women in the Church. Several of the early Fathers of the Church (e.g., St. Irenaeus, St. Epiphanius, St. Ambrose, St. Augustine) call it an heretical error to admit women to the office and dignity of the priesthood."[20]

6. *The Ecclesiastical Law Argument*—Some authors attest that the exclusion of women from orders is of divine law and can never be changed; others feel that the exclusion is of ecclesiastical law and change is possible. One author who seems to uphold the "ecclesiastical law" argument is Raoul Naz in a commentary on canon 968. Naz claims that both the order of widows and the order of deaconesses occupied a place in the ecclesiastical hierarchy. Granting that women did receive even one of the sacramental orders at some time in the history of the Church, it follows, to Naz, that the exclusion from the sacrament of orders is an ecclesiastical (not a divine) law.[21]

7. *The Hierarchic Argument*—While Yves Congar has reassessed some of his earlier opinions as expressed in *Lay People in the Church*,[22] still his thinking on the hierarchical "order" of creation is still around. In this concept Congar sees the economy of God on earth as patterned on the same hierarchical structure as "the eternal mystery of God." He applied the same principle to the man-woman relationship: "We are told in Genesis that man was made in God's image. The woman is made in the image of the man, for she is derived from him, dependent on him, and, so to say, his 'opposite number,' his fellow creature and his partner . . ." and he sees in this relationship (mirrored also between God and man), the law of divine economy "whereby a principle of help and fulfillment is joined to a principle of authority or hierarchy."[23] Such a theory fits in beautifully with a static notion of creation, a notion which seems to be no longer acceptable even to Congar himself.

In summary, the seven theories presented (and many others could be given) are not all mutually exclusive. They reveal at least one thing: the issue of woman's exclusion from orders is not a minor issue; it touches the very heart and structure of the ecclesiastical Church, and rationalizations have been forthcoming from every quarter.

Orders and Jurisdiction in the Codex Iuris Canonici

At the time of the writing of the *Codex*, the Church was conceived almost exclusively as a "perfect society," with its own public order and structure. The concept of "perfect society" seems basic to the distinctions between orders and jurisdiction found in the Code. Perhaps the canons that indicate this are canons 108 and 109 at the introduction to the laws concerning the clergy; and canons 218 and 219, concerning the Roman Pontiff.

Canons 108 and 109 contain the following ideas: those who have been assigned to the divine ministry at least by first tonsure, are called clerics. They form a sacred hierarchy made up of different grades in which some are subordinate to others. The sacred hierarchy of orders consists of bishops, priests and ministers.[24] The hierarchy of jurisdiction, on the other hand, consists of the supreme pontificate and the "subordinate" episcopate. Persons who are received into the ecclesiastical hierarchy are constituted in the degrees of the power of orders by sacred ordination; they are not accepted by the consent or at the call of the people or of the secular power. In the supreme pontificate, the person legitimately elected and freely accepting the election, receives jurisdiction by the divine law itself. All other degrees of jurisdiction are received by canonical appointment.

Canons 218 and 219 are more specific about the primacy of jurisdiction received by the Roman Pontiff, who at the time of his acceptance of legitimate election receives "the full power of supreme jurisdiction by divine right." Such bodies as ecumenical councils (canon 222), cardinals (canon 230), curial departments (canon 242), etc., share the supreme authority "by ecclesiastical law." Bishops are described as having "ordinary power under the authority of the Roman Pontiff" (canon 329).

What seems to be evident, is that there is an intimate relationship between orders and jurisdiction. Both are seen as of divine institution and for a supernatural end: the eternal salvation of souls. Jurisdiction presupposes orders (canon 118), and moderates its exercise (canon 879). However, their source or origin is different: order is conferred by rite of ordination (canon 109); jurisdiction is conferred by canonical mission (canon 109) except in the case of the Supreme Pontiff. Again, their particular end is different: order is to sanctify the individual; jurisdiction is to govern the faithful.

By canon 118, only clerics can obtain the power of either order or ecclesiastical jurisdiction; and by canon 968 only men may be clerics. Women, therefore, are excluded from orders which give the power to transmit to others the means of salvation, and they are excluded from jurisdiction, the power of ruling the faithful in order to attain the end of the

Church. Moreover, they are excluded by canon 118 from occupying any ecclesiastical office or from receiving benefices and pensions related to clerical offices. And as the power of order and jurisdiction comprised the main ecclesiastical structure of the Church, women might be considered as having no part in the ecclesiastical structure *per se.*

Woman's relationship to orders and jurisdiction has a direct bearing on her relation to all the sacraments. In particular, women (who comprise over half the membership of the Church) have the juridic capacity to receive only six sacraments; and while canon 737 describes baptism as "the door and foundation of all other sacraments," no footnote is added that when baptizing a female the formula should read, "the door and foundation of all the sacraments except holy orders."

In regard to the "six" sacraments and in cultic worship, a woman can be the ordinary minister of matrimony (though no canon acknowledges this power); and she can be the extraordinary minister of baptism in accord with canon 742, though "a man is to be preferred to a woman . . ." A woman may be sponsor or witness of baptism, confirmation, and matrimony (canons 764, 793, 1094), and a woman has the juridic capacity to receive all six sacraments in accord with the norms. In connection with the divine office ordained for divine cult, canon 2256 limits this to clerics. By such canons as 813 (the server at Mass) and canon 1262 (the separation of the sexes for divine services with the women "modestly dressed,") women are not treated on a par with men as equivalent members of the laity; and it might be said that women have less proximity than men even to the "six" sacraments because of their exclusion from orders and jurisdiction.

So far, in this review of the Code, orders have been considered mainly under the aspect of power, and in relation to jurisdiction. There are still aspects to be considered under the concept of holy orders as sacrament which are significant for women.

It has already been noted that canon 968 states that sacred ordination can be validly received only by a baptized man. From the structure of the sentence, *Sacram ordinationem valide recipit solus vir baptizatus*, it is not clear whether it is the nature of the sacrament itself that demands masculinity; or whether it is the nature of the male that gives the capacity for orders. Few commentators do more than refer to tradition as the reason. But perhaps even more than rationale, the question of the *source* of the law is important. Canon 948 states that the sacrament of holy orders by Christ's institution *distinguishes* the clergy from the laity in the Church for the government of the faithful and the ministry of divine worship. Here, the divine law seems responsible for the *division* between clergy/laity accomplished by holy orders. However, canon 968 does not mention any divine ordinance but stresses the validity of the sacrament when received by the male. The question is, whether the canons state clearly that the *source* of women's exclusion is of divine law? The answer is that the canons do not state this; and in canon 968 where the male-qualification for orders is stated, there is no assertion that this qualification is of either divine or ecclesiastical law. It may be assumed that the setting up of qualifications falls within the realm of ecclesiastical law. It would follow that if the male-qualification is of divine origin, such should be stated; especially as the prohibition affects all women and because we are dealing with an important grace-giving sacrament particularly ordained to worship and service.

Pressing the question of source still further: assuming that the prohibition against women *is* of divine origin, it follows that the Church possesses the power only to interpret such a law and to enjoin its observance as of obligation. Also, such a divine law would apply to all peoples, all Christian Churches, and even to all infidels. Assuming that the prohibition is *not* of divine, but of ecclesiastical origin, the law then would apply only to members of the Catholic Church, and dispensation would be possible.

To declare the prohibition as of divine origin, there would be some difficulty with early ecumenical council legislation; for instance canon 15 of the Council of Chalcedon stated, "A woman is not to be ordained deaconess before she is forty years of age, and then only after a careful examination." There would be difficulty, too, with the Eastern tradition in which deaconesses were ordained and constituted an ecclesiastical order. There would be difficulty for the ecumenical goals in the acceptance of traditional and current practices of ordaining women in other Christian Churches. To declare the prohibition as of ecclesiastical law, recalls the dictum that by natural law every human being is capable of enjoying certain inalienable rights which are not subject to direct remission by positive law. And to summarize this examination of canons 948 and 968, it is clear that until the Church makes a declaration on the matter, it is at least an ecclesiastical law that women are excluded from holy orders. However, the theological questions remain open as to the source of the exclusion, and even the Church's authority to attach invalidating ecclesiastical restrictions should any human right be in question.

New Perspectives: Second Vatican Council and Post-Conciliar Documentation

The conciliar documents teach the basic equality of men and women and the dignity of each human person; they affirm a dynamic-evolutionary perspective on *humanitas* in which men and women find self-actualization in mutuality and communion; they proclaim that while God makes the future possible, men and women are made jointly responsible for that future.

The main traits of the human person, that must be respected in order to contribute to the dignity of each man and woman are the dignity of the mind, the dignity of the moral conscience, and authentic freedom.[25] Whatever should be affirmed for the male in these areas, should (in like manner) be affirmed for the female.

Many of the ideas presented so far, while retaining a certain validity, are presented in the documents of Second Vatican Council and in postconciliar legislation from new perspectives. Some of the new trends have deep meaning in the life and mission of the laity and for women. Among the concepts that have undergone development must be numbered those connected with the Church as perfect society, the hierarchy, orders and jurisdiction. The perfect-society concept has given place to the Mystery of the Church, a community of faith, hope, and charity expressed in a visible structure through which Christ communicates truth and grace to all (cf. L.G. n. 8). The hierarchy as sole guardian of the "deposit of faith," has given place to the hierarchical communion which is found in a juridical form in the episcopal body (L.G. n. 22) but extends to the *presbyterium* which "requires hierarchical communion with the order of bishops," (P.O. n. 7); and extends also to the whole people of God for "since the priestly ministry is the ministry of the Church itself, it can be discharged only by hierarchical communion with the whole body," (P.O. n. 15).

The Church is still considered as society in the conciliar documents, but the perspective is different. In *Lumen Gentium* the doctrine of the nature of the Church is first set forth as Mystery: "the Church or in other words the kingdom of Christ now present in mystery, grows visible in the world through the power of God," (L.G. n. 3). The Church, then, is both community and structure, but it is the structure that serves the community. As a more comprehensive recognition is given to the role of the "hierarchic community," a more realistic concept of power and jurisdiction will emerge, especially with the deepening awareness that the body of the faithful as a whole, "cannot err in matters of belief," (L.G. n. 12). This recognition of a totally integrated community "of faith, hope, and love," begins to take shape in Chapter 3 of *Lumen Gentium*, "The Hierarchical Structure of the Church." However, there appears to be one slight oversight: the women of the Church do not seem to appear in the structure.

Chapter 3 of *Lumen Gentium* deals with the ordained ministers in the Church and contains important doctrinal affirmations of the sacramentality of episcopal consecration and the collegiality of bishops. The Council teaches that the bishop is not just a priest with greater powers of jurisdiction, but that he receives through sacramental consecration the fullness of the power of orders involving power to sanctify, teach, and govern (L.G. n. 21). The main doctrinal point is set forth in Article 22. All bishops who are united to the pope and their fellow bishops by hierarchical communion, constitute a collegial body enjoying supreme power in governing the Church. Such supreme power is exercised not only when the college is united in an ecumenical council but also through other forms of appropriate collegiate action which is not specified, though the episcopal synod is seen as an example. The Council makes it clear that the canonical mission by which a bishop is assigned to a particular task or diocese need not in every case come by the positive activity of the pope (*L.G.* n. 24), although in the Latin Church this is the normal procedure. The priests, as "prudent cooperators" with the episcopal order, as well as its "aids and instruments," are called to serve the people of God (*L.G.* n. 28). At a lower level of the hierarchy are the deacons, upon whom hands are imposed, "not unto the priesthood, but unto a ministry of service," (*L.G.* n. 29).

Article 29 goes on to make provision for the restoration of the diaconate as a permanent grade in the churches of the Latin rite and for the eventual ordination of married deacons of mature years. It is in the last paragraph of this Chapter that the exclusion of women at the diaconate level is mentioned: "With the consent of the Roman Pontiff this diaconate will be able to be conferred upon men of more mature age (*viris maturioris aetatis*), even upon those living in the married state," and it may also be conferred upon suitable young men (*iuvenibus idoneis*).

It would seem that the "Hierarchical Structure of the Church" is totally male-oriented. Though the theory of hierarchical-communion is used throughout the Chapter, it is the adjective "hierarchical" that becomes the determinant of the structure, not the noun, "communion." The strict division between clerics and laity has been maintained under more pastoral language. And among the laity, the males are at least open to the call of service in the structure; the females are still "more radically" excluded than the lay men of the Church.

From the positive side, jurisdiction and orders (though distinct) are no longer seen as having two principles but are rooted in the pneumatic oneness of the Church; a pneumatic oneness that in theory extends to the whole People of God.

The Second Vatican Council has opened up many new doctrinal perspectives. Among these is the clear teaching that the assumption of the subordination and inferiority of women (evident in the *Codex Iuris Canonici*) is no longer tenable. A review of the conciliar documents shows that the theory of non-discrimination is strongly affirmed and that sex-discrimination is specifically mentioned in most of the affirmations. There are at least seven strong declarations to this effect in *Gaudium et Spes*, and several in *Lumen Gentium*; and to quote but one: "Hence, there is in

Christ and in the Church no inequality on the basis of race or nationality, social condition or sex, because 'there is neither Jew nor Greek; there is neither slave nor freeman; there is neither male nor female. For you are all one in Christ Jesus' (Gal. 3:28, Greek text; cf. Col. 3:11)," (*L.G.* n. 32).

With the doctrinal base of the pneumatic oneness of the Church and the principle of non-discrimination of sex seen as the characteristic of Christ and the Church, it yet remains to transform these theories into structural realities.

Post-Conciliar Documentation—In the decade following Second Vatican Council there has been an abundance of ecclesial documentation affecting nearly every area of the life and mission of the Church. Here, the references will be limited to documents which are affecting the ministry of women:

Extraordinary Ministers of the Eucharist—The question of "extraordinary ministers of the Eucharist," has been chosen to illustrate one manner of implementing the conciliar doctrine of non-discrimination in sex used during the past decade.

By 1966 the question of extraordinary ministers began to receive attention. In the instruction *Fidei Custos*, norms for the obtaining of the faculty and qualifications of the minister of eucharistic communion were issued. Among the norms it is stated that the recipients of the ministry "must be of the male sex," however in urgent need "the superior or superioress" of a religious institute is permitted to distribute the eucharistic bread to his/her fellow religious and to the lay persons present. Within a short time, the episcopal conferences of several countries applied, indicating in all cases that reputable lay men would receive the mandate. However, in 1971, the president of the episcopal conference of the United States, broadened the petition and asked the faculty for "qualified persons." Though the word "woman" is not used, the request is made that all "mature laity" be given the opportunity. An affirmative answer was received from the Sacred Congregation of the Sacraments, with a few precautions added; and the stipulation that "in other matters," the instruction *Fidei Custos* is to be followed. Two years later, in May of 1973, revised guidelines were approved for the Archdiocese of Chicago, and among other norms for extraordinary ministers, it is stated that "candidates may be men or women and should be, in the judgment of the pastor and his staff, exemplary Catholics."[26]

It would seem that through a legitimate pastoral need and in accord with norms, laymen are given the privilege to be extraordinary ministers, and in some places the same privilege is extended to laywomen. The evolution of outlook in regard to women ministers, as it centers upon this privilege, might be interesting and instructive for future changes in the ministry of women. Even in *Fidei Custos* the superioress could obtain the privilege, so there is no question about a woman's "capacity" to serve, and thus the subordination principle is removed. The extension of the privilege, however, is another matter, and might be considered as an educative procedure. The gradual evolution from allowing women to read certain passages of scripture from outside the santuary to functioning as extraordinary ministers of the eucharist (and that without conditions, precautions, or warnings concerning sex) is a significant change from canon 813. While the server at mass is not equated with the extraordinary minister, still there are certain similarities in duties. In 1973, the instruction *Immensae Caritatis* from the Sacred Congregation of the Sacraments, extended the privilege of extraordinary ministry to both lay men and women.

Lay Ministries in the Church—Perhaps an even more significant development for women is in regard to the institution of lay ministries in the Church. Basically, the new norms affect some of the canons from 948 to 978. In an apostolic letter *Ministeria Quaedam* issued August 15, 1972, Pope Paul VI suppressed the traditional orders of first tonsure, minor orders and the subdiaconate. As introduction to this change in a "long-standing discipline," reference was made to the fact that in ancient times functions of "sacred liturgy and charity," were entrusted to the "faithful," although in time some of these functions came to be considered as preparatory steps for minor orders. In place of the suppressed orders, the letter established the lay ministries and readers and acolytes for those "not considered clerics or candidates for holy orders." In addition, "the establishment of other lay ministries is left to the proposal of episcopal conferences." Several important distinctions are made between lay and clerical ministries. The conferral of lay ministries should not be called ordination, but "installation," and only those who receive the diaconate are considered clerics. Thus, "ministries can be entrusted to Christian lay persons with the result that they are not to be considered as reserved to candidates for the sacrament of orders." Then, after a more detailed description of the ministries of lector and acolyte, the much-publicized norm 7 appears:

> The installment of lector and acolyte, in accord with the venerable tradition of the Church, is reserved for men.[27]

On the same date, the *motu proprio Ad Pascendum* was promulgated, in which "some norms concerning the sacred order of the diaconate" were established in accord with the wishes expressed by Second Vatican Council and implemented as regards the permanent diaconate in the *motu proprio Sacrum Diaconatus Ordinem* in 1967. Though there is no specific norm that states that the diaconate is reserved for men, yet "candidates for the diaconate, whether permanent or transitional, and for the priesthood, must receive the ministries of lector and acolyte." Therefore, norm 7 of *Ministeria Quaedam* applies, and women are excluded from the diaconate.

For women, however, the fact that ministries can now be entrusted to Christian lay persons, and that such ministries are not reserved to candidates for holy orders, is of importance; as is the fact that in addition to the offices common to the Latin Church (lector and acolyte), nothing prevents "episcopal conferences" from petitioning the apostolic see for other needed ministries. Thus despite the exclusion of women from the ministries of lector and acolyte, and with the door still closed to diaconate and priesthood, the possibility of evolution in the area of official ministries for women can be envisaged.

Pope Paul VI: Champion of Women's Equality with Men—Although Pope Paul VI has a primary role in all post-conciliar legislation, his stand on women's equality with men must not be lost sight of. Many examples could be given but the establishment of the special Commission to study the role of women should be noted. In 1973, at the request of the 1971 Synod of Bishops, the Pope created a Commission to study the question. The final plenary session of the Commission was held on January 31, 1976, and speaking to the members on that occasion, the Pope said that instead of thinking in terms of an end of the work of the Commission, the programs that were drawn up by the members "must now be progressively realized in deeds." The Pope reiterated what he has said before, that "men and women are equal before God: equal as persons . . . equal in dignity, equal also in their rights." He pointed out that authentic Christian advancement of women is not limited to the claiming of rights, for it also "obliges men and women alike to remember their proper duties and responsibilities."[28] While questions might arise as to just what is meant by "proper" duties and responsibilities and whether sex-discrimination might not actually continue if duties and responsibilities are labelled "masculine" or "feminine," still the affirmation of equality is unequivocal and again asserts the conciliar stance of the Church in decrying not only the subordination of women but any inferences of woman's "inferiority."

The special Commission was not assigned to consider the ordination of women; that task was given to a Pontifical Biblical Commission with terms of reference "to study the role of women in the Bible . . . to determine the place that can be given to women today in the Church."[29] Some of the findings of the Commission about the "eventual ordination of women to the priesthood," should provide some understanding of the current outlook on this matter. A summary of part of the report follows.

To begin with, the "masculine character of the hierarchical order which has structured the Church since its beginning," seems attested to by scripture. But the report immediately raises the question: "Must we conclude that this rule must be valid forever in the Church?" And another question is asked: "What is the normative value which should be accorded to the practice of the Christian communities of the first centuries?" The report sees the primordial role of the "leaders" of the communities in the New Testament, in the field of "preaching and teaching." No biblical text defines the leaders' charge "in terms of a special power permitting them to carry out the eucharistic rite or to reconcile sinners." But given the relationship between the sacramental economy and the hierarchy, "the administration of the sacraments should not be exercised independently of this hierarchy." It is within this perspective that "we must consider the issue of eucharistic and penitential ministry."

The report states that two texts (1 Cor. 14:33-35 and 1 Tim. 2:11-15), "forbid women to speak and to teach in assemblies." However, the report continues, "without mentioning doubts raised by some about their Pauline authenticity, it is possible that they refer only to certain concrete situations and abuses." Thus it is possible that "certain other situations call on the Church to assign to women the role of teaching which these two passages deny them and which constitute a function belonging to the leadership." This raises the question for the Commission: "Is it possible that certain circumstances can come about which call on the Church to entrust in the same way to certain women some sacramental ministries?" They point out that this has already been the case in regard to baptism which, though entrusted to the apostles (Mt. 28:19 and Mk. 16:15 f.), can now be administered by women. Is a similar evolution possible for the ministry of the eucharist and reconciliation, "which manifest eminently the service of the priesthood of Christ?"

The crux of the report is that it "does not seem that the New Testament by itself alone will permit us to settle in a clear way and once and for all, the problem of the possible accession of women to the presbyterate." The two outlooks that might stand in the way of the possibility of women's ordination are then given: "Some think that in the scriptures there are sufficient indications to exclude this possibility, considering that the sacraments of eucharist and reconciliation have a special link with the person of Christ and therefore with the male hierarchy as borne out by the New Testament." And others wonder "if the Church hierarchy, entrusted with the sacramental economy, would be able to entrust the ministries of eucharist and reconciliation to women in light of circumstances, without going against Christ's original intentions."[30]

It would seem that the rationale against the ordination of women has been reduced to two: the priest as symbolic of the "male" Christ; and the argument of the "will of God."

Ecumenical Ramifications—The last documentation to be considered is concerned with the ecumenical ramifications of ordaining women to the priesthood. A series of four letters (July 9, 1975 to March 23, 1976) between Anglican Archbishop Donald Coggan of Canterbury and Pope Paul VI seems to add a few insights into the ecumenical issue.[31]

The correspondence was released by the Anglican primate during a general synod of the Church of England held in July at York, England. The series began when Archbishop Coggan wrote to Pope Paul as well as to Orthodox and Old Catholic leaders, to inform them "of the slow but steady growth" of a consensus within the Anglican Communion that there are "no fundamental objections in principle to the ordination of women to the priesthood." In his reply Pope Paul said that the position of the Catholic Church is "that it is not admissible to ordain women to the priesthood for very fundamental reasons." These reasons are here summarized:

1. The example of Christ choosing his apostles only from among men.
2. The constant practice of the Church which has imitated Christ in choosing only men.
3. The living teaching authority in the Church has consistently held that the exclusion of women from the priesthood is in accord with God's plan for his Church.

The letter ends with appreciation expressed that "the fundamental theological importance" of the question is mutually acknowledged. In reply, Archbishop Coggan reiterated his adherence to "the goal which we jointly seek," which is "that visible unity of the Church for which Christ prayed." He then states, "We believe this unity will be manifested within a diversity of legitimate traditions because the Holy Spirit has never ceased to be active within the local churches throughout the world." The response of Pope Paul VI on March 23, 1976, recalled the ardent hopes that had been experienced in the past, that the Holy Spirit "would lead us along the path of reconciliation," and "this must be the measure of the sadness with which we encounter so grave a new obstacle and threat on that path."

From this correspondence, it would appear that in the mind of Pope Paul VI, the question of the ordination of women is of such grave moment that the great advances towards reconciliation between the Anglican and the Catholic Church are imperilled. It is also to be noted that the rationale given against the ordination of women by the Pope may be reduced to the imitation of Christ and the argument of God's will.

Jurisdiction in Post-Conciliar Documentation

The important changes in jurisdiction as set forth in *Lumen Gentium*, Articles 21 and 22 have been noted. Here, jurisdiction in relation to orders is based in the pneumatic oneness of the Holy Spirit operating in the Church, and the episcopal consecration in hierarchical communion integrates the power of order and jurisdiction without obliterating the distinction. In general, in post-conciliar legislation, there seems to be a trend to speak of the "social authority" in the Church, and former distinctions between the so-called dominative power of superiors or religious women (see canon 501) and jurisdiction are not maintained. There are also examples of jurisdiction being granted to lay men to act as judges in ecclesiastical tribunals;[32] and to lay persons to preach. In regard to the office of preaching, the Sacred Congregation of Clergy in November of 1973, in reply to the bishops of the German Federal Republic, allowed experimentation for lay persons, in accord with norms, to preach in the Church and in extraordinary cases, to give the homily at Mass.[33] The designation throughout the documentation is for "lay persons," so women are included.

Recapitulation and Current Issues

In approaching the question of "Women in Relation to Orders and Jurisdiction," a brief historic perspective was attempted. The point stressed was that concepts of order and of jurisdiction have evolved over the ages. This evolution was not seen as a steady progress and clarification of the two concepts; but at different times in history the very understanding of the functions and missions of bishops, priests, and deacons underwent substantial changes. Changes were also perceived in concepts of jurisdiction; especially in the understanding of the source of jurisdiction and in the relationship of jurisdiction to the sacrament of orders. In regard to the ministries of women in the Church, there is a tradition of the Eastern Church attesting the laying-on of hands in the ordination of deaconesses; and the Western Church has a tradition of ecclesiastical institutions of widows and of deaconesses, at least in the early ages. In the West, however, the ministries of women have remained largely un-institutionalized.

The *Codex Iuris Canonici* states that holy orders can be received only by a baptized man, and as only clerics can receive jurisdiction, women are exluded from both order and jurisdiction. A survey of the Code reveals that while no canon *per se* states that sex is a juridic fact, and that women because of their sex are "subordinate and inferior," nevertheless the canons that relate to women are based on an assumption of women's subordination. And even within the status of laity, women are not accorded equivalence with men; and this to such a degree that the inferiority of women is implied.

The documents of Second Vatican Council place great emphasis on the dignity of the human person, and non-discrimination on the basis of sex is strongly affirmed. These teachings are so emphatically asserted that the assumption of the subordination and inferiority of women can no longer be maintained.

In post-conciliar documentation, Pope Paul VI emerges as a champion of human rights and the equality of men and women, though he seems to maintain that women have a "proper" role in life which bespeaks a differentiation rather than a basic mutuality of rights and duties in respect to both men and women. On the question of the ordination of women, Pope Paul strongly affirms the exclusion of women to the priesthood, in accord with the "plan of God" for his Church. The Biblical Commission, appointed by Pope Paul to look into the issue of women's ordination from a biblical stance, concludes that the New Testament by itself does not permit the question to be settled in a clear and definitive way.

This summary may help to single out at least some of the current issues connected with the ordination of women in the Catholic Church today. Here, mention will be made of only five such issues in need of further research and development.

1. *Discernment in Scriptural Norms*—This issue centers on Christ's *will* to have/not to have, women in the priesthood. Research in this area would build on the findings of the Biblical Commission already noted and deal with the significance of the "masculinity" of Christ in the Christian message and dispensation, as well as the normative value that can be attached to actions of Christ in the absence of any positive divine ordinance against the ordination of women.

2. *The Source of Law in Canon 968*—The canonical issue of the *source* of the male qualification for the validity of the sacrament of holy orders, whether of divine/ecclesiastical law is important. Should the source be seen as ecclesiastical, the further problem would arise of the right of ecclesiastical authority to attach invalidating restrictions for a sacrament solely on the basis of a person's sex.

3. *Distinctive Charisms of Office*—The theological issue of clarifying the *essential* aspects, qualifications, and/or functions of the priest as distinct from those of deacon/lay minister, is basic for an understanding of long-standing divisions in the Church: clergy/laity, and the male/

female division in the public life of the Church. Here, the origin and evolution of the offices are to be recalled, as well as the new perspectives on the lay person (priest, prophet and king) with a mandate to mission from Christ himself.

4. *The Authenticity Issue*—There is a question as to whether the male-oriented orders and ministries (as sacramental signs of inner reality) give authentic expression of the Christian reality in which there is neither "male nor female."

5. *The Dimorphic Issue*—Should Christianity be dominantly conceived and structured from the male outlook? From the female outlook? Do women (in general), need or want to express their life and mission in the traditional male-oriented orders and ministries? Or, to state this more positively, how best can dimorphic *humanities* (male and female) respond to God's call to holiness and transcendence of nature, and thus in partnership and mutuality, set about the task of renewing the face of the earth?

While these five issues might indicate that both men and women have a long road to travel before Christ is manifested through the ordained ministries of men and women (signs of the "new creation" in Christ), still the future is hopeful if assessed from today's vantage. It took but ten short years to change the "subordination" of women (maintained for over nineteen hundred years) to a recognition of women's equivalence with men. We may look forward with confidence in the Holy Spirit.

NOTES

1. Historic References used: W. J. O'Shea, "Ordinations in the Roman Rite," in *New Catholic Encyclopedia*, 10, p. 727-734; R. J. Banks, "Jurisdiction, Canon Law," in *N.C.E.*, 6, p. 61-62; S. E. Donlon, "Power of Jurisdiction," in *N.C.E.*, 6, p. 62-63.

2. See W. O'Shea, "Ordinations in the Roman Rite," *op. cit.*, p. 727, 728.

3. *Ibid.*, p. 728, 729.

4. *Ibid.*, p. 729, 730; Also Joseph Lecuyer, C.S. Sp., *What is a Priest?* London, Burns & Oates, 1959, p. 30.

5. *Ibid.*, p. 31.

6. *Ibid.*

7. *Ibid.*, p. 32.

8. *Ibid.*, p. 33.

9. *Ibid.*, p. 42, 43.

10. *Ibid.*, cf. p. 48, 49.

11. *Ibid.*, p. 52; 56-60.

12. *Ibid.*, p. 64-67.

13. See J. Daniélou, "The Ministry of Women," in *La Maison Dieu*, 61(1960), p. 10, 17, 19.

14. *Ibid.*, p. 22, 30, 31.

15. See Robert L. Benson, "Plenitudo Potestatis: Evolution of a Formula," in *Studia Gratiana*, IV, p. 196.

16. Cf. A. M. Stickler, *Ius Canonicum*, XV/29, p. 45-74.

17. S. Donlon, "Power of Jurisdiction," in *N.C.E.*, 6, p. 63.

18. See René van Eyden, "The Place of Women in Liturgical Functions," in *Concilium*, 4(1968), p. 75.

19. Witney J. Oates, ed., *Basic Writings of Saint Augustine*, New York, Random House Publishers, 1948; see "The Confessions," 13:XXXII, p. 253-254.

20. Stanislaus Woywod, ed., *A Practical Commentary on the Code of Canon Law*, New York, Joseph F. Wagner, Inc., 1957, p. 578.

21. Raoul Naz, ed., *Traite de Droit Canonique*, III, p. 230.

22. See Yves Congar, "My Path-Findings in the Theology of the Laity and Ministries," in *The Jurist*, 1972, p. 169-188.

23. Yves Congar, *Lay People in the Church*, Westminster, Maryland, Newman Press, 1965, p. 284.

24. The term "ministers" is not defined in canon law; but commentators tend to limit the term to the diaconate.

25. See especially *Gaudium et Spes*, no. 12 to 22.

26. James O'Connor, ed., *Canon Law Digest*, 7, New York, Bruce Publishing Co., p. 645-652.

27. *Ibid.*, p. 694.

28. See "Pope Paul VI: Women/Balancing Rights and Duties," in *Origins*, Feb. 19, 1976, p. 549-552.

29. See "Biblical Commission Report: Can Women be Priests?" in *Origins*, July 1, 1976, p. 92-96.

30. *Ibid.*, p. 96.

31. See "Women's Ordination: Letters Exchanged by Pope and Anglican Leader," in *Origins*, Aug. 12, 1976, p. 129-132.

32. See *Canon Law Digest*, canon 1573, "Lay Persons on Ecclesiastical Tribunal" (Sig. Apost., 11 July, 1968, Private, p. 929 f.)

33. See *Canon Law Digest*, Supplement through 1974, c. 1342, "Preaching by Lay Persons," S.C. Cler., 20 Nov., 1973, Private, p. 1-4.

Changing Forms of Ministry in the Early Church

HAMILTON HESS

The Catholic Church of the 1970's is beset with a restlessness regarding the expression of its faith, its ways of worship, the patterns of its life and the forms of its ministry. The mood of restlessness is shared to one degree or another by the majority of Christian Churches. Even as this paper is in preparation, the American Episcopal Church has approved in General Convention the ordination of women to the priesthood. The radical significance of this action in the face of twenty centuries of Christian tradition can scarcely be overstressed.

The current restlessness is born of cultural pressures, of a sharpened historical awareness and of changing aspirations of the human spirit. Restlessness leads to change, and change in the Christian community inevitably finds itself in tension with tradition and in potential conflict with principles which are accounted to be essential to the Church's message, mission or self-understanding.

This paper is concerned with changing structures in the Christian community and with changing forms of ministry. Its focal point is not change in the present but change in the past. We are concerned with the process which led to the formation of the ecclesial structures and ministerial forms which we have inherited, with the causes of this process, and with the concepts of the Christian community and ministry that are involved. It is hoped that in considering these matters we may more fully appreciate the issues which presently face us and may be assisted in discerning the principles of community and ministry that should apply. The present paper lays no particular claim to originality. For the most part its purpose is to draw together certain findings and conclusions of modern scholarship as they relate to structure and ministry in the early church.

For the Christian Church, the twentieth century is showing signs of being comparable to the fourth. Both are periods of significant and rapid change, rivaled only by the first century as the foundational period and by the 16th century as the age of the Protestant reform. Seen as the focal point of the somewhat broader time frame of 250 to 500 AD., the fourth century is in many ways one of the most crucial periods in the history of the Christian Church. During this time the classical doctrinal formulations common to East and West received their basic shape, the major liturgical rites were fundamentally established and the organizational structure and ministerial functions of the Christian community assumed the form which has essentially persisted up to the present time.

In terms of position in the community and possibilities for service, the consequences of the fourth century changes in ecclesial structure and ministerial form were immense for lay people in general, and for women in particular. A distinctly clerical class emerged within the community and all ecclesial functions effectively passed into its hands. The fact that the class was male precluded Christian females from even the limited participation in leadership and distinctive service within the community which they had previously exercised.

During the first few centuries the local Christian community was served by a variety of functionaries who together carried forward the total life of the Church. The community believed itself to be the arena of the workings of the Spirit of God, and the operations of leadership and service performed within it were regarded as functional charisms received from the Spirit. Some functions were structured within the community and were recognized by ratification or appointment with the laying on of hands. Some were totally unstructured "happenings" in the Spirit, and some were established functions of service recognized or conferred by forms of appointment less formal than the laying on of hands.

While the later distinctions between "ordained" and "non-ordained" may be meaningfully applied to the first and second groups, they do not apply with any precision at all to the third. For this reason, the concept of ordination must be used with care, for a proper understanding of ecclesial functions in the early Church does not allow a clear distinction to be drawn between the first and third groups, nor for that matter does it disallow an overlap between the first and second groups or the second and the third. It is clear, in fact, that no absolute distinctions can be made.

The first group is composed of bishops, presbyters, and deacons, and is distinguished from other functions both by formality of appointment and by the pre-eminence of leadership which its representatives exercised within the community. It is this group which has been consistently referred to as the threefold "Apostolic ministry" by Catholic and Anglican writers during the past century, with the assertion of its foundation within the Church by Jesus and the Apostles. It need not detract from either the authority nor the antiquity claimed for the group to point out that during the first century it seems impossible to draw firm distinctions between those who were called bishops and those who were called presbyters, that the specific ecclesial functions under these titles had not yet stabilized, and that the diaconate as a formalized function within the community seems to have been established no earlier than about 70 A.D. Furthermore, we may cite two clear examples of overlap between this group and the second group, which for practical purposes may be said to be composed of prophets and confessors. At least in the Church of Antioch during the late first or early second century, a prophet was entitled to preside at the Eucharist in place of the bishop.[1] At Rome in the late second or early third century a confessor who had suffered imprisonment for his faith, was to be admitted to the office of presbyter or deacon without formal ordination.[2]

The third group was by far the largest and was composed of functionaries who were centrally involved in the life of the second and third century community in capacities both subordinate and auxiliary to the liturgical, pastoral, disciplinary and teaching leadership of the bishops, presbyters and deacons. The members of this group are widows, deaconesses, subdeacons, readers, acolytes, healers, and doorkeepers. They are of particular interest to our study, for their ministerial services were gradually assimilated by the clerical class which emerged during the fourth century. The male functionaries, while surviving in name as clerical novices and trainees, ceased to be significant within the life of the community, and the female functionaries disappeared entirely.

We have noted that the concept of "ordination" must be carefully qualified when applied to ministerial functions in the Church of the first three centuries. This does not mean that concepts of ministerial authority were lacking nor that specific operations of the Spirit were not seen to be focussed in particular ministries. Ignatius of Antioch bears clear witness to these concepts in the second decade of the second century. Concerning bishops, presbyters and deacons, he writes,

> I exhort you to strive to do all things in harmony with God: the bishop is to preside in the place of God, while the presbyters are to function as the council of the Apostles, and the deacons, who are most dear to me, are entrusted with the ministry of Jesus Christ.[3]

All authority regarding the liturgical celebration of the Christian mysteries is committed to the bishop:

> It is not permitted without authorization from the bishop either to baptize or to hold an agape; but whatever he approves is pleasing to God. . . . Let that celebration of the Eucharist be considered valid which is held under the bishop or anyone to whom he has committed it.[4]

It has been argued that this Ignation view of ecclesial leadership is anomalously authoritarian and structured for its times. Ignatius may well have been in the vanguard of such developments, but he was not alone, for the Ignatian pattern was already widespread in Syria and Asia Minor and was universally established in the Church within four or five decades of his own time.

Ministry during the first three centuries was, however, understood as a function of service within a spirit filled community in which all members shared in the life of the Spirit, each exercising the particular gifts, or charisms, with which he or she had been endowed. At the end of the second century, Irenaeus is clearly expressive of this understanding as he states,

> "For in the Church," it is said, "God hath set apostles, prophets, teachers," and all the other means through which the Spirit works. . . For where the Church is, there is the Spirit of God; and where the Spirit of God is, there is the Church, and every kind of grace.[5]

The ministries which flow from these gifts are, as St. Paul tells us, "for the equipment of the saints, for the work of ministry, for building up the Body of Christ."[6] Second century models of the Church such as "the high priestly race of God" or the "brotherhood" strongly reflect this notion of communitarian sharing in the gifts and functions of the spirit.

Although there is no articulation of a theology of the conferral of charisms (in later terms, a theology of ordination), the gifts of the spirit in service to the community seem to have been regarded as both given by God and ratified or authenticated by the community within which they were exercised. Authentication took the form of either recognition alone or supplication for the conferral of gifts upon a person who was recognized as having been called to receive them. In certain situations the clear manifestation of a spiritual charism or gift of service is taken as a sign of divine conferral, and no action is taken by the community. This is the case with the healer in Rome in the early third century,[7] and the prophet and the possessor of the gift of knowledge as well as the healer are given the same recognition in a fifth century Syrian document which reflects earlier practice.[8] We have previously noted this recognition of extraordinary gifts in the confessor who had suffered imprisonment, which qualified him for the presbyterate or diaconate without formal appointment. Concerning virgins, the *Apostolic Tradition* of Hippolytus and the *Testament of Our Lord* tell us that "The virgin is not appointed but voluntarily separated and named. A virgin does not have an imposition of hands, for personal choice alone is that which makes a virgin."[9] Clearly, the Church acknowledged that some charisms were regularly conferred directly by God without community action and that others (apparently all with the exception of the episcopate) could be so conferred in circumstances of an extraordinary nature. The divine action was, however, understood normally to take place through the cooperative action of the community.

These concepts are illustrated by the ordination prayers for bishops, presbyters and deacons in the early third century *Apostolic Tradition* of Hippolytus of Rome. The bishop is to be "chosen by all the people," and the appointment is to take place in their presence, "together with the presbytery and such bishops as may attend." The bishops are to lay hands upon the chosen one and "All [the whole assembly] shall keep silence praying in their heart for the descent of the Spirit." Then one bishop "at the request of all" shall lay his hand on the one being ordained and shall pray to the Father:

". . . and now pour forth that Power which is from Thee of 'the princely Spirit' which thou didst deliver to thy Beloved Child Jesus Christ, which he bestowed on the holy Apostles . . . grant upon this thy servant whom thou hast chosen for the episcopate to feed thy holy flock and serve as thine high priest . . . and that by the high priestly Spirit he may have authority to forgive sins according to thy command, to assign lots according to thy bidding . . ."[10]

The prayer for the ordination of the presbyter calls also for the "power which is from thee, of 'the princely Spirit' ", which is in this case identified as the "spirit of grace and counsel, that he may share in the presbyterate and govern thy people in a pure heart."[11] With reference to the deacon, it is stated that "he does not receive the Spirit which is common to the presbyterate" (the "Spirit of seniority" as it is described by the Arabic version of Hippolytus' work found in an Egyptian collection.) The prayer at the deacon's ordination calls upon the Father for "the Holy Spirit of grace and earnestness and diligence upon this thy servant whom thou hast chosen to minister to thy Church."[12]

Three points illustrated by this material call for our attention. First, the bishop, the presbyter and the deacon are regarded as charismatic functionaries in service to the community to which they are appointed, each receiving a different "spirit"; the bishop the "princely spirit" and the "high priestly spirit," the presbyter also the "princely spirit" but uniquely this "spirit of grace and counsel," and the deacon the "spirit of grace and earnestness and diligence," but explicitly not the spirit common to the presbyters. Second, it is stated of the bishop and deacon—and presumably intended with regard to the presbyter also—that the recipient of the Spirit has been chosen by God, although it is clear that in the case of bishops and presbyters the selection has been made by the ecclesial body. The implicit attribution of divine determination to community choice is indicative that election by the community is itself regarded as the exercise of a corporate charism. Third, the function of the bishop "to assign lots according to thy bidding" is a reference to his powers to ordain or to confer charisms according to the divine will. The term *clerus* (Greek *kleros*), or "clergy," which is used in the Apostolic Tradition and elsewhere in reference to major ministerial functionaries, seems to be derived from its use in Acts 1:17, in which this first ministerial appointment of the infant Church, in the person of Matthias, was made by lot (*kleros*), through which the choice of God was made manifest.

The unique importance of each ministry within the community, and the fact that each was understood as the expression of an individual and separate charism is further illustrated by the custom of the direct appointment of persons to ministerial functions, irrespective of other functions that they may or may not have previously exercised, St. Cyprian, for example, was ordained presbyter and later bishop, without having held a lesser ministry. Although it was common practice at Rome to select the bishop from among the deacons, Pope Fabian (d. 250) was a layman at the time of his election. General custom provided for the selection of candidates for the higher ministries from among those who had proven their worthiness by serving the community in lesser capacities, but any notion of progression through an ascending scale of ministries, each possessing the ministerial powers of the one below it, was not only lacking but antithetical to the concept of a multiplicity of distinctive and complementary charisms operative within the Spirit-filled community.

The ministries which have been described had their place within a communitarian ecclesial structure. It has been argued by scholars of the evangelical traditions that the Church of the earliest decades was virtually without structure, and that the original ideal of the Christian community allowed for the unhampered freedom of the charisms of the Spirit. Structure, ministerial offices, and the establishment of a lineage of leadership, it is argued, were false to the unhampered freedom in the spirit by which the Christian movement was characterized.

On the contrary, it would seem that the followers of Jesus very quickly structured their communal life, and that they used the organizational model which was familiar to them as Jews and which would quite naturally be utilized by those who considered their religious movement to be the fulfillment of Judaism and themselves to be the New Israel. Their organizational model was the synagogue congregation under the leadership of a board of elders (presbyters) who were chosen from the membership of the community and who were ultimately responsible for all aspects of its life. While Paul does not mention presbyters in his epistles, the salutation to the bishops at Philippi in Philippians 1:1 is probably a reference to ruling elders, and there is no reason to dispute the account of Paul's farewell address to the presbyters of Ephesus in Acts 20:17. These allusions would indicate an established presbyteral structure in these churches in 60-63 A.D., and as early as 52 A.D. Paul refers to the rulership in the Church at Philippi as "those who are over you in the Lord."

The list of charismatic functionaries which Paul gives in Corinthians 12 (52-55 A.D.), Romans 12 (58 A.D.) and Ephesians 4 (early 60's) are instructive. Not only do we find those gifted with the utterance of wisdom, the utterance of knowledge, faith, healing, miracles, prophecy, distinguishing of spirits, speaking with tongues, the interpretation of tongues, service, exhortation, and financial contribution, but we are also told that there are apostles, evangelists, teachers, helpers, pastors, and administrators. The latter three in particular represent functions of authority and reflect an organizational structure within which the more spontaneous charisms can operate in cooperative interrelationship.

The Church of the first three centuries continued to be characterized by the synagogal structure as well as by the charismatic concept of ministry, but a number of subtle and gradual changes were taking place throughout this period which were in fact preparing the way for a radical shift from the charismatic concept and communitarian structure to a different understanding of ministry and the application of a different organizational model.

Evangelical Christian critics of the "early catholicism" exhibited in the Pastoral Epistles and in the letters of Ignatius of Antioch are correct in their discernment of a gradual crystalization of ecclesiastical offices from an earlier plasticity of function within the Christian community. The eucharistic presidency and sacramental and pastoral ministry which appertained uniquely to the bishop on a universal basis by 150 A.D. had presumably been previously exercised severally among the ruling presbyters of the Christian congregation. The diaconate seems to have been universally established as a formal ministry by 70 A.D., with the drawing together of a number of services, liturgical and otherwise, which had previously been provided by a greater number of persons within the community. The public reading of scripture in the Christian assembly was evidently practised from the beginning of the Church's liturgical life, but it was not until the latter part of the second century that the office of lector became established. The subdeacon, as designated assistant to the deacon, first appears in about 250, as does the acolyte, to whose office a variety of minor liturgical tasks were assimilated.

The trend is clearly one of the upward absorption of ecclesial functions to increasingly prestigious and frequently powerful ministerial offices. By the fourth century, for example, the deacons wielded immense influence as immediate assistants to the bishop. Canon 18 of the Council of Nicea indicates that at least in some regions deacons rivaled presbyters in prestige and honor, and they are bidden to observe the duties and prerogatives of their own station. Common tendencies toward organizational complexification and toward an inflation of the authority of established offices are apparent throughout the pre-Nicene period.

Before we consider other factors leading to the fourth century shifts in ministry and ecclesial structure, it is appropriate to consider the early ministries of deaconesses and widows. Not only do they appertain directly to the theme of this symposium, but in the widow especially we find an example of a communitarian function which grew in prestige as a specific ministry in the second and third centuries and which eventually disappeared as a result of the shifts of the fourth and the fifth.

Both the deaconess and the widow occupied positions and performed functions within the community which were analogous to those of male counterparts but which were at the same time modified in accordance with the generally inferior position of women in contemporary culture. The prestige and functional roles of the female minister seem to have varied from area to area. Such variations presumably resulted from subcultural differences and modifications of custom resulting from local circumstance and the influences exercised by specific personalities.

Women ministers who gave service (*diakonía*) within the community are described as early as c. 58 A.D. in the reference to Phoebe in Romans 16:1. I Timothy 3:11 witnesses to "the women likewise" who with male deacons must be serious, temperate and faithful. The earliest description of the duties of the deaconess are given in chapter 16 of the *Didascalia Apostolorum*, written as a book of ground-rules for a community in Syria in the early third century. The appointment and duties of deacons and deaconesses are treated together. The bishop is instructed: "Those that please thee out of all the people thou shalt choose and appoint as deacons: a man for the performance of most things that are required, but a woman for the ministry of women." Women deacons are to be sent to minister to believing women in pagan households, they are to anoint women in baptism and to instruct women in keeping the baptismal seal, they are to visit the sick and to minister to those in need.[13] Deaconesses seem generally to have shared the deaconal ministry with men except for the functions performed by male deacons in the Eucharist, although certain liturgical duties also were performed by deaconesses in the Nestorian and Monophysite churches of the fifth and sixth centuries. The eighth book of the

Apostolic Constitutions, presumably representing fourth century Syrian practice, gives an ordination prayer for the deaconess which is quite parallel to that for the deacon, and, as with the deacon, she is to be ordained with the laying on of hands in the presence of the presbyters and deacons (and in her case, the deaconesses).[14]

The widowhood seems to have been confined throughout its existence to membership by those who were widows indeed. In I Timothy 5:9-10 it is stated that only those are to be "enrolled" as widows who are sixty years of age or more and well proven in good deeds and piety. Their position in the community is apparently that of worthy and respected recipients of charitable assistance. A century and a half later, the Syrian *Didascalia* shows widows to have taken on a specific role with the community. As elder women of proven character and devotion, they are respected intercessors for those who contribute to their support and for the whole Church. They pray over the sick and also lay hands upon them. Widows are not to curse anyone, "for they have been appointed to bless," and are grouped in this function with the bishop, the presbyters and deacons. However, they are to be subject to the deacons as well as to the bishop, and as with all women (presumably including deaconesses) they are not to teach.[15] The roughly contemporary *Apostolic Tradition* of Hippolytus of Rome speaks of the widow in analagous fashion. She is not to be ordained because she does not have a liturgical ministry. She is "appointed for prayer, and this a function of all Christians."[16] The early fourth century Egyptian *Apostolic Church Order* directs that three widows be appointed, "two to devote themselves to prayer on behalf of all who are tempted, and to revelations to whatever extent is necessary, and one to succour women who are sick."[17]

The details of their position are not as important as the fact that the widows have risen as a class to exercise functional roles within the community which is fundamentally derived from their prestige as its female senior members. This suggests a position analagous to that of the presbyter, and this suggestion is borne out by a number of sources in the third and fourth centuries. Origen, preaching in Palestine during the earlier part of the third century, links bishops, presbyters, deacons and widows as "ecclesiastical dignitaries,"[18] and his contemporary, Tertullian, writing in Roman North Africa groups these four classes of functionaries together as "the clergy."[19]

The fifth century *Testament of Our Lord*, written in Syria, shows the widowhood at the apparent apex of its development. It directs that there are to be thirteen widows "who sit in front," meaning in the seats reserved for the clergy. During the celebration of the Eucharist they are to stand "immediately behind the presbyters on the left side of the bishop," while the deacons stand behind the presbyters on the right hand side of the bishop. The *Testament* provides an ordination prayer for the widow in which it is asked that God may send the "spirit of strength upon this thy servant and strengthen her in your truth, that fulfilling your precepts and laboring in your sanctuary, she may be an honorable vessel"; further on in the same prayer it is asked, "give to her, Lord, the spirit of humility, virtue, patience and kindness, that taking up your yoke with unspeakable joy she may persevere in her work."[20] Her "work" is described in the *Testament* as prayer and spiritual ministry and leadership among the women.

The widow's role is significantly parallel to that of the presbyter. Both are the elder spiritual dignitaries of the Christian community, and it is from this that their ministries derive. As we shall note below, the presbyter's function did not inherently involve a liturgical or sacramental ministry, although he increasingly exercised these roles during the third century. Similarly, the widow is frequently found to be performing duties of the deaconess, such as assisting at the baptism of women, but these are not associated with the charisms of the Spirit which are given to her. The presbyter leads through governance and has an overall responsibility for the welfare of the Christian community. The widow leads through prayer and has an overall responsibility for the women of the congregation. She is the "altar of God"[21] to the community, fulfilling a ministry of prayer and Christian example. The roles of both the presbyter and the widow will disappear as the Church takes on a new organizational structure.

We have noted the gradual upward absorption of ecclesial functions during the pre-Nicene period from an initially broad base of participation within the Christian community to a relatively small number of officially designated ministers. This is one of the preparatory factors underlying the shifts of the fourth century. Other factors must be discussed as well.

The first of these is the gradual decline of the sense of the charismatic which is evidenced from the early second century onward. The magnificent statement of Irenaeus quoted above concerning the Spirit in the Church is paralleled by other late second and third century writers, but the Church of the second century lacked the sense of the dynamism of the Spirit in the community that is present in the first, and this decline is even more evident in the third. Enthusiasm and spontaneity within the Christian movement inevitably became tempered with time, and the discernment of authentic manifestations of the Spirit became a problem.[22] The Montanist movement in the late second century was partially a revivalist trend which was attempting to recapture the spiritual enthusiasm of earlier decades. Ironically, Montanism itself caused the further suppression and institutionalization of the Spirit as the main stream of Christianity reacted against its excesses.

The diminished sense of the dynamic presence of the Spirit within the Christian community inevitably led to a shift of attention from the charisms expressed in its varied ministries to the ministries themselves, and from the Spirit whose charisms they were to the offices within which they were exercised. Ministry gradually came to be viewed as a function of the Church rather than as a function of the Spirit who chooses his own functionaries as he wills, both through the action of the community and independently from it. In the middle of the third century Cyprian develops a theology of the episcopate considerably beyond that of Ignatius when he writes:

> Thence have come down to us in course of time and by due succession the ordained office of the bishop and the constitution of the Church, forasmuch as the Church is founded upon the bishops and every act of the Church is subject to these rulers.[23]

Here the continued existence of the Church itself becomes dependent upon the episcopate. Cyprian further expresses the notion of the episcopate as a foundational office when he states, "The episcopate is one, each part of which is held by each one for the whole."[24] The theological model of ministry has been altered from operational charisms within a Spirit filled community to the exercise of the ministry of Jesus Christ by delegation from those whom he has sent. This was certainly not a new idea,[25] but in becoming the dominant model it provides a theological foundation for the hierarchical structuring of ministerial offices in the century to follow.

The growth of the Church's membership and the spread of Christianity from the cities and larger towns to the smaller towns and villages during the latter part of the third and early fourth centuries brought conditions which resulted in rapid organizational change. In the Church of the second and third centuries, each local congregation was led by its own bishop and college of presbyters. The bishop was the celebrant of the Eucharist and sacraments, and this ministry was not normally shared by presbyters, who had their own specific functions of governance. There is evidence for the occasional celebration of the Eucharist by presbyters in the bishop's absence, but this seems to have been by specific delegation rather than by prerogative of office.[26] As daughter churches began to multiply in the regions surrounding the original Christian communities, bishops were appointed to preside over them. In both Asia Minor and in the West in the early fourth century we hear of "country bishops" and the problems connected with them.

The alternative which was rapidly adopted in both East and West was the delegation of presbyters on a regular basis to serve as eucharistic and sacramental ministers, and soon as permanent pastors in the outlying congregations. This entailed radical changes in organizational structure and ministerial function. The presbyter was no longer a ruling elder within a community exercising his own unique function and the bishop was no longer the pastor of a single flock. The presbyter was a delegate of the bishop exercising the bishop's ministry, and the bishop lost his personal relationship with his people and became the ruler of a diocese. The presbyter, who had been an "elder of the people" within the congregation was not replaced, except perhaps by a brief experiment in North Africa under the title "Senior of the Church."

These changes took place rapidly in some localities and more gradually in others, but the evidences provided by fourth century synods and councils indicate that they were universally in progress during the first half of the century. The canons of several synods of the period bear witness to the presbyter celebrant,[27] and canons 6 and 15 of the Council of Sardica assume the existence of parishes in which a presbyter is resident as pastor. Canon 6 which deals with the problem of "country bishops," forbids the ordination of bishops for communities in which presbyters would suffice. Presbyter pastors are also presumed by canons 47, 49, 50, 52 and 58 of the spurious series known as the "Canons of the Apostles," which was composed in the East during the latter half of the fourth century.

The functions and position of the deacon and the lesser ministers within the community were affected in turn by the new roles of the bishop and the presbyter. The deacon, having been the chief assistant to the bishop, now undergoes a two-fold transition as he either moves upward with the bishop and becomes a diocesan administrator or remains an assistant in the parish community in service under the presbyter-priest. In both cases the importance of the diaconate diminished. The positions of diocesan administrators, while frequently retaining the diaconal title (e.g. the cardinal deacons of Rome), gradually became filled by presbyter-priests, and the deacons in the parishes lost considerable prestige.

The Church of the fourth century found itself in a new situation following the legalization of Christianity by Constantine in 313. Political freedom for Christians within the Empire brought theological disputes into the market place and created a need for mechanisms for their resolution on a regional or global basis. A rapid growth of the Church's membership with the influx of large numbers of social and political converts lowered the level of Christian commitment and the degree of popular participation in the life of the Church and accelerated the emergence of a distinctly clerical class. The changing roles of bishops and presbyters called for new structures of leadership. The manipulation of the Church by the imperial power brought internal problems and tensions which called for centralized leadership and mechanisms for dealing with rival factions. The structure of the Church of the first three centuries, as a loosely knit association of functionally independent communities, was inadequate in face of these new demands.

A new ecclesial model was ready at hand in the institutions of the Roman state. The imperial model was not chosen as a consciously deliberated alternative, but its organizational forms were spontaneously adopted and modified in relation to the particular and urgent needs of the Church. As city pastors with responsibility for a family of flocks, the newly emerging diocesan bishops became the counterparts of city magistrates. The bishops of provincial capitals became metropolitan bishops with recognized authority over the bishops of the province[28] as counterparts of the provincial governor. A similar development in the hierarchicalization of structure is seen in the emergence of patriarchal jurisdiction,[29] and the development of the papal office during the fourth and fifth centuries was significantly influenced by the application of the same model.[30] The new model also fostered an understanding of ecclesial authority in terms of binding jurisdiction in contrast to the charismatic, morally suasive leadership of the earlier centuries. The agreements reached at the synods and councils of the fourth and fifth centuries gradually came to be regarded as ecclesial law, and were gathered together into a corpus analagous to the imperial civil code. The synods and councils themselves were a form of governance significantly influenced by the Roman senate and its provincial parallels.

The new ecclesial structure was essentially vertical. The functionaries within it were interrelated in a chain of command in which appointment to office tended to be upward from the lowest to the highest. In contrast to the earlier mode of appointment by which office holders were appointed directly to the function which they were to exercise, canon 13 of the Council of Sardica (343) directs that no man shall be appointed bishop unless he has passed successively through the offices of reader, deacon and presbyter and has been found worthy. During the fourth century the readership in both East and West became a probationary office for young aspirants to higher ranks in the ministry.

The crystalization of a vertically structured hierarchical ministry accelerated the upward absorption of ecclesial functions and also assisted in creating a chasm between clergy and people which had not existed in earlier centuries. Whereas formerly the term *laos* had appertained to the whole people of God as a term of dignity, it now became a term distinguishing the common Christian from the *kleros*, or clergy, with whom the active affairs of the Church were exclusively identified. Although popular suffrage in the election of bishops was suppressed with difficulty, the trend toward suppression is clear in canons 19 and 23 of Antioch (330), which introduce the provincial synod as the appointing body, and in canon 13 of Laodicea which directs that "the election of those who are to be appointed to the priesthood is not to be committed to the multitude." Canon 44 of Laodicea forbids women to go to the altar, and canon 69 of the Council "in Trullo" at Constantinople two centuries later (692) forbids lay men as well to enter the sanctuary or to teach.

Canon 11 of Laodicea prohibits the appointment of "presbytides" or "female presidents" in the churches. The meaning is obscure, but it is probably expressive of the general movement toward the suppression of the widow as female counterpart to the presbyter. The office of deaconess was ordered to be suppressed by the Councils of Epaon (517) and Orleans (533) in the West, but survived with respect somewhat longer in the East. The ordination of deaconesses is mentioned, for instance, in canon 14 of the Council "in Trullo," but is also associated with the monastic life in canon 48 of the same council. The future of women's roles in the active life of the Church was soon to be confined entirely to the monastery in both East and West.

The fourth century changes in the structures of the Church and forms of its ministry were brought about by internal conditions and external pressures which demanded rapid resolution. The Church's response to the situation was in certain ways tremendously successful, but success was procured at a price which is still being paid. The emergence of an all male, vertically structured clerical class which became the official Church has resulted in the exclusion from meaningful and effective ministry those members of the People of the Spirit, both female and male, whose charisms of service could have immeasurably enriched the life of the Christian community and enhanced its mission during the centuries to follow. Our own century is a time of reappraisal and it will undoubtedly be a time of further change in response to the pressures of our own age. It is hoped that we may be assisted in the tasks which we will face by the Spirit of perspective, of insight and of responsibility to the whole people of God and to the community of humankind.

NOTES

1. *Didache* 10
2. Hippolytus, *Apostolic Tradition*, 10
3. *Magnesians*, 6
4. *Smyrneans*, 8
5. *Adversus Haereses*, 3.24.1

6. Ephesians, 4:12
7. Hippolytus, *Apostolic Tradition* 15
8. *Testament of O.L.*, 47
9. Quotation from *Apostolic Tradition*, 13; See *Testament of Our Lord* I.46
10. Chapters 2 and 3
11. Chapter 8
12. Chapter 9
13. Chapter 16
14. Chapters 17-20
15. Chapter 15
16. Chapter 11
17. Chapter 21
18. *Homily on Luke* 17
19. *On Monogamy* 11.1,4; 12.1
20. Book 2, Chapter 41
21. Polycarp, *Philippians* 4; *Didascalia* 15
22. See I John 4:1 and *Didache* 11
23. *Epistle* 33.1
24. *On the Unity of the Church* 5
25. See Clement of Rome, I *Corinthians* 42 and 44; also Irenaeus, *Adversus Haereses* 3.3.1.
26. Presbyters under Cyprian celebrated the Eucharist for confessors in prison. Cyprian, *Epistle* 5.2; *Epistle* 34.1. Ignatius allows that the bishop may entrust the celebration of the Eucharist to others.
27. Canon 1 of Ancyra (312); canon 19 of Neoceasarea (c. 315); canon 4 of Gangra (341); canon 6 of Sardica (343), canons 10 and 11 of the African Code.
28. See for example canon 4 of Nicaea (325); canons 16, 19, and 20 of Antioch (330); canons 6, 9 and 14 of Sardica; canons 17 and 19 of the African Code; and canon 19 of Chalcedon (451).
29. See canon 6 of Nicaea, canon 3 of Constantinople (381), and canon 28 of Chalcedon.
30. Canons 3, 4, and 7 of Sardica recognize the bishop of Rome as the highest authority for purposes of appeal.

Tradition, Hermeneutics, and Ordination

FRANCINE CARDMAN

In what is now very familiar history, Archbishop Joseph Bernardin, President of the National Conference of Catholic Bishops, in advance of the Ordination Conference held in Detroit in November, 1975, declared that, "Throughout its history the Catholic Church has not ordained women to the priesthood. Although many of the arguments presented in times gone by on this subject may not be defensible today, there are compelling reasons for this practice."[1] The most compelling reasons that Archbishop Bernardin could find to cite were those offered in a 1972 report from the NCCB Committee on Pastoral Research and Practices entitled "Theological Reflections on the Ordination of Women."[2] According to this report, revelation is made known both by Tradition and Sacred Scripture (understood as two distinct entities); any theological reflection, therefore, on the ordination of women must "look to the life and practice of the Spirit-guided Church." The "constant practice and tradition" of that church (i.e., the Catholic Church) "has excluded women from the episcopal and priestly office." This "constant practice and tradition of the Catholic Church against the ordination of women, interpreted . . . as divine law, is of such a nature as to constitute a clear teaching of the Ordinary Magisterium of the Church." Although the 1972 report concedes the possibility of a "contrary theological development," it by no means considers this likely. Constant practice and tradition are seen as holding the day.

What then is to be done about the growing conviction—a conviction that is theological, ecclesiological, sociological, and even political/cultural in its basis—that women not only can be but in fact are being called to the priesthood in the Roman Catholic Church? What is to be made of the recent decision of the Episcopal Church in the United States at its General Convention in Minneapolis to ordain women to the priesthood? What, finally, does "constant practice and tradition" mean? How is it to be recognized historically and how is it to be interpreted in the present historical situation in which the church finds itself today?

In examining the possibility of the ordination of women to the priesthood in the Roman Catholic Church today, several areas of theological reflection and historical interpretation must be taken into account. Accordingly, this paper will investigate first the meaning of "tradition" in its various senses, asking not only about the distinction between these senses, but also about the ways in which tradition is shaped and handed on. The hermeneutics necessary for understanding tradition in any contemporary situation will then be explored. And finally the question of the ordination of women will be taken up in light of the historical-theological considerations already offered.

I. THE MEANINGS OF TRADITION

In order to ascertain what the "constant practice and tradition of the Catholic Church" both is and means, it is necessary first to define the terms of the discussion, particularly the sensitive and difficult term "tradition." Only when the various senses of this term have been carefully distinguished is it possible to proceed to an inquiry into the significance of the historical facts of church practice and teaching and the means of arriving at an understanding of these facts as they relate to the present life of the church, particularly in regard to the question of the ordination of women.

There are numerous ways in which one might go about defining "tradition," but the most profitable of these are reflected in two recent studies which might, for the sake of convenience be labelled as Catholic and "ecumenical." The first is the lengthy historical and theological work of Yves Congar, *Tradition and Traditions: An Historical Essay and a Theological Essay.*[3] The second is the fruit of a long process of ecumenical consultation and study by the Faith and Order Commission of the World Council of Churches. The end product of that process (though by no means the end of the discussion) is the report from Section II of the Fourth World Conference on Faith and Order (Montreal, 1963) on "Scripture, Tradition and Traditions."[4] Neither study is entirely satisfactory in itself, but when taken together and placed in the context of other contemporary discussions, it is possible to come to a sense of the question that approximates a theological consensus. It is necessary to distinguish between Tradition, tradition (or apostolic tradition), and traditions. The familiar but imprecise distinction between "Scripture and tradition" would fall under the category of tradition on this analysis.

Some Definitions

Tradition is the Gospel itself, transmitted from generation to generation in and by the church. It is, in a sense, Christ himself present through the Holy Spirit in the life of the church.[5] This understanding of the centrality of the Gospel is reflected in the opening verses of Paul's letter to the Christians at Rome (Rom. 1:1-6):

> Paul, a servant of Jesus Christ, called to be an apostle and set apart for the gospel of God, which he promised beforehand through his prophets in the holy scriptures, the gospel concerning his Son, who was descended from David according to the flesh and designated Son of God in power according to the Spirit of holiness by his resurrection from the dead, Jesus Christ our Lord, through whom we have received grace and apostleship to bring about the obedience of faith for the sake of his name among all the nations, including yourselves, who are called to belong to Jesus Christ.

It is this same gospel, the Tradition of Jesus Christ in the Church, of which Paul can say (Rom. 1:16), "I am not ashamed of the gospel: it is the power of God for salvation to everyone who has faith, to the Jew first and also to the Greek." Further, "in it the righteousness of God is revealed through faith for faith" (Rom. 1:17).

Thus Congar can conclude that there are two aspects to the gospel, a *noetic* aspect that gives knowledge and a *dynamic* aspect that produces an effect.[6] The Gospel that is the power of God for salvation by means of faith is therefore the reality which the First Vatican Council identifies as the *salutiferem redemptionis opus*.[7] On this view it is also possible to say simply that "the Gospel is Jesus Christ" and is present when Christ is present through the Holy Spirit and actively communicating his life.[8] Tradition, then, is restricted to the meaning of the whole Gospel and its transmission in the church; it is the *paradosis* of what R. Geiselmann refers to as the Word, and it comes close to what J. Ratzinger identifies as revelation.[9]

In distinction to Tradition, the meaning of *tradition* without a capital embraces what is often referred to as "apostolic tradition." The Montreal report leaves a gap here when it defines tradition simply as the traditionary process and traditions as the varieties of expression of Tradition or the various confessional traditions.[10] The emphasis on the traditionary process is well placed, certainly, for the very historicity of human experience binds everything up in tradition in this sense, making it difficult to distinguish the process from that which it hands on (Tradition).[11] The gap in the understanding of tradition offered by the Montreal report is due in part to the tendency (never fully realized) to equate Tradition with the Scriptural and written word. It results as well in a relegation of everything included under "traditions" to the realm of the relative and the relatively

unimportant, thus failing to convey fully the complexity of the relationship between Tradition and its expressions in the church's history
through the traditionary process. In order to reflect both the historical situation and the reality in which the Tradition is still experienced today, it
is necessary to define an intermediate sense of "tradition" that would fall
between the terms of the Montreal analysis.

To speak of *tradition* in the lower case is thus to speak of the apostolic tradition and to make an essential connection between tradition and
Tradition. This connection is well expressed by Congar's broad sense of
tradition as being both a) the act of transmitting and b) the content which
is thus transmitted (passive or objective tradition).[12] To define tradition in
this manner is to embrace and in a certain sense overcome the familiar
distinction between Scripture and tradition. (Because this distinction is so
familiar, however, reference to it cannot always be avoided, except at the
expense of being incomprehensible; but whenever it is referred to in this
restricted sense it will be enclosed in quotation marks.)

For the sake of clarity it is perhaps better to think of tradition as the
traditionary process as it manifests itself in the apostolic tradition; this apostolic tradition in turn consists of both Scripture and what has been fa-
miliarly and inexactly referred to as "tradition." The primary sense of
tradition that is important here is the fullness of the apostolic tradition. It
corresponds generally to Congar's widest sense of apostolic tradition,
namely "everything the Apostles have passed on to help the people of God
to live in the truth of the divine covenant relationship sprung from Jesus
Christ."[13]

Within the tradition, it is the scriptural witness to Tradition that
holds pride of place.[14] Although it springs from tradition (i.e., from the
handing on of the oral testimony of the Apostles which is then written
down and handed on), in its final written state Scripture possesses a normative value in relation to all subsequent tradition. There is, as Congar
maintains, "an absolute normative value" to the Scriptures,[15] for they are
the formulation of the church's *paradosis* and are given to the church so
that it might preserve the Gospel (i.e., Tradition).[16]

Taken in its more common and less precise sense, "tradition" is often
related to Scripture in such a way that it includes everything else (other
than the Scriptures) which comes from the apostles. Under this somewhat
truncated sense of "tradition" fall several meanings isolated by Congar: the
usage and reading of Scripture from the viewpoint of the Christian mystery—i.e., Scripture read christologically, ecclesiologically, and eschatolog-
ically; the meaning given to the realities transmitted within the group or
community which is committed to share them (especially eucharist and
baptism); and, though it is always linked to Scripture, dogma understood

as the attempt to understand the Tradition as conveyed by the Scriptures and the church's life.[17] Even on this understanding, Scripture and "tradition" are in actuality quite closely related. They are, in fact, but two aspects of the same reality, namely the tradition in its broadest and most useful sense. Thus Scripture and "tradition" are significant realities only in the context of the church. Scripture, "tradition" and church are inseparably related; apart from each other they are insufficient and even, Congar admits, inconsistent.[18]

Much of the earlier Protestant-Catholic polemic about the relationship of "Scripture and tradition" can be resolved by distinguishing the various senses of Tradition and tradition. To make these distinctions is also to enter more deeply into the church's historical tradition (taken here in its non-technical sense), which has generally held a more unified view of the relation of Scripture, "tradition" and church than either of the polemical positions formulated during the Reformation controversy.[19] By distinguishing more carefully than has previously been done in the context of controversy, it is possible to leap the horns of the "Scripture-tradition" dilemma by seeing it for what it is: a false dilemma. The old terms of debate are thereby rendered meaningless or at least no longer relevant.

In addition to Tradition and tradition (the latter in the more inclusive sense in which I have defined it), it is possible and perhaps helpful to use the term *traditions* to indicate other aspects of the church's life that have not been covered explicitly by the other terms. These would include particularly the traditions of ecclesiastical disciplines, institutions, liturgical customs, and so on—those things that Congar refers to as "monuments."[20] In a subsidiary sense one could also speak of confessional traditions, as does the Montreal report, but clarity would be aided by use of some other term, perhaps "denomination" or simply "confession."

To understand the distinctions between Tradition, tradition, and traditions suggested here is also to reflect more accurately the complexity of the relationship between Tradition and tradition and the difficulty encountered in attempting to make clear-cut distinctions between the two in any given historical situation. Tradition can only be expressed in tradition, that is, in the traditionary process that hands on the message and eventuates in the written Scriptures preserved and interpreted in the life of the church. Scripture has a privileged position both in the traditionary process and in relation to the Tradition, though it is not itself simply identical with that Tradition.[21] The relationship of other aspects of tradition to Traditions is somewhat more ambiguous. This ambiguity results from the fact that Tradition itself is not an isolated reality but is the Gospel of Jesus Christ made present in the Church by the Holy Spirit, that is, the Tradition is made known only in the context of the historical life of the church in which the traditionary process occurs and the tradition is lived.[22] Because the church itself exists only in the context of culture, a further element of ambiguity is added to the Tradition-tradition relationship. The church is in continuous interaction with its culture and this interaction occurs in continuously changing ways. In its efforts to express the Tradition, tradition must find different forms suitable to changing historical situations.

The relationship between the Tradition and its expression in the tradition is therefore a subtle one; clear lines of demarcation between the two cannot be drawn. Some elements of the tradition (aside from Scripture) are in closer relationship to the Tradition than others. Some elements shift in and out of relationship to the Tradition, approaching it more or less directly depending on the historical context. Even those aspects of tradition that at one time might seem closest to the Tradition can in principle change their relationship to it. They can certainly, at the least, change the forms of their expression, and in this respect, as Schillebeeckx observes, they also change their relation to Tradition.[23]

An Image

As a means of visualizing the relationship between Tradition and tradition, a relationship which is at once both complex and flexible, the amoeba suggests itself as a helpful image. Like all metaphors, it is imprecise—no strict analogy between the two objects of contemplation is envisaged—yet it can perhaps convey a sense of what is involved in the ambiguity of relationship between Tradition and tradition.

An amoeba is a one-celled organism consisting of protoplasm and membrane organized by and around a nucleus. The amoeba itself has no definite shape but changes its form as it moves through its environment (its "culture"), extending pseudopods in one direction or another; it can also engulf and digest other organisms in its environment. What is most significant about the amoeba is a trait that it shares with other cells: simple substances can pass back and forth across its semi-permeable membrane by a process of osmosis. To exist at all in its environment, then, the amoeba must have some basic substances in common with its culture—it could not exist in an acid medium, for instance. Other substances capable of passing through the membrane may be present in varying concentrations in the environment and in the protoplasm. But when the concentration of one of these substances outside the amoeba reaches a critical level, the laws of osmosis take effect and that substance tends to pass into the protoplasm in order to equalize concentrations on both sides of the membrane. The reverse process also holds. Because the membrane is, as a result of genetic (i.e. nuclear) determination, semi-permeable, there is a kind of natural selectivity in regard to what may or may not enter the amoebic protoplasm.

The point of this elementary biology lesson is simple and, I hope, by now obvious. The church is brought into being and maintained in being by its organizing nucleus, the Tradition. This nucleus, however, is not an independent entity capable of existing by itself; rather, it is dependent on the surrounding protoplasm for its continued existence. The forms which the church takes can (and have) changed as it carries the Christian faith through its historical environment. The metaphor breaks down somewhat at this point, or at least has to do double duty. In the first place, the passage of substances back and forth across the membrane suggests the way in which tradition and traditions can move in and out of relationship to the Tradition, assuming a position nearer to or farther away from the nucleus. In the second place this process of osmosis also suggests the way in which tradition and culture, hence also Tradition and culture, are related. When the concentration of a "substance" in the culture reaches the critical point—say, for instance, the demand for the abolition of slavery (disregarding for now the ultimate origin of the impulses that have led to this demand)—then this cultural "substance" must pass into the church. Likewise, if the concentration of such a "substance" is high in the church but no longer so in the culture, it must pass out of the church and be dispersed into the environment. The nucleus of the amoeba determines the selectivity of its membrane, which will not permit harmful substances to pass through it by any natural process. The Tradition performs a similar function for the church. Because of human freedom and sinfulness, however, the exclusion of essentially alien and harmful substances is not as "mechanically" guaranteed as with the amoeba. Yet for the church there is a far more important guarantee at work: the divine promise that ultimately the gates of hell would not prevail against it. Though at times the church may be more culture-bound than others, it will never finally so lose its identity as to betray the Tradition.

Tradition and the Church

The church exists to embody the Tradition, which is the constitutive factor of its identity. It is called into existence as a community and maintained in existence by the common memory and common hope (the Tradition) in which all its members share and which they attempt to realize both individually and collectively.[24] The Tradition from which the church derives and in which it lives surpasses all expressions of it, even Scripture itself. It is a *mystery* that transcends all attempts to express it and which continually calls the church (and all humanity) to the future fulfillment of that mystery. While Tradition is normative, tradition is relative. Although the Tradition is finally mystery, it is nevertheless conveyed to us in and through the relative. To the extent that the divine absolute is made known, it is made known through the relativity of human history. Therefore tradition is authoritative for the church's life, though never in an absolute way. Because the fulfillment of the promise of the mystery is in the future, it is important that there be a place in which that promise is presently being made known. Therefore, changing historical situations are significant: the proclamation of the Gospel—the Tradition in the church—will take on different forms in different situations, even though every form will finally fall short of the promise until the time of its fulfillment. The Tradition must be continually reappropriated, reformulated and reconceptualized in terms that can speak to present situations. New responsibilities for actualization of the Tradition in the tradition always remain open as long as the historical life of the church continues.

There is a certain amount of discontinuity in this conception, since history makes for discontinuity, but even in what seems to be radical discontinuity the absolute or the divine (the Tradition) is made present. It is Tradition itself that provides the continuity, bridging the gulf between past and present and looking to that future in which the saving work of redemption is fulfilled.[25]

Change across the whole spectrum of tradition is not only possible but necessary on this view—and necessary precisely in order to remain faithful to the Tradition. Change in traditions, practice, interpretation of dogma, and interpretation of Scripture are all theoretically conceivable and have in fact taken place throughout the church's history. Consider only a few examples. Perhaps the most dramatic example of change in the history of the church is the Gentile mission: in its radical discontinuity not only with Judaism but with the previous understanding and practice of the Christian community, it has few rivals; yet it nevertheless represents continuity by virtue of its faithful response to the Tradition that calls all persons to its promise. The understanding of the impossibility of a further forgiveness of sins after baptism (except by martyrdom) gave way to the possibility of one additional repentance, and finally of many. Cyprian was mistaken about the sacramental understanding of baptism and ultimately his views had to be corrected by Augustine, who was himself wide of the mark in regard to predestination but to the point about grace. The development of a sacramental system of seven sacraments and the theological rationale for it were hardly straight-forward. The dogma of the Immaculate Conception represents an obvious change and correction of most of the previous theological reflection on the subject, though it was somehow in touch with at least the piety of the faithful. In the realm of discipline and practice, examples could be multiplied well beyond necessity. Consider only the questions of communion in both kinds or Mass in the vernacular. And in that shadowy area where doctrine and discipline interact, consider the halting progress of demands for clerical celibacy as revealed in church orders, canons, and decrees of Popes.[26]

The only real constant in "tradition and practice" has been change.[27] Yet change in the church is never for novelty's sake, but for the sake of the realization of the Tradition in the Spirit-guided life of the church. Because the relationship between Tradition and tradition is seldom unambiguous, change is not to be undertaken hastily or haphazardly. It is in helping to discern and direct the course of change that the magisterium has its particular importance in the church's life.

Magisterium, however, is not simply to be equated with the teaching office of Pope or bishop in either its infallible or its ordinary exercise. The reduction of the concept of magisterium to this hierarchical and jurisdictional teaching office is the result of a theory of tradition that originated with Roman theologians in the last half of the nineteenth century and was widely taught in the first half of the twentieth.[28] Aside from an unfortunate identification of magisterium and tradition (and with the limited understanding of tradition that it entailed), this theory is responsible for separating the work and authority of bishops from that of theologians, to the point that the latter are virtually ignored in the teaching functions of the church. It would be more reflective of the historical reality, and more helpful in the church's present situation to speak, as Dulles does, of two magisteria, that of pastors and that of theologians, complementary and mutually corrective.[29] Neither of these magisteria, however, has significance apart from the full life of the church, including the *sensus fidelium*. For this reason Dulles urges that magisterial statements should "ordinarily express what is already widely accepted in the church, at least by those who have studied the matter in question."[30]

Because most changes or developments in doctrine, dogma, or interpretation need to receive confirmation at some point by the magisterium if they are to be fully incorporated into the life of the church, it is important to have a clear understanding of what constitutes magisterium. But even with a more adequate conception of magisterium, the problem of change and reinterpretation remains: how is the church to interpret its tradition in light of new questions and new situations? To ask this is to raise the question of hermeneutics.

II. HERMENEUTICS

It is in the tradition—in the historical church guided by the Holy Spirit—that the Tradition is proclaimed and handed on. Although Tradition is apprehended in tradition (however partial and incomplete this apprehension may be), the manner of its apprehension is by no means immediate or direct. Rather, the tradition and particularly its Scriptural witness must be grasped and interpreted in each new situation. Although interpretation need not be done *de novo* in every historical moment, a certain degree of critical reflection is required in any appropriation of the Scriptures or any other aspect of the tradition. The process of interpretation presents a hermeneutical question: how and by what principles can the gap between text and reader be bridged?[31] In regard to Scripture, a generally accepted hermeneutical understanding already exists.[32] But in regard to the other aspects of tradition, there is as yet no common hermeneutical understanding. Many of the elements for constructing a hermeneutics of tradition or history are already at hand, however, in the work that has been done on the interpretation of dogmatic and magisterial statements by Rahner, Schillebeeckx, Dulles and others.[33] What I propose to do is to expand the inquiry which they have begun and ask about the interpretation of tradition in both its inclusive and its restricted sense.

Because hermeneutics is generally understood to relate to the interpretation of texts, its use in regard to Scripture and even to dogmatic or magisterial statements is readily understood. But in order to speak of a "hermeneutics of history" (Schillebeeckx's formulation) or a hermeneutics of tradition, it is necessary to extend the notion of "text" so that it refers to the traditionary process (in both its aspects—as that which is handed on, and the process of handing on) and the efforts, whether past or present, to interpret and understand it.[34] Since a text is "a document whose real meaning can only be understood beyond its literal meaning,"[35] any present understanding of tradition must go beyond mere literal repetition of words or practices.[36]

The question of interpretation is also unavoidably a question about the significance of culture. As the sociologists of knowledge have made clear, reality is to a large extent "socially constituted." That is, our subjective perceptions of reality are given coherence and structured into an "objective" universe by our language, our social values, and our norms. Reality is thus experienced and perceived in and through culture: knowledge is, in its broadest sense, socially defined.[37] Both the message which the church proclaims (the Tradition) and the means by which it proclaims and perpetuates it (the tradition) are therefore intimately related to culture, although, given the transcendental or divine aspect of the Tradition, neither it nor tradition are ever identical with culture. Because the Tradition is conveyed in tradition, there must be a continual reinterpretation of this tradition in light of the present hermeneutical situation. The way in which tradition understands and expresses the Tradition must change with changing historical situations, or otherwise the same thing (the Tradition) would not continue to be understood.[38]

In formulating and applying a hermeneutics of tradition, the extremes to be avoided are an excessive reliance on either the past or the present. K. E. Skydsgaard, in a World Council of Churches study on "Tradition as an Issue in Contemporary Theology," characterizes the extremes of scriptural interpretation (which apply equally well to the interpretation of tradition) as either fundamentalist or illuminationist.[39] Dulles describes the extremes in regard to the interpretation of dogma (again, equally applicable to tradition) as either archaist or evolutionist.[40] He also takes note of the tension between past and present as the locus of interpretation when he observes that the lack of equation between the Word of God and the words of man frees us from the limitations of any cultural period: "the present liberates us from the tyranny of the past, the past from idolatry of the present."[41] And Schillebeeckx stresses the value of an openness to the future that will not permit the present to be the only significant moment (contra the Bultmannian existentialist view which "de-eschatologizes history" by regarding the present as the eschaton).[42] At the same time, however, he also insists that a proper emphasis on the present as the locus for understanding a text precludes any attempt simply to retreat into historical reconstruction or return to an original period.[43] Another way of putting what all these views seek to convey is to say that the present and the past are given significance—i.e., interpreted—by the future. For the Christian, then, as Schillebeeckx asserts, the "eschatological kerygma of Christ" is a constant that cannot be superseded.[44] Yet that kerygma is made known only in the tradition, hence the past is significant; the tradition is always appropriated in the present, hence the significance of the present hermeneutical situation. One can conclude with Schillebeeckx that "a present-day understanding in faith cannot take place outside this dialogue with Scripture and the whole tradition of faith."[45]

The hermeneutical process thus has the double thrust of viewing both past and present critically. This twofold aspect of a hermeneutics of tradition is described by Schillebeeckx as consisting of *demythologizing* (i.e., demolishing earlier structures of truth) and then *mythologizing* (or re-mythologizing, i.e. constructing new concepts).[46] His analysis of the hermeneutical process applies to the appropriation of tradition in general as well as it does to the interpretation of dogma. It is similar also to P. Ricoeur's delineation of a "hermeneutics of suspicion" or demystification and a "hermeneutics of restoration" or reappropriation.[47] In the process of faithful listening to the tradition, one undergoes what Ricoeur terms an "ascesis of reflection," which by the "extreme iconoclasm" of allowing itself to be "dispossessed of the origin of meaning" makes possible the "restoration of meaning."[48] The restored meaning is not identical with the original text or (in Ricoeur's terminology) symbol; but it is not finally discontinuous with it either, for the second meaning resides somehow in the first.[49]

In terms of Tradition and tradition, the newly reappropriated meaning of tradition that the hermeneutic process makes possible remains in touch with the Tradition that guarantees all meaning and all continuity, even in the face of apparent discontinuity. "Orthodoxy" is thus understood as the living interpretation of the promise (the Tradition) as it has been realized in the past (the tradition), and it becomes the "basis of orthopraxis."[50] In this sense interpretation is the "hermeneutics of praxis."[51] What can be expected from this is that "God will be in the future as he was in the past and is now, always unexpected."[52]

What, then, of the ordination of women in the Roman Catholic Church?

III. Women and Ordination

If by the power of the Holy Spirit the Gospel of Jesus Christ is made present in the church—if Tradition is expressed and responded to in tradition—then it is necessary to consider the possibility that the current crisis of priestly ministry in the church (as revealed particularly, but not only, in declining numbers), the cultural movements toward the liberation of many groups of people, and even the confusion about sexuality may all be converging toward a moment of *kairos*. Such a moment offers both opportunity and judgment, and calls for response. Reading the signs of the times is always a risky matter. What might be termed the "Gamaliel principle" (cf. Acts 5:34 ff.) of non-interpretation at least has the advantage of "benign neglect" for those to whom it is applied; it is the least one can expect from those in a position to exercise it. There are, however, historical situations which call Christians to attempt, in faith, to interpret the signs of the times insofar as such interpretation is necessary for commitment.[53] For women in the church this crisis of interpretation is already at hand, and as more and more women actualize the risk of interpretation, the crisis will become a crisis for men as well—that is to say, a question for the whole church. For even though interpretation is in the first instance personal, it is not meant to remain a mere private opinion.[54] Interpretation of the signs of the times must be confirmed, amended or rejected by the common body of Christ. In confidence Christians trust that the Lord will keep his people in all truth. Yet it must also be noted, not as a threat but as an indication of the seriousness of the issues that affect women (hence also men), that unless women can both hear and experience the Good News within the body of Christ, their participation in that visible body will become increasingly problematic.

The question of the ordination of women to the priesthood in the Roman Catholic Church is only one of a complex of issues that concern women in the church and in society. But it presents a specific occasion for taking some steps in the reshaping of Christian thought and life that is going on in this century. How does one faithfully interpret the tradition in light of this present hermeneutical situation?

Interpretation becomes a difficult problem and hermeneutics takes on a particular significance when the church is in a period of transition from an earlier interpretation to a new one.[55] The present question of women's ordination is certainly to be situated in the midst of a process of reinterpretation. The factors calling for new interpretation themselves suggest that the situation ought to be viewed in an even broader framework, namely that of a time of theological revolution, the beginning of a "paradigm shift" in theology.[56] Revolutions in Christianity, representing major shifts in thought and life, "occur when the Christian story is organized and utilized in markedly different ways in order to structure and interpret new life worlds and new thought worlds."[57] Such revolutions are not necessarily good or even representative of "progress." There are good and bad theological revolutions: "an authentic theological revolution . . . is one which comprehensively affirms the heritage even while reformulating, redirecting, and extending it into new domains of experience and reality."[58] Even in the midst of a paradigm shift, therefore, the process of interpretation begins with a return to the sources.

The tradition becomes an object of the "ascesis of reflection." It is critically examined from the perspective of suspicion in order eventually to achieve a restoration of meaning. This recovered meaning is what any new or emerging paradigm must, at the least, be able to account for and affirm.

In regard to the ordination of women, I want here only to suggest the major elements of an "ascesis of reflection" as it relates to the tradition and history of praxis that has so far excluded women from ordination in the Roman Catholic Church. I then want to point out those elements of the tradition that might be sources for a renewed interpretation and a restoration of meaning.

The Scriptures

Since Scripture has a privileged place in the witness to the Tradition, it is the logical starting point in the process of reflection. The task here is surprisingly easy. Not only is there a considerable amount of material dealing with the scriptural sources that relate to the question of women's ordination.[59] There is also a report on this subject from the Pontifical Biblical Commission which concludes (on a 12-7 vote) that "it does not seem that the New Testament alone will permit us to settle in a clear way and once and for all the problem of the accession of women to the presbyterate."[60] The report takes notice of the dignity and equality of women and men in both the Gen. 1 and Gen. 2 creation accounts; the use of feminine imagery in the Old Testament; the remarkable attitude of Jesus toward women; and the striking newness of his teaching in their regard. The report also emphasizes the necessity of investigating the sociological condition of woman according to biblical revelation and to her "ecclesial condition." The critical question, however, is this: "What is the normative value which should be accorded to the practice of the Christian communities of the first centuries?"[61]

In answering this question the authors of the report were divided. There is apparent agreement on the fact that although the New Testament makes no explicit connection between hierarchy and sacramental economy, this connection must nevertheless be assumed. There also seems to be agreement that despite a specific injunction to the contrary (1 Cor. 14:33-35 and 1 Tim. 2:11-15) it might in certain circumstances be possible to allow women to preach. Nevertheless, there is no agreement on the possibility of entrusting the sacramental ministry to women—despite the fact that there is no specific New Testament reference to entrusting this ministry to anyone, male or female.

The significance of the disagreement at this point must be weighed against the warning at the beginning of the report that questions of priesthood and eucharistic celebrant represent a "way of looking at things which is somewhat foreign to the bible."[62] This is why such questions cannot finally be resolved by appeal to Scripture. What is clear, both from the report and from a consideration of hermeneutics is that to attempt to identify the "will of Christ" in regard to priesthood and sacrament on the basis of the apparent facts ("apparent" because facts do not speak for themselves and cannot be taken in isolation as fragments of pure truth) that Jesus called only twelve males (Jewish at that) to be his apostles, or that he did not include his mother among them and constitute her a priest as well, is to read Scripture in a fundamentalist and ahistorical manner.[63] Interpretation of this sort is at odds with a genuinely Catholic (and catholic) appropriation of the tradition through the Scriptures.

I have examined the report from the Biblical Commission at some length because of its significance as a recent statement from the church, but also because it is an apt illustration of what the Scriptures *cannot* tell us in the present discussion. It is possible to be considerably briefer in suggesting what they *can* tell us.

Two recent studies point to the way in which Scripture can inform current thought on the ordination of women, namely by providing paradigmatic understandings of ministry and the basic structures of the church's life.[64] In the first of these Edmund Schlink seeks to discern the "dynamic basic structures" that underlie the diversity of church life and ecclesiological thought in the New Testament.[65] He isolates six basic structures: the structure of the church's relationship to the history of salvation; of the worship gatherings; of the relation between church and world; of church order; of church unity; and of theological reflection about the church (ecclesiology). Each of these structures is in some sense basic to the church, yet each of them manifests itself in a variety of ways during the New Testament period. Thus the question of the preservation of the church in history is raised.[66] In answer to this question Schlink concludes that: the church is always threatened by false doctrine and secular powers, in ever-changing forms of attack, yet it is promised indestructibility because Christ will remain with it; in every changing historical situation the church must remain true to the fundamental apostolic witness, and to do so it must continually distinguish true from false, preaching Christ in a new way in new situations, adapting church order as it progresses; by remaining in Christ while also pushing forward, the church assures its basic unity; both change of structures and correction of such changes are necessary as the church continues in history.[67]

From its beginning, then, the church has lived out of a paradigm of change even in regard to its most basic structures. Reginald H. Fuller's study of the ordination of women in the New Testament reinforces this point. After examining the evidence from Jesus, the earliest church, Paul, and "emergent Catholicism" in regard to women and ministry, Fuller concludes that "adaptation and flexibility were the keynotes of ministry in the New Testament period."[68] He argues further:

> If in Paul's churches women were allowed to exercise a full ministry of the word (and perhaps even of sacrament), though under a single restriction of being veiled, and if in the sub-apostolic age women were silenced; if too in Paul's churches there was no ordination, and if by the time there was ordination there was no ministry of women apart from the widows, the New Testament says to us that the church is free to adapt its ministry to the needs of the age.[69]

The conclusions reached by Fuller and Schlink are by no means unique, but represent what could be called a consensus, or at least an emerging consensus, of biblical scholarship in regard to the ordination of women.

The Tradition

Just as there is the possibility of a fundamentalist reading of Scripture, there is equally the possibility of a fundamentalist reading of tradition. This position can best be characterized by the argument that what the church has done for nearly 2,000 years must represent Christ's will for his church for all time.[70] Even when proponents of this position acknowledge some kind of historical development in "what the church does," this development is without contingency—i.e., it is regarded as homogeneous in its course and content and normative in its concluding state, whenever that is reached. Such a view is basically unhistorical; to understand the "will of Christ" in regard to the details of the church's life is to violate that genuine historical perspective that looks to the future fulfillment of God's promises and so realizes that present and partial experiences of that future promise cannot represent the *telos* of Christ's will.

It is therefore necessary to approach the historical evidence through a "hermeneutics of suspicion," questioning the tradition about the sources of women's exclusion from ordination. Without tracing in detail here either the nature of women's ministries in the church or the disciplinary and doctrinal developments that led to the restriction of such ministries and finally to their prohibition altogether in the exclusion of women from priesthood, I want to outline the major factors that contributed to this situation.

After the New Testament period, which gives evidence of considerable "apostolic" and ministerial activity of women, the ministry of women in the early church was basically that of deaconess. While subject to some kind of ordination, the deaconesses were clearly subordinate to the deacons, presbyters, and bishops.[71] Deaconesses assisted at the baptism of women, catechized female converts to the degree thought suitable for women, visited and sometimes anointed sick women, and performed a number of order-keeping functions at the liturgy. Although there are some ambiguities in the evidence of the early church orders,[72] it is clear that the role of deaconess was limited, much more popular in the East than in the West, restricted to spheres in which males could not easily or appropriately function, and was soon relegated to unimportance. The factors that effected this restriction and led to the exclusion of women from both ministry and priesthood, were basically two: the development of clerical celibacy and the emergence of a Christian priesthood.[73]

Early attempts to require celibacy of the clergy were related to a growing spirit of asceticism in the church, an exaltation of the virtue of virginity, and a confusion of virginity (particularly as expressed in monasticism) with the qualities and charisms necessary for church office. The history of canonical legislation in this period is an impressive witness to the difficulties of trying to require continence of the already married among the clergy and celibacy of those seeking to be ordained.[74] Along with the development of clerical celibacy and the limitations this put on the ministry of women, the emergence of the notion of a Christian priesthood modeled after the Old Testament levitical priesthood[75] further inhibited the association of women with the clergy and positively prevented them from membership in the clerical ranks. A Christian priesthood on Old Testament lines was necessarily male and was concentrated on ministry at the altar of sacrifice, service of which required ritual purity.[76] Emphasis on the offering of sacrifice as the major role of the male Christian priesthood led as well to concentration on the maleness of Jesus Christ rather than on the generic nature of the humanity that he took upon himself in the incarnation.

The history of theological reflection on woman mirrors these developments.[77] Women tend to be seen as weak by nature, inferior in creation, easily deceived and led into sin, and subject to man in the punishment meted out after the Fall. The canonical history of the exclusion of women from orders also reflects the various factors enumerated here. The process by which canon 968 of the present Code of Canon Law was first incorporated into Gratian's *Decretum* and through it transmitted to the present day was a process basically uncritical in regard to sources and significance; they are much more the result of the developments sketched above than of critical theological reflection and reception.[78]

In the history of the exclusion of women from orders, disciplinary developments took on theological justifications which helped in turn to reinforce practices and elevate them to the status of "tradition." Yet such developments and their rationales are not expressive of the full sense of genuine tradition. While the evolution of celibacy and the priesthood of a male clergy is one instance of the interaction of discipline and doctrine, it is an expression of the discipline-doctrine connection in regard to only certain doctrines—and perhaps at the expense of other more basic doctrines.[79] In concentrating on the levitical priesthood and ministry at the altar of sacrifice as an understanding of both Christ's ministry and the Christian ministry, it is easy to lose sight of more fundamental trinitarian and christological beliefs. In seeking to recover these doctrines—having been provoked to do so by the exercise of suspicion and the asking of new questions—a "hermeneutics of restoration" comes into play.

The Restoration of Meaning

Here I can only suggest two areas which would reward further exploration. Taking the Trinity as the image of God in human beings one is led to expect that the most intimate aspect of trinitarian relations—namely the mutuality of the persons of the Trinity—will be reflected in human experience, particularly in the relations between men and women.[80] The history of the relationship of celibate male clergy to women has shown little of this mutuality; neither have man-woman relations in general. Yet if the doctrine of the *imago Dei* is to mean anything, must not the mutuality of the persons of the Trinity be what persons are trying to embody in all aspects of human life, whether in the so-called secular world or, especially, in the church?

Similarly, a serious and critical attempt to reappropriate the christological decisions of the early church would lead one to understand that what was at stake in the conflict between Nestorius and Cyril was whether it was generic humanity which the Word of God assumed (Cyril) or a specific, individual manhood (Nestorius). If the latter, the *maleness* of Jesus Christ would be of peculiar importance. But if, as was the case, the former position was maintained, then it is the *humanity* of Jesus Christ that is significant. Whether representing Christ to the church or the church to Christ,[81] this representation is best achieved by a clergy that includes men and women (i.e., all of redeemed humanity).[82]

By a critique of the doctrinal traditions related to the exclusion of women from priesthood, it is possible to restore some important and neglected aspects of the central trinitarian and christological doctrines on which all other Christian doctrines depend. This restoration of meaning is beneficial in several ways: it offers the possibility of a resymbolization of evil[83]—i.e., of ceasing to see woman as a symbol and source of evil, and looking instead for other and more appropriate symbolic expressions of the nature of evil; it further makes possible an expanded vision of priesthood and ministry and an increased appreciation of the uniqueness of Jesus Christ's priesthood; and finally it can enable women to live more fully the eucharistic mystery as it both expresses and builds the community of the body of Christ at the same time that it anticipates the fulfillment of this community in the time of God's promise.

As applied to the tradition as the bearer of Tradition, the exercise of a hermeneutics of suspicion and restoration makes it possible to reappropriate some of the central scriptural affirmations about life in the new community that is the body of Christ. For any one who is in Christ is a new creation (2 Cor. 5:7 ff.), and his/her life is shaped by the fundamental Christian experience of "the grace of the Lord Jesus Christ and the love of God and the fellowship of the Holy Spirit" (2 Cor. 13:14). It is this trinitarian experience that baptism represents in a particularly vivid and efficacious way. In this context Paul's allusion to a baptismal formula or fragment of liturgy in Gal. 3:27-29 takes on particular significance. For in the new community, the new creation, the barriers of division have been and are being broken down, and there is neither Jew nor Greek, slave nor free, male nor female. Although it has been quoted so often in recent discussion that it seems trite, this baptismal formula cannot fail to have impact as long as it is seen for what it is: not a statement of Paul's individual theological opinion but an expression of the Christian community's very life and identity. The baptismal affirmation of faith in the paschal mystery provides a perspective of interpretation that is at once christological, ecclesiological, and eschatological.[84] It calls the church and the individual Christian into the future of God's promise while making it possible to live from that promise in every present situation.

Although the Roman Catholic Church has not in the past ordained women to its sacramental priesthood and ministry, it can certainly do so in the present or the future. "For freedom Christ has set us free; stand fast therefore and do not submit again to a yoke of slavery" (Gal. 5:1).

NOTES

1. United States Catholic Conference. News Release, Oct. 3, 1975.

2. Committee on Pastoral Research and Practices, National Conference of Catholic Bishops, The Most Rev. John R. Quinn, Chairman. The text of the report is reprinted in *Journal of Ecumenical Studies* 10, n. 4 (Fall 1973), pp. 695-99.

3. London: Burns and Oates, Ltd., 1966.

4. *The Fourth World Conference on Faith and Order: The Report from Montreal 1963*, ed. P. C. Rodger and L. Vischer, pp. 50-61.

5. Montreal, p. 50. See also Alexander Schmemann, "The Orthodox Tradition," in *The Convergence of Traditions*, ed. Elmer O'Brien (New York: Herder and Herder, 1967), pp. 22-27; and John Meyendorff, *Orthodoxy and Catholicity* (New York: Sheed and Ward, 1966), pp. 91-106, on "Tradition and Traditions." For Orthodox theology especially the role of the Holy Spirit in tradition is particularly important.

6. Congar, pp. 280-282. For a basic scriptural instance of the combination of the noetic and dynamic, see I Cor. 11:23-26. See also Joseph R. Geiselmann, "Scripture, Tradition, and the Church: An Ecumenical Problem," in D. Callahan, H. Oberman, and D. O'Hanlon, eds., *Christianity Divided*, p. 56.

7. Congar, p. 282. See Vatican I. *Pastor Aeternus*, First Dogmatic Constitution on the Church of Christ (Denzinger, XXXIV ed., 3050).

8. Congar, p. 272.

9. Geiselmann, p. 54; Joseph Ratzinger, "Revelation and Tradition," in *Revelation and Tradition*, ed. with K. Rahner, Quaestiones Dis-

putatae 17 (London: Burns and Oates, 1966), pp. 35-40. This sense of "Tradition" corresponds to Congar's first and broadest meaning of "tradition" —see pp. 287, 296-97.

10. Montreal, p. 50.

11. J. Geiselmann, *The Meaning of Tradition,* Quaestiones Disputatae 15 (London: Burns and Oates Ltd., 1966), p. 82.

12. Congar, pp. 287, 297.

13. Congar, p. 300. While Congar's definition is perhaps too sweeping, the use of the term "apostolic tradition" has a practical function— namely in distinguishing the meaning of tradition that I am proposing here from other uses of the word (such as that which would set it in contradistinction to Scripture)—as well as a more substantive function of emphasizing that Scripture is itself a result and a part of tradition and cannot make much sense or be of much value apart from that tradition. The Scriptures are "apostolic" only in the loose sense in which the early church felt them to possess that authority which the apostles represented in the church. Likewise various aspects of the church's life are "apostolic" only in this loose sense of being faithful to or in harmony with the apostolic witness to the Gospel. Just as specific books of the New Testament cannot be traced reliably to specific apostles (nor need they be), so too with other aspects of the church's tradition. The notion of "apostolicity" is significant as a link between the Tradition and the various attempts of the church to express that Tradition in its tradition. In this sense "apostolicity" is, in most cases, more like the "Good Housekeeping Seal of Approval" than a label guaranteeing that "this product was made in first century Palestine by Apostles."

14. Congar, p. 305.

15. Congar, p. 422.

16. Geiselmann, *Meaning,* pp. 35-37.

17. Congar, pp. 288, 301.

18. Congar, p. 423. Cf. Geiselmann, "Scripture," pp. 54-55; Montreal, pp. 51-53; Karl Rahner, "Scripture and Tradition," *Theological Investigations* VI (Baltimore: Helicon Press, 1969), pp. 98-112.

19. Geiselmann, "Scripture," pp. 44 ff.; Congar, p. 423.

20. Congar, p. 288.

21. Congar, pp. 422, 305.

22. See, for instance, Rahner, in *Revelation and Tradition,* pp. 9-25, esp. 20-21; "The Historicity and Theology," *Theological Investigations* IX (New York: Herder and Herder, 1972), p. 71.

23. Edward Schillebeeckx, "Toward a Catholic Use of Hermeneutics," in *God the Future of Man* (New York: Sheed and Ward, 1968), p. 12, applies as well to tradition as to dogma; Avery Dulles, *The Survival of Dogma,* pp. 198-99; Rahner, "Historicity," pp. 67-68.

24. Josiah Royce, *The Problem of Christianity,* Vol. II (Chicago: Henry Regnery Company, 1968—originally published 1913), pp. 57-103.

25. Schillebeeckx, pp. 39-40, 41; Dulles, pp. 189, 202-203; Rahner,

"Revelation," pp. 12-14; Rahner, "Historicity," p. 79; Geiselmann, *Meaning*, pp. 41-43.

26. John E. Lynch, "Marriage and Celibacy of the Clergy: The Discipline of the Western Church: An Historico-Canonical Synopsis," *The Jurist* (1972), pp. 14-38, 189-212. See also Roger Gryson, *Les origines du célibat ecclésiastique* (Gembloux: Duculot, 1970).

27. On the possibility of error in theology, see Rahner, "Historicity," pp. 74-80; on reversibility of dogma, see Dulles, pp. 192-212; for documentation of examples of change in doctrinal positions by the magisterium, see Raymond Brown, *Biblical Reflections on Crises Facing the Church* (New York: Paulist Press, 1976), pp. 109-118.

28. A. Dulles, "What is Magisterium," *Origins*, Vol. 6, n. 6 (July 1, 1976), p. 84. See also two recent articles by Congar: "Pour une histoire semantique du term "magisterium," and "Bref historique des formes du "magistere" et de ses relations avec les docteurs," *Revue des Sciences Philosophiques et Théologique* 60 1976), pp. 85-98 and 99-112, respectively. There are surveys of the historical development of this position in Gabriel Moran, *Scripture and Tradition: A Survey of the Controversy* (New York: Herder and Herder, 1963) and James P. Mackey, *The Modern Theology of Tradition* (New York: Herder and Herder, 1962).

29. Dulles, "Magisterium," pp. 85-86, with reference to Thomas Aquinas' distinction between *magisterium cathedrae pastoralis* and *magisterium cathedrae magistralis*. See also the articles by Congar. Dulles' formulation in *Survival*, p. 211, is also helpful.

30. Dulles, "Magisterium," p. 86.

31. Schillebeeckx, p. 20.

32. "The Significance of the Hermeneutical Problem for the Ecumenical Movement," in *Faith and Order Studies 1964-67* (Geneva: World Council of Churches, 1968), pp. 35ff. See also Vatican II, *Dei Verbum*, art. 11-12 (Dogmatic Constitution on Divine Revelation), in Walter M. Abbott, ed., *The Documents of Vatican II* (New York: Guild Press—America Press—Association Press, 1966).

33. Rahner, "Historicity"; Schillebeeckx, "Toward a Catholic Use of Hermeneutics"; Dulles, *Survival*, esp. chapts. 11-12.

34. See Paul Ricoeur, *Freud and Philosophy. An Essay in Interpretation*, trans. Denis Savage (New Haven: Yale University Press, 1970), p. 25. The possibility of applying Ricoeur's work to the present problem was first suggested to me by Joseph A. Komonchak's brief references to the "hermeneutics of suspicion" and "hermeneutics of restoration" in his essay on "Theological Questions on the Ordination of Women," in *Women in Catholic Priesthood: An Expanded Vision*, Proceedings of the Detroit Ordination Conference, ed. Anne Marie Gardiner, S.S.N.D. (New York: Paulist Press, 1976), p. 255.

35. Schillebeeckx, p. 18.

36. Schillebeeckx, pp. 8, 19; Dulles, p. 206.

37. Peter L. Berger and Thomas Luckman, *The Social Construction*

of Reality; A Treatise in the Sociology of Knowledge (Garden City, New York: Doubleday Anchor Books, 1967), pp. 66-68.

38. Cf. Schillebeeckx, p. 31.

39. Skydsgaard, in *The Old and The New in The Church.* World Council of Churches Commission on Faith and Order (Studies in Ministry and Worship [London: SCM, 1961]), p. 34.

40. Dulles, *Survival*, p. 189; cf. R. Brown on "blue-print" vs. "erector-set" ecclesiologies, pp. 52-57.

41. Dulles, *Survival*, p. 189.

42. Schillebeeckx, p. 37.

43. Schillebeeckx, p. 30; cf. Robert Wilken, *The Myth of Christian Beginnings* (Garden City, New York: Doubleday Anchor Books, 1972).

44. Schillebeeckx, p. 30; cf. Rahner, "Historicity," pp. 68, 71; Wolfhart Pannenberg, "Dogmatic Theses on the Doctrine of Revelation," in *Revelation as History*, ed. Pannenberg, et al., trans. David Granskou (New York: Macmillan Company, 1968), p. 133 ("it is not so much the course of history as the end of history that is at one with the essence of God") and pp. 143-144 (on "the inexhaustibility of the event of revelation as an eschatological event" and the provisionality of all forms of Christian life in this world).

45. Schillebeeckx, p. 34.

46. Schillebeeckx, p. 40.

47. Ricoeur, p. 27 ff.

48. Ricoeur, p. 27.

49. Ricoeur, p. 31.

50. Schillebeeckx, p. 36.

51. Schillebeeckx, p. 37.

52. Schillebeeckx, p. 37.

53. "God in Nature and History," *Faith and Order Studies 1964-1967* (Geneva: World Council of Churches, 1968), p. 29.

54. Ibid., p. 30.

55. Schillebeeckx, p. 12.

56. George A. Lindbeck, "A Battle for Theology: Hartford in Historical Perspective," in *Against the World For the World; The Hartford Appeal and the Future of American Religion*, ed. Peter L. Berger and Richard John Neuhaus (New York: The Seabury Press, 1976), pp. 31 ff. Lindbeck uses T. S. Kuhn's *Structure of Scientific Revolutions* as the basis of an analysis of "theological revolutions."

57. Lindbeck, p. 35.

58. Lindbeck, p. 36.

59. See, for instance, the bibliographies in *Anglican Theological Review*, Suppl. Series n. 6 (June 1976), by Barnhouse, Fahey, Oram, and Walker, pp. 87-94; *Women and The Priesthood; A Selected and Annotated Bibliography*, compiled by Patricia A. Kendall (published by The Committee to Promote The Cause of and to Plan for the Ordination of Women to the Priesthood, The Episcopal Diocese of Pennsylvania, 1976).

60. "Can Women Be Priests," Biblical Commission Report, in *Origins*, vol. 6, pp. 92-96.

61. Ibid., p. 95.

62. Ibid., p. 92.

63. See, for instance, John R. Sheets, "Ordination of Women: The Issues," *American Ecclesiastical Review* 169 (January 1975), pp. 17-36, esp. p. 29 ("the sole reason is the will of Christ and consciousness of his will in those who were chosen to continue his ministry.").

64. Edmund Schlink, "The Unity and Diversity of the Church," in *What Unity Implies: Six Essays after Uppsala*, ed. R. Groscuth, World Council Studies n. 7 (Geneva: World Council of Churches, 1969), pp. 33-51. Reginald H. Fuller, "Pro and Con: The Ordination of Women in the New Testament," in *Toward a New Theology of Ordination; Essays on the Ordination of Women*, ed. Marianne H. Micks and Charles P. Price, Virginia Theological Seminary (Somerville, Mass: Greeno, Hadden and Company, Ltd., 1976), pp. 1-11.

65. Schlink, p. 38.

66. Schlink, p. 45.

67. Schlink, pp. 45-46.

68. Fuller, p. 9.

69. Fuller, p. 9.

70. E.g., Sheets, *art. cit.*

71. See, for instance, the *Apostolic Tradition* of Hippolytus; the *Didascalia Apostolorum*; and the *Apostolic Constitutions*. See also Roger Gryson, *Le ministere des femmes dans l'Eglise ancienne* (Gembloux: Duculot, 1972), for a thorough review and evaluation of the early evidence.

72. Gryson, *Ministere*, p. 107, "Deaconesses are part of the clergy," in ref. to *Apostolic Constitutions* 8.28.6.

73. I have sketched in slightly more detail than is possible here the outlines of this interpretation in "Women, Ordination and Tradition," *Commonweal* CII, n. 26 (Dec. 17, 1976), pp. 807-810, and hope to develop it more fully elsewhere. For some of the evidence pertinent to these historical developments, see the essays in this volume by Katharine Meagher, S.C., "Women in Relation to Orders and Jurisdiction," and Hamilton Hess, "Changing Forms of Ministry in the Early Church."

Rather disappointing both in its use and evaluation of the sources and in its estimation of the current situation is Agnes Cunningham's brief study for the Ad Hoc Committee for Women in Society and the Church of the USCC, "The Role of Women in Ecclesial Ministry: Biblical and Patristic Foundations" (Washington, D.C.: United States Catholic Conference, 1976), 29 pp.

74. Gryson, *Célibat*; Lynch, *art. cit.*

75. For documents, see James A. Mohler, *The Origin and Evolution of the Priesthood* (Staten Island, New York: Alba House, 1969). For historical analysis see Bernard Cooke, *Ministry to Word and Sacraments* (Philadelphia: Fortress Press, 1976), pp. 525-573.

76. See Gryson, *Célibat*; Bernard Verkamp, "Cultic Purity and the Law of Celibacy," *Review for Religious* 31 (1971), pp. 199-217.

77. See, for instance, Rosemary Ruether, "Misogynism and Virginal Feminism in the Fathers of the Church," *Religion and Sexism*, ed. Ruether (New York: Simon and Schuster, 1974), pp. 150-183; George Tavard, *Woman in Christian Tradition* (Notre Dame: University of Notre Dame Press, 1973), pp. 1-122.

78. Joan Range, "Legal Exclusion of Women from Church Office," *The Jurist* 1/2 (1974), pp. 112-127; Ida Raming, *Der Ausschluss der Frau vom priesterlichen Amt: Gottgewollte Tradition oder Diskriminierung? Eine rechts historisch-dogmatischen Untersuchung der Grundlagen von Kanon 968.1 des Codex Iuris Canonici* (Cologne: Bohlau, 1973). Raming's work is now available in translation: *The Exclusion of Women from the Priesthood: Divine Law or Sex Discrimination?*, trans. Norman R. Adams (Metuchen, N.J.: Scarecrow Press, 1976).

79. Cf. Vatican II, *Unitatis Redintegratio*, art. 11, in Abbot.

80. See Margaret Farley, R.S.M., "New Patterns of Relationships: Beginnings of a Moral Revolution," *Theological Studies* 36, n. 4 (December 1975), pp. 640-643 especially; also "Moral Imperatives for the Ordination of Women," in *Women and Catholic Priesthood*, p. 47.

81. Edward J. Kilmartin, S.J., "Apostolic Office: Sacrament of Christ," *Theological Studies* 36, n. 2. (June, 1975), pp. 243-264.

82. Richard A. Norris, Jr., "The Ordination of Women and the 'Maleness' of the Christ," *Anglican Theological Review*, Suppl. Series, n. 6 (June 1976), pp. 69-80.

83. Farley, "Moral Imperatives," pp. 44-45, 47-48.

84. Schillebeeckx, p. 288.

Woman in Vatican Documents 1960 to the Present

NADINE FOLEY, O.P.

In the past twenty-five years documents issued from Vatican sources have frequently included references to women, particularly in texts dealing with social doctrine. This same period is roughly that of escalation in what is often called the movement for women's liberation, particularly among North American and European women. This movement has its starting point, as have other so-called liberation movements, in experience, in this case the experience of women, identified and made the object of critical reflection. Among Christian women the process of reflection necessarily involves them in examining their experience in the light of the Gospel of Jesus Christ and that doctrine which develops from it in successive periods of the Church's history as official teaching. As important new developments take place in human consciousness, it is appropriate that the import of such trends become matter for inclusion in the continuing experience of a living Church, as well as for comment and interpretation by a teaching Church. For, as Vatican Council II has acknowledged, cultural transformation is ongoing as a process in which all people are involved. It brings forth new aspects of human reality for the incarnating mission of a Church always in need of reformation.

What then do official texts say about women? Are their contents compatible with the emerging realizations to which women themselves are coming as they subject their experience to critical examination in the light of the Gospel? These are the questions this paper addresses. In the first part representative statements from Vatican documents of the past twenty-five years are examined for the implicit "ontology of woman" which informs them. In the second part insights pertinent to the nature, status and roles of women from other sources are discussed for purposes of evaluation.

I. THE "ONTOLOGY OF WOMAN" IN VATICAN TEXTS

A critical reading of the allusions to women which are made in contemporary writing from official Roman Catholic sources seems to allow the following organization of the material. A. Rapid changes in the contemporary world call for new declarations of fundamental human rights and concerted efforts of all persons to insure them. B. One of the evident features of contemporary socio-cultural life is the changing status and roles of women. C. The Church looks with approval on these new developments while expressing concern that the dignity of women be protected. D. The nature of women is unique, divinely established and manifested in characteristics proper to women in their social roles. E. Roles appropriate to women in the ministry of the Church correspond to their specific nature and complementary relation to men.

A. Rapid changes in the contemporary world call for new declarations of fundamental human rights and concerted efforts of all persons to insure them.

The most influential documents which have come from Vatican sources in the past twenty-five years have enunciated the dignity and freedom of human persons, especially as a context for setting forth the Church's developing social doctrine. Pope John in *Pacem in Terris* states the basic premise in terms of what is intrinsic to human personhood.

Any human society, if it is to be well-ordered and productive, must lay down as a foundation this principle, namely, that every human being is a person, that is, his nature is endowed with intelligence and free will. Indeed, precisely because he is a person he has rights and obligations flowing directly and simultaneously from his very nature. And as these rights and obligations are universal and inviolable so they cannot in any way be surrendered (9).

On this basis the encyclical continues with an enumeration of the fundamental rights of human persons: to life, to an appropriate standard of living, to respect for one's person, to good reputation, to freedom of expression, to information about public events, to education, to worship according to individual conscience, to choose one's state of life freely, to protection of the family in society, to parental support for and education of children, to work, to proper working conditions, to a just wage, to private property, to freedom of assembly and association, to emigrate and immigrate, to active participation in public affairs and to protection under the law (10-27).

Not only has the Church declared in this way its concern for basic human rights in a generic way, but it has also given voice to what must be guaranteed to individual persons. Pope Paul speaks in this vein in *Populorum Progressio.*

In the design of God, every man is called upon to develop and fulfill himself, for every life is a vocation. At birth everyone is granted, in germ, a set of aptitudes and qualities for him to bring to fruition. Their coming to maturity, which will be the result of education received from the environment and personal efforts, will allow each man to direct himself toward the destiny intended for him by his Creator. Endowed with intelligence and freedom, he is responsible for his fulfillment as he is for his salvation. He is aided, or sometimes impeded, by those who educate him and those with whom he lives, but each one remains, whatever be these influences affecting him, the principal agent of his own success or failure. By the unaided effort of his own intelligence and his will, each man can grow in humanity, can enhance his personal worth, can become more a person (15).

Given the form of this kind of discourse it can be inferred that such a design of God applies universally to all human persons signified by the English word *man* (Latin *homo*). Yet within the extensive tracts on human rights and personal freedom characteristic of contemporary ecclesial social teaching there occur special paragraphs on women. A number of these will be cited in this paper.

The radical nature of the social change which typifies the present time may well dictate the singling out of women for special concern in the area of human rights. Nevertheless there is also the possibility that women require separate treatment because, in the minds of those who author Church documents, what is said of "man" generally does not apply to women without distinction. The task of verifying that in truth this possibility in fact is impeded by language—those modern languages, such as English, in which the generic word for humankind is also the specific word for the male person; and the "dead" Latin language, whose meanings can be nuanced by the modern words derivative from them. The problem of language in this respect is present in much of what is presented here.

B. One of the evident features of the contemporary socio-cultural life is the changing status and roles of women.

The approach to women evident in the texts reviewed is nonetheless guided by an important operative principle. Pope John XXIII gave expression to it in *Mater et Magistra*. Recalling the social teaching of Leo XIII, Pius XI and Pius XII, he acknowledged that the circumstances contemporary to the concerns of his predecessors no longer prevailed. New trends were evident and called for further elaboration of social doctrine to meet the emergent circumstances. *Mater et Magistra* commemorated

Rerum Novarum of Leo XIII but it was issued also, said Pope John, "in the light of changed conditions, . . . to set forth the Church's teaching regarding the new and serious problems of our day" (50).

The principle that fundamental truths related to the nature of human persons and their social institutions must be brought into a continuing relation with issues which emerge in a developing human history is an important one. It was expanded in the opening paragraphs of *Gaudium et Spes*, ". . . the Church has always had the duty of scrutinizing the signs of the times and of interpreting them in the light of the Gospel. . . . We must therefore recognize and understand the world in which we live, its expectations, its longings, and its often dramatic characteristics" (4). In reawakening the Church to an acknowledgment of its continuing need for reformation in the light of new challenges presented to it by ongoing human development, Pope John and Vatican Council II made undoubtedly the most profound contribution to a renewed ecclesial self concept. The starting point of the indispensable process of *aggiornamento* is to be found in the experience of peoples and societies which calls the Church to an ever renewed reflection upon the import of the Gospel and of the Church's capacity to respond to new demands upon its mission of proclaiming the kingdom of God. It seems important to acknowledge this principle for the purposes of this paper since it functions in the very fact that issues relating to women are attracting the attention of and provoking responses from those who assume responsibility for the Church's magisterium. New dogmatic statements about women do not arise from the Church's exploration into the liberating message of Gospel alone, but because an emergent consciousness of human reality in the experience of both women and men calls forth a reflective response.

Pope Paul VI acknowledged the principle, as well as the new problem when, on December 8, 1974, he addressed the Convention of the Union of Italian Catholic Jurists. Significantly, he traced the origin of the social and cultural phenomena evident in the changing position and roles of women today to the economic shift which marks the modern historical era, though he makes no allusion to the currently popular notion that we may be participating in the movement into a post-industrial age.

Neither we nor any other observer of the contemporary scene are unaware of the sociocultural transformation that has caused, among other things a remarkable change in the position and roles of women. A rather rapid transition has brought us from a primarily agricultural society to a new type of society characterized by industrialization and its satellite phenomena: urbanization, population mobility and instability, and a revolution in domestic life and social relations.[1]

The fact of women's changing situation in the contemporary world is remarked upon in numerous other places. In *Gaudium et Spes* the conciliar fathers speak of "new social relationships between men and women" (3), and note that "where they have not yet won it, women claim for themselves an equity with men before the law and in fact . . ." (9), and further that "Women now engage in almost all spheres of activity" (60). *Humanae Vitae* states, "A change is also seen both in the manner of considering the person of woman and her place in society" (2). These selected instances, typical of many, are cited for the purpose of indicating the starting point of the official Church's awareness of new trends in women's experience, namely, as a phenomenon occurring in the cultural history of peoples.

Observation of these and other phenomena led Pope John to identify three distinctive characteristics of our age in *Pacem in Terris*. The first was the growing ascendancy of the working classes and the third, the achieving of independence by increasing numbers of nations. The second is pertinent here.

> . . . it is obvious to everyone that women are now taking part in public life. This is happening more rapidly perhaps in nations of Christian civilization, and more slowly but broadly, among peoples who have inherited other traditions and cultures. Since women are becoming more conscious of their human dignity, they will not tolerate being treated as mere material instruments, but demand rights befitting a human person both in domestic and in public life (41).

Summarizing these trends, Pope John encompassed all three in one principle: "Thus in very many human beings the inferiority complex which endured for hundreds of thousands of years is disappearing, while in others there is an attenuation and gradual fading of the corresponding superiority complex which had its roots in social-economic privileges, sex or political standing" (43). The much studied and admired *Pacem in Terris* proceeds with an extensive treatment of rights and obligations affecting persons and societies in the economic and political spheres of life, but does not specifically address the second of the characteristics it had signalled as typifying our age. It is noteworthy, however, that the point of observation taken by Pope John is not merely of the external changes in "women's roles" but something occurring within the consciousness of people. Unfortunately, in subsequent documents the phenomenon of contemporary experience has rarely been addressed on this level.

Nevertheless, as one peruses the official documents of this period there is repeated recognition of what is happening to women in contemporary society. The earlier statements seem to address the issue as it exists in social institutions outside the Church. The later ones begin to address roles and responsibilities of women within the Church itself.

Thus *Gaudium et Spes* could say "Women now engage in almost all spheres of activity. . . . It is incumbent upon all to acknowledge and favor the proper and necessary participation of women in cultural life" (60). In the 1971 Apostolic Letter *A Call to Action*, Pope Paul could note approvingly that ". . . in many countries a charter for women which would put an end to an actual discrimination and would establish relationships of equality in rights and of respect for their dignity is the object of study and of lively demands" (13). He could also identify sex as a basis for discrimination. "Among the victims of injustice—unfortunately no new phenomenon—must be placed those who are discriminated against in law or in fact, on account of their race, origin, color, culture, sex or religion" (16). Later in the same year the synodal document *Justice in the World* brought concern for women's participation into the household of the Church. "We also urge that women should have their own share of responsibility and participation in the community life of society and likewise of the Church."[2]

C. *The Church looks with approval on these new developments while at the same time she expresses concern that the dignity of women be protected.*

Perhaps one of the clearest indicators of this generalization is found in the following from Pope Paul VI.

If we were to reduce to a few brief essentials these brief indications concerning the place women should have in a renewed society, we might say: Let us willingly vote for
(1) the recognition of the civil rights of women as the full equals of men, whenever these rights have not yet been acknowledged;
(2) laws that will make it really possible for women to fill the same professional, social and political roles as men, according to the individual capacities of the person;
(3) the acknowledgment, respect and protection of the special prerogatives of women in marriage, family, education and society;
(4) the maintenance and defense of the dignity of women as persons, unmarried women, wives and widows; and the help they need, especially when the husband is absent, disabled or imprisoned, that is, when he cannot fulfill his function in the family.[3]

The first two of these "essentials" are among the clearest unqualified statements of the rights of women to be found in any official text. Some of the implications of the context provided by the third and fourth points are appropriate to the material in the next section of this paper.

A major concern about women, due to their increased presence in the labor force and professions, is for their economic rights. *Mater et Magistra* includes among the duties of the state the safeguarding of ". . . the rights of all citizens, but especially the weaker, such as workers, women and children" (20). *Pacem in Terris* states, "Women have the right to working conditions in accordance with their requirements and their duties as wives and mothers" (19). This concern is echoed in *Gaudium et Spes*. ". . . it too often happens, even in our day, that in one way or another workers are made slaves of their work . . . Such is especially the case with respect to mothers of families, but due consideration must be given to every person's sex and age" (67). Reference to the role of women in the family here is key to the fundamental position of the Church on women, from which notions of feminine nature and distinguishing characteristics are derived. Official Church teaching repeatedly addresses the place of the woman in the family. Vatican II idealized the family as a "school of deeper humanity," and continued,

> But if it is to achieve the full flowering of its life and mission, it needs the kindly communion of minds and the joint deliberation of spouses, as well as the painstaking cooperation of parents in the education of their children. The active presence of the father is highly beneficial to their formation. The children, especially the younger among them, need the care of their mother at home. This domestic role of hers must be safely preserved, though the legitimate social progress of women should not be underrated on that account (*Gaudium et Spes*, 52).

Yet developments in our times continue to place the domestic role of women in the family in jeopardy. One effect of rapid social transition, according to Pope Paul, has been . . . to put women at the center of a yet unresolved crisis in institutions and culture with critical implications for their relationships within the family, their educational mission, their very identity as women, and their "specific way" of sharing in the life of society through work, friendships and the help and comfort they give to others. Even the religious outlook and practice of women have been affected, he observes. He then enumerates four developments of enormous importance:

1. the equal rights given to women, along with their increasing emancipation from the control of men;

2. a new conception of their roles as wives, mothers, daughters and sisters;

3. the ever greater availability to them of a vast and expanding range of specialized professional occupations;

4. their growing tendency to prefer jobs outside the home, with its effects on the marital relationship and, above all, on the education of children who are prematurely freed from the authority of parents and especially of the mother.[4]

While the Holy Father is concerned about the dangers to woman's dignity and her place in the family he does not take a totally negative view of the new developments.

The new situation is evidently not wholly negative in its impact. In these new circumstances the woman of today and tomorrow will perhaps be able more easily to develop her full potential. Even the misguided experiments of the present time can be useful, if the sound universal principles of conscience take firmer root in society and lead to a new balance in family and social life.[5]

The context of these kinds of statements indicates official concern that what is regarded as woman's essential role of nurturing in the family be guarded because it is intrinsically related to her special nature.

D. The nature of women is unique, divinely established, and manifested in characteristics proper to women in their social roles.

There is a consistency in the way in which affirmations about woman in Vatican texts are qualified by references to her nature. *Gaudium et Spes* continues, after observing the fact that women are now employed in almost every area of life, with the following: "It is appropriate that they should be able to assume their full proper role in accordance with their own nature" (60). Women were singled out, along with rulers, men of thought and science, artists, the poor, sick and suffering, workers and youth for a special message at the close of Vatican Council II. They were told, ". . . the Church is proud to have glorified and liberated women, and in the course of centuries, in diversity of characters, to have brought into relief her basic equality with *man*." Women were further directed:

You women have always had as your lot the protection of the home, the love of beginnings, and an understanding of cradles. You are present in the mystery of a life beginning. You offer consolation in the departure of death. Our technology runs the risk of becoming unhuman. Reconcile men with life and above all, we beseech you, watch carefully over the future of our race. Hold back the hand of man who, in a moment of folly, might attempt to destroy human civilization.[6]

Presumably this role for women is conformable to her position at the heart of the family and within society of which Pope Paul speaks in *A Call to Action*. After approving the idea of a charter for women that would put an end to discrimination against them he continues.

We do not have in mind that false equality which would be in contradiction with woman's proper role, which is of such capital importance, at the heart of the family, as well as within society. Developments in legislation should on the contrary be directed to protecting her proper vocation and at the same time recognizing her independence as a person, and her equal rights to participate in cultural, economic, social and political life (13).

In his address to Italian Catholic Jurists in December of 1972, Pope Paul identified the appropriate role of woman and qualified the nature of her equality with men when he said, ". . . women's authentic liberation does not consist in a formalistic or materialistic equality with the other sex, but in recognizing what the female personality has that is essentially specific to it: woman's vocation to be a mother."[7] In the 1975 document *The Role of Women in Church and Society: Disciples and Co-Workers*, Pope Paul referred to complementarity of roles, ". . . to speak of rights does not resolve the problem, which is much more profound; it is necessary to aim at an effective complementarity, so that men and women bring their *proper* riches and dynamism to the building of the world, not levelled and uniform, but harmonious and unified, according to the design of the Creator, or, to use the terms of the Holy Year, renewed and reconciled."[8]

Pope Paul expresses his concern for women's proper place in society and in the Church in his statement on *Women/Balancing Rights and Duties*. He says in part, "The panorama of the apostolic activities of women is already an impressive one in those places where an effort has been made to enable them to take on the responsibilities *that can be theirs*." (emphasis added) And further, "Authentic Christian advancement of women is not limited to the claiming of rights. The Christian spirit obliges all of us, both men and women, to remember always our *own proper duties and responsibilities*. (emphasis added) Today it is especially a question of achieving a greater and closer collaboration between men and women in all society and in the Church."[9] In this same document the Holy Father urges a seeming kind of restraint in efforts to promote women in positions of increased responsibility. ". . . we cannot fail to emphasize the fact that in the most highly developed countries the ascension of women to posts of reflection and decision making which conditions all spheres of life in society needs to progress with wisdom and realism." In a similar vein he urges women to remain alert to needs that manifest themselves with the caution that it would be vain and illusory to increase experiments indefinitely. "It is rather a question of totally taking on responsibilities that you have accepted, not in a spirit of competition or vanity, but in a spirit of collaboration and evangelical humility."[10]

The Holy See itself has taken some cautious steps in involving women in its organization. Pope Paul observes,

Effectively for several decades, a great many Christian communities have benefitted from the apostolic commitment of women, most especially in the prime area of pastoral work with families. At present certain women are even called upon to participate in sessions of pastoral reflection, either on the level of the dioceses, or on that of parishes and deaneries. It goes without saying that these new experiences need to mature. The Apostolic See, as you know, has itself called some particularly qualified women to take places on certain working groups.[11]

A number of texts point to the unique qualities or traits of women that derive from their special nature. In Vatican II's closing address to women they are given the vocation to save the peace of the world. "Women, you who know how to make truth sweet, tender and accessible, make it your task to bring the spirit of this Council into institutions, schools, homes and daily life. Women of the entire universe, whether Christian or nonbelieving, you to whom life is entrusted at this grave moment in history, it is for you to save the world."[12] The qualities of women are divinely bestowed as Pope Paul maintains in his discourse on "Reconciliation/the Way to Peace" delivered at Christmas time in 1974.

We rejoice especially on the eve of International Women's Year, proclaimed by the United Nations, at the ever wider participation of women in the life of society, to which they bring a specific contribution of great value, thanks to the qualities God has given them. These qualities of intuition, creativity, sensibility, a sense of piety and compassion, a profound capacity for understanding and love, enable women to be in a very particular way the creators of reconciliation in families and in society.[13]

In a similar vein in April of 1975 Pope Paul spoke of the need to obtain for women equality of rights and their full integration in the worldwide effort of development. He cited their growing contribution to the strengthening of peace among peoples. He concluded,

Yes, Christian women, the future of civil society and of the ecclesial community expects much of your sensitivity and of your capacity for understanding, of your sweetness and of your perseverance, of your generosity and of your humility. These virtues, so well in accord with feminine psychology, and magnificently developed in the Virgin Mary, are also the fruits of the Holy Spirit. This Holy Spirit will guide you surely into the full development, into the promotion that you seek, that we all seek.[14]

A somewhat different approach to specifically feminine qualities is found in the document *The Role of Women in Evangelization* from the Pastoral Commission of the Vatican Congregation for the Evangelization of Peoples. Some anonymous women missionaries are quoted as having said, "A woman is better suited to all that relates to life rather than to structures. She is better equipped for acting in the area of personal relations." This observation is then declared subordinate by the same women to three more general principles. The document affirms that the basic charism for both men and women is the gift of faith and baptism. Accordingly, a life lived in accordance with the gospel constitutes true witness and supersedes any subsequent differentiations. Furthermore, spiritual depth, consistency between preaching and one's way of life, the equilibrium and joy in the Spirit that results from this consistency are charisms that have no boundary and can be equally shared by men and women. There then follows a lengthy discourse on specifically feminine qualities. It deserves quotation in full.

On the other hand, women themselves, and men who observe them at work, recognize that certain human qualities are more specifically feminine and are a precious resource for evangelization.

As fashioners of life, women are aware of the conditions that this slow germination of persons, according to both nature and grace, demands of them and develops in them. They show a great capacity for loving what is to come, and for living in hope, in spite of delays, disappointments and trials.

"That human beings may have life," full life and especially that of the soul through grace, "that they may have life more abundantly," through the gospel, the sacraments and the Church, women are capable of giving themselves without counting the cost.

Their devotedness is often more intuitive than that of men; they are better able to grasp the aspirations and distress, even when unexpressed, of mankind and to sense what response ought to be made. Their intuition spontaneously produces practical initiatives: "Man is a being of ideas, woman a being of action," it has been said, though the antithesis should not be exaggerated.

A woman reacts with more continuity and fidelity than a man to life as it presents itself. Her faith in life sustains her faith in grace and gives her the patience necessary for the work of natural and supernatural education. As the sanctuary in which each living person begins to grow, women have a more alert sensitivity to and a deeper respect for the individual person and his special qualities; they are better judges of character, and better able to bring to flower the seeds of good that lie latent in every well-disposed soul.

In the complex work of evangelization they show a special capacity for establishing contacts through a delicate sympathy, for patiently sowing the seeds of faith, and building up the family of God's children in countless ways.

Finally, in the face of the varied and often unforeseen demands of the actual life of social groups and ecclesial communities, experience shows that women give proof of a great capacity for personal adaptation, which enables them, even in difficult circumstances, to ensure the survival and progress of evangelization.

In fact, the history of the missions has for a long time borne witness to the very large role played by women in the evangelization of the world.

The Church can never thank them enough; and, at this particular moment of history, the best form of gratitude would probably be a more serious and more open reflection on the future of women in evangelization.[15]

It is difficult to imagine a Vatican text detailing the characteristics of males in a corresponding way, nor certainly a statement of the Church's gratitude to its male members. One cannot escape the impression that such detail is required about those who are deviant from the norm and who are marginalized in the Church and considered as a category without differentiation.[16]

E. Roles appropriate to women in the ministry of the Church correspond to their specific nature and their complementary relation with men.

Having taken up the cause of justice in the world, the Church has declared what this mission requires of her own institutions.

> The Church, indeed, is not alone responsible for justice in the world; however, she has a proper and specific responsibility which is identified with her mission of giving witness before the world of the need for love and justice contained in the Gospel message, a witness to be carried out in Church institutions themselves and in the lives of Christians.[17]

The Pontifical Commission for Peace and Justice reflects this realization. "If her evangelical mission is to be effective, the Church must first and foremost stimulate in the world the recognition and promotion of the rights of the human person, beginning with an act of self-examination, a hard look at the manner and degree in which fundamental rights are observed and applied within her own organization."[18] In an uncharacteristic phraseology this document later states, "All persons are made in the image of God, the Father of all. They thus feel themselves, and indeed truly are, brothers and sisters equal in dignity and freedom."[19] Quite as noteworthy as the use of the phrase "brothers and sisters" is the acknowledgment that equality in dignity and freedom is something felt or experienced by persons today.

It is perhaps in the light of the admitted demands of justice upon the Church itself that in the past year several documents have addressed the roles of women in the Church, especially the statement on "The Role of Women in Evangelization" from the pastoral commission of the Vatican Congregation on the Evangelization of Peoples (October 19, 1975), and Pope Paul's text "Women/Balancing Rights and Duties" (January 1, 1976). The operative principles applied in these statements are those of woman's specific feminine nature, her unique qualities as a woman, and her *appropriateness for* serving in auxiliary, nurturing ministerial roles.

"The Role of Women in Evangelization" is a case in point. Basic premises are contained in the first two paragraphs. First the universality of the Christian call to participation in evangelization is declared. "The work of evangelization belongs to every Christian, regardless of sex, age or condition. By virtue of their baptism Christians are not only called and enabled to possess the faith, but also to radiate and transmit it."[20] The text then continues with a principle of differentiation.

The motivations and forms of this work, which is basically the same for all, are differentiated according to groups and individuals, and one of these differentiations obviously derives from the nature, masculine or feminine, of the persons concerned.[21]

The authors then declare their intent to examine the feminine group while admitting that both "categories" have "features appropriate to each" which merit study. There is no indication that a companion document on "men's role" and evangelization is contemplated. The approach is based on an "attentive study" of the Bible which, it is stated, is easier now than in the past. There is, however, little to suggest the application of contemporary exegetical methods in the following.

In noting that God created human beings male and female, Genesis, at the beginning of the sacred text, indicates briefly but clearly the complementary nature of the two sexes; that is to say, their likeness, difference and convergence in every human enterprise, including therefore evangelization.[22]

Once again, relying curiously on "dozens of groups of women missionaries" as noted earlier, the "traditional occupations" of women missionaries in hospitals, schools and welfare services are recommended as essential. The anonymous women missionaries suggested other areas for the expansion of women's ministry—catechetical work, active home visiting, active contribution to retreats and spirituality sessions, counselling, the teaching of religion "including theology when one has the necessary qualifications," activity in the social communications media. There is confidence that, with a presupposed deep faith and "appropriate pedagogical preparation," women "will bring to their task their own special gifts of sensitivity and finesse."[23]

The document then spells out two groups of parish activities in which feminine qualities will be useful, the first called "roughly" *administrative*, the second directly pastoral. To the first it is envisioned that women will bring "the precious contribution of their sense of concrete reality, their methodical and personal diligence and their practical creativity." For the pastoral duties which, it is cautioned, do not constitute ministries in the strict sense, "women have a special educational role to play, which men cannot lay claim to."

Preparation of people for sacraments is as open to women as to priests. Hope is expressed that priests who are "often overburdened in this area will find women to be valued associates in it." They are advised to give women the responsibility and independence due to "their personal qualifications." The document remarks with approval that long experience in some cases and the success of new initiatives by women in other instances have taken women into areas previously reserved to priests. It adds, "Some of these were previously reserved to priests, but are not of their nature sacerdotal and so may be made the object of a 'diakonia' or service on the part of women."[24] Examples cited are the presiding over Sunday and weekday assemblies in the absence of a priest, exhortation and instruction of the faithful in their Christian duties, distribution of the blessed sacrament though the allusion here is to a "sister." More extraordinary are the cases in which, with a bishop's authorization, a sister is in charge of a parish, administers baptism and presides as the Church's official witness at marriages. Given the possibility of these responsibilities for women, the following line is surprising. "Other functions, such as the prayer for the sick and at funerals, are also urgent, but the role of women in them should be the object of further precise study."

Another observation contained in this text is worth quoting here.

> It is certain that sisters often suffer deeply at the sight of the neglected state of Christian communities, threatened by loss of vitality and death. Their requests to be entrusted with greater pastoral responsibilities spring from this anguish and not from a spirit of pretension, and should be examined with sympathy and urgency required by the circumstances.[25]

Though the context does not seem to imply women's requests for authorization to perform sacramental ministry the description corresponds to the kind of experience which leads many women to consider such a possibility for themselves. The writers can only hope . . . "that, to the consecrated women's offer of their service, the authorities will reply with the full range of possibilities, which are many."[26]

The continued reference here to "sisters" raises questions about the involvement of lay women in evangelization. In the introductory background to the text the lay women Pauline Jaricot and Jeanne Bigard are cited as founders of the first mission-aid societies. Apart from the sections dealing with women's characteristics in general, the remainder of the treatise seems to imply that its concern is with women religious and their roles in evangelization. Though this may be only an impression, it is sufficiently strong to cause women who are not members of apostolic religious institutes to question the real possibility of their being encouraged to carry on the work of evangelization which belongs to them by virtue of their baptism.

Pope Paul's statement on "Women/Balancing Rights and Duties" echoes the concern that women in the Church contribute to the immense task of evangelization their special talents, both human and divine. He is especially concerned, however, that "Women should be encouraged and assisted in the role of prime importance which they take on in their families."[27] He includes a word of warning against some of the pitfalls in current strivings for equality.

The equalizing of rights must not degenerate into an egalitarian and impersonal leveling. Egalitarianism, which is blindly pushed by our materialistic society, is little concerned with the specific welfare of persons, and contrary to appearances it takes no notice of what is suitable or not suitable for women. It thereby runs the risk either of "virilizing" them or depersonalizing them. In both cases, it does violence to women's deepest qualities. Egalitarianism can even favor certain forms of hedonism which are a threat to the spiritual and moral integrity of women and to their purely human dignity.[28]

The corrective for the dangerous consequences of an unrestrained egalitarianism is predictable. "Authentic Christian advancement of women is not limited to the claiming of rights. The Christian spirit also obliges all of us, both men and women, to remember always our own proper duties and responsibilities."[29]

The Apostolic Letter *Ministeria Quaedam* issued on August 15, 1972, perhaps implicitly carries this kind of reasoning through to its conclusion. The letter which revised Church discipline on first tonsure, minor orders and the subdiaconate opened the offices of lector, acolyte and subdeacon to the laity. The rationale cited in the letter is quoted from the Vatican II *Constitution on the Sacred Liturgy* as follows.

Mother Church earnestly desires that all the faithful should be led to that full, conscious, and active participation in liturgical celebrations which is demanded by the very nature of the liturgy. Such participation by the Christian people as 'a chosen race, a royal priesthood, a holy nation, a purchased people' (1 Pt. 2, 9; see 2, 4-5) is their right and duty by reason of their baptism. In the restoration and promotion of the sacred liturgy, this full and active participation by all the people is the aim to be considered before all else; for it is the primary and indispensable source from which the faithful are to derive the true Christian spirit; and therefore pastors of souls must zealously strive to achieve it, by means of the necessary instruction, in all their pastoral work (14).[30]

Phrases such as "all the faithful," "the Christian people," "right and duty by reason of their baptism," "participation by all the people," are inclusive seemingly of all baptized Christians, men and women. They are nonetheless at odds with the statement occurring in norm 7 of the letter: "In accordance with the venerable tradition of the Church, installation in the ministries of lector and acolyte is reserved to men." This statement is also in evident contradiction with the developing practice in the contemporary Church whereby women competently assume the roles of acolyte and lector in parishes in growing numbers, to say nothing of the expanded responsibilities of women cited in *Women in Evangelization.*

This text particularly must cause reflective women to ask seriously whether or not the authors regard them as included among all the faithful, among Christian people, among those who have rights and duties by reason of their baptism. A casual reference to the Church's "venerable tradition" in such a context is inadequate and ambiguous and can only raise questions about the meaning of a tradition that is inconsistent with such basic ecclesial concepts as inclusion among the people of God and the consequences of baptism.

Conclusion

This survey of selected texts from official Vatican documents of the past twenty-five years supports the conclusion that they are informed by a distinctive "ontology of woman." This ontology is distinctive for one category of human beings because by implication women's nature has a specificity revealed through a unique set of personal traits evident in her behavior. These characteristics are interpreted as necessarily flowing from the woman's child bearing function in procreation which in turn dictates her primary and indispensable role in nurturing children in the family. It is a role of complementarity with men whose educative influence in the family is necessary but secondary. The familial role of women is essential and normative. All other possibilities which may open to women through sociocultural development are legitimate for her to the extent that her complement of unique "feminine" qualities can be expressed in a nurturing supportive capacity. The rights of women are those compatible with her nature understood in this way. The championing of these rights, which is to say in another way the preservation of women's dignity, is taken as a special responsiblity of the Church. This follows from the conviction that the ontology of woman may be expressed philosophically, but its final guarantee is in the divine order of things. The theological foundation is claimed to be ultimately rooted in the revelation contained in the first two chapters of Genesis. It is thus deemed to be absolute and unchangeable.

II. AN ONTOLOGICAL OPTION

The official teaching of the Church on women revealed through formal statements from the Vatican, while possessing a certain inner logic which can be elucidated, nonetheless does not resonate with the conclusions to which many women today have come after reflection upon their growing experience. Consequently, thoughtful women are challenging the ontological and theological presuppositions upon which such a doctrine, incompatible with their emerging self concepts, is founded. That biological differences established in the divine order of creation must be definitive of women and their social roles is not immediately evident in the existential order of human reality. In fact this option for designating the roles of women and men is only one of a variety of possibilities which might be suggested.

Peggy Ann Way, surveying the several ontological approaches to sexual differences taken by various persons and groups, suggested that they are five,

1. There are fixed sex roles in the orders of creation. The male is superordinate; the female, subordinate.
2. Biology determines the crucial shapes which masculine and feminine experiences take. The male-female duality is complementary on this basis.
3. There is no sexual difference in the nature of things. Culture wholly transcends biology.
4. There are polarities of human existence which have been called masculine and feminine polarities but which are not determinative of sexual roles.
5. New cultural experiences should speak for themselves. There is not enough data on what is masculine and what is feminine, especially since feminine possibility is new and needs time for fuller realization.[31]

In this schema the official Roman Catholic position would seem to encompass the first and second options with emphasis upon what has been established in the divine order of things. The third option attributes all gender differentiation to the influences of acculturation in the course of time, while the fifth seems not to accord value to the cultural experience of the past.

The fourth option is the one having the most to recommend itself to those interested in a holistic view of human persons. It allows for the fact that individual persons manifest a unique complement of human characteristics, that on a continuum of human potentialities from what has been called "masculine" to what has been viewed as "feminine" individual men and women would fall in various places. Operationalizing such an option would involve affirming people for what they are individually without requiring them to conform to sex role stereotypes. It is an ontological option which accords well with Pope Paul's statement on the rights of individual persons when he speaks generically in the passage quoted from *Populorum Progressio* above, p. 84.

The problems which arise when individual persons are required to fit their behavior to stereotyped expectations of what it is to be a man or a woman have been widely identified and discussed. The data accumulated in psychological and sociological studies is a record of human experience and is in contradiction with the ontology represented by option one. But even these sciences are inadequate to the extent that they share with theology the tendency to deal with an abstract category *woman*. "Despite thousands of years of concern, something important has eluded the grasp of philosophers and scientists. Somehow in our eagerness to know and understand women as a group, we have overlooked women as individuals. We have forgotten that a woman is, above all else, a person. We have surrounded women with myriad restrictions and demands, assuming that what is good for some women is good for all. The individual woman, as a person, has been ignored."[32] This nicely summarizes a pervasive problem in the Church's centuries old treatment of women. It is epitomized in the model of Mary constantly held up for imitation by women.[33]

Part of the difficulty in understanding the mind of the Church on women is due to the ambiguity experienced in trying to relate the treatment of human persons (*man* used generically) to those which treat of women specifically, especially in the absence of any corresponding special tracts on male persons. It is evident that among human persons women are singled out as a distinct category and described as such without allowance made for differentiation of the individual traits of personality which women experience in themselves. It is in this respect that the presumed essential function of woman at the heart of the family is a critical issue for interpretation. This is the factor which repeatedly surfaces with urgings that women's role in it be protected especially so that proper attention be given to the rearing of the children. There are no extended treatises on the man's role in the family, apparently because his major area of responsibility is elsewhere.

There is an assumption in all of this, namely, that in a family as traditionally structured, indispensable human values are insured. The family is viewed therefore as a stable social organization to be preserved in a proven pattern of relationships. There is considerable evidence to the contrary, however, especially as the family with its traditional sex roles is subjected to the pressures of rapidly changing economic structures. "The sociological, anthropological, or social theories all seem to point—ultimately—to changes in the requirements of the economic system as the prime moving forces of shifts in sex roles or changes in the status of women."[34] Social organization within the family was a product of a long agricultural era;[35] it changed with the advent of the industrial age; it continues to adjust to the assaults of a world moving faster than its powers of assimilation toward post-industrialization. As women and men are caught up in the confusion of contemporary life many have come to question the traditional division of labor in the family and roles in society. A significant trend toward "dual-career" families has come about, for example, as more women have entered the labor market.

The dual-career family is one in which both "heads" pursue careers. It is not only a situation of dual careers but of acknowledged dual family responsibility.

The implication is not, as with the concept of women's two roles, that men do not also have two roles. Both men and women, in the dual-career family, have both career roles and familial roles, and with the exception of pregnancy and childbirth, there is no assumption that any of the activities are inexorably sex-linked. This is not to say that there are categorically no biologically linked sex differences in the capacities of men and women to perform specific activities, e.g. "mothering." The probability is that there are "overlapping curves" of characteristics such that some men may have more of one attribute (say, nurturance) than some women and, conversely, some women may have more of an attribute (say, mechanical skills) than some men (Riesman 1965). At the same time more women may turn out to be more nurturant biologically than most men and more men may turn out to be more "mechanical" than most women.[36]

This sociological analysis of the sex role differentiation appropriate to the dual-career family reflects the fourth ontological option described earlier. It further points to a better foundation for speaking of equality in the relation of spouses within the family. When each has a career and when each has a designated role to play in the family according to individual capabilities there is a foundation for genuine complementarity of shared participation in carrying out mutual responsibilities. The possibility of a kind of complementarity that shields a superiority-inferiority relationship is removed. Respect for the uniqueness of persons is operationalized.

What this might mean in terms of the Vatican mentality is that special sections on women peripheral to documents on human rights might be obviated in favor of needed expositions on the family, with broader concerns for the complementary partnership of the adult persons who form that social unit to achieve its ends. Complementarity of persons is not complementarity of sexes. But that such a new approach might be adopted seems unlikely if a principle enunciated by Pope Paul continues to be applied as it is at present, namely, "In the exercise of Our apostolic ministry, We move beyond sociological situations and problems and adopt a theological and spiritual viewpoint."[37] This raises the issue of appropriate theological method and the relation of the human sciences to theological reflection in the matter of sex role differentiation as in all other areas of theological concern. Not only do Vatican pronouncements on women appear to be made in isolation from the kinds of data available from such sciences as anthropology, psychology and sociology, but they are also made in isolation from the insights of modern biblical scholarship.

One of the tasks of biblical interpretation is to recognize and take into account the fact that the biblical materials are themselves products of acculturation. As Raymond Brown points out, "Since the Bible contains the word of God *in the words of men*, these texts reflect the sociology of God's people respectively in the first century A.D. and the eleventh century B.C. They cannot be repeated as normative today in a different sociology without first investigating whether the change of social condition does not require a different expression of God's will for his people."[38] This principle applies certainly to the first two chapters of Genesis so frequently invoked as precedent for a view of divinely established differences in the natures of men and women.

Evidence of the kind of painstaking work required to exegete the meaning of Old Testament texts pertinent to the issue is found in the recent report of the Pontifical Biblical Commission on the ordination of women.[39] The report notes at the beginning that "in general the role of women does not constitute the principal object of biblical texts." As a consequence investigators must rely on "information given here and there."[40] The members of the pontifical commission indicate the scope of the inquiry in the survey of both Old Testament and New Testament texts reviewed briefly in their document. They make a careful distinction between the equality of men and women in the spiritual domain and the moral area, which is the teaching of the Bible, particularly the New Testament, and the social condition of women which is a sociological problem. This problem, the report states, must be treated as such:

1. In terms of the laws of sociology: physical and psychosomatic data of feminine behavior in an earthly society;
2. In terms of the history of the societies in which the people of God lived during and after the composition of the Bible;
3. In terms of the laws of the Church of Christ, his body, whose members live an ecclesial life under the direction of a magisterium instituted by Christ, while belonging to other societies and states.[41]

The application of the first two of these criteria is less evident in current official teaching about women than the influence of the third.

The Pontifical Biblical Commission points out a direction for theological inquiry involving biblical texts which is a continuing requirement for a Christian community in bringing its faith into relation with developments taking place in contemporary society. A simplistic use of long standing assumptions about the meaning of the scriptures is a failure in the kind of responsibility to be expected from a Church which takes its teaching function seriously.

> It is from the perspective of their freedom that man and woman discover not only their equality and their complementariness but also the paradox of their freedom. The Bible does not contain a ready answer to the question of the role of women in the Church or in society. Many questions related to this role remain for contemporary theologians to investigate. Biblical faith, however, from Abraham to Jesus Christ, lays the basis of a theology of womanhood which goes counter to the traditional attitudes and practices of Christendom and challenges the Church of today to rethink critically and creatively the functions of man and woman.[42]

Those who accept such a challenge in the name of the Church and her official teaching must include women who alone can bring a requisite reality testing to this area of study. Yet there is little evidence of even a few women being recognized as "highly qualified" for the task. This will remain a consistent problem in a male dominated Church, customarily alluded to in female terms, but habitually couching its formal pronouncements in a male idiom.

The seeming impossibility of gaining admission to the exclusively male preserve of theologizing for a reconsidered doctrine leads some women to look for other ways to bring their experience into the mainstream of movements that have potential for a Church renewal which will remove them from their present status of a marginated category of persons. In the post Vatican II tension among varying ecclesial self concepts, especially those of hierarchy and people of God, many concerned Christian men and women forsake the privileged domain of the former for the real possibilities present in the latter. For the Church as people of God is accessible and large segments of it are open to new initiatives of leadership for the exploration of faith and the renewal of ministry. Increasing numbers of women find acceptance and creative possibilities for testing their own newly discovered potential in opportunities for Christian service in response to genuine needs with which they are confronted.

In this respect women are in a good position to do something advocated by theologian Letty Russell who recalls that it is the liberating and saving action of God that opens up future and hope. This, she says, is the key to creation and not the other way around. "Those who begin with creation, without first gaining a new perspective are likely to lose sight of the eschatological dimension of partnership as seen in the *koinonia* creating presence of Christ in their lives."[43] The new perspective comes from considering the meaning of two words most frequently used in the early Church to connote partnership, namely, *koinonos* and *metochos*. Commenting on the more familiar *koinonia*, she says "The emphasis of *koinonia* or community is on a two-sided relationship of giving or receiving, participation, impartation, fellowship."[44] We are set free for others by a new focus of relationship in a common history of Jesus Christ. *Koinonia* enables us to come to a new theological understanding of partnership of women and men and of all sizes and groupings of Christians. "A new event of God's traditioning action in Jesus Christ results in a focus of *koinonia* that sets us free for *diaconia*.[45] Russell proposes that instead of perpetuating the hermeneutical debate over Genesis 1-3, Christians would be better advised to begin exploring the meaning of the New Humanity in Jesus Christ as *anthropos* (human), not just *aner* (male). She says ". . . as important as sexuality is in the lives of each of us, the bearer of the image of God is servanthood (*diakonos*), not sexuality, and is best expressed in many varieties of partnership (*koinonos*)."[46]

When the emphasis is upon the service made possible through partnerships of whatever numbers of persons, it is easier to see that personal gifts are neither equally distributed nor sex-linked.

Every human partnership, of whatever kind is based, not on equality of gifts, but on a relationship of mutual trust that allows each to find his or her best forms of service and affirms this in others. To assume we know a person's gifts simply because of her or his biological sex is a form of "heresy," because the Spirit works in many ways through people.[47]

Russell suggests a model for praxis that is already in effect within the Church. Women, lay and religious, along with men who share their vision, have begun to form relationships and pool talents for the sake of services they perceive to be needed. In them can be found an opting for the priority of mission over structure in the Church.

This is a hopeful sign for the future of the Church. Women, all "lay" people, married and single, indeed all Christians who desire to be responsible for their role in evangelization will, by the power of the Spirit dwelling in them, come to an ever deeper realization that it is to his mission that the Lord calls them, that the forms and structures of the Church have no other purpose than to serve and facilitate that mission, that in the freedom Christians enjoy they will form life-giving partnerships witnessing to the unifying and reconciling mission of the Lord. Many will come to the threshold of sacramental ministry without the requisite empowerment to carry it out. This will perpetuate the pain to which the document on "Women and Evangelization" alludes with such apparent insensitivity. But it will not be in vain. The Spirit of the Lord in bringing in a new future cannot be contained.

Conclusion

However limited the scope of an inquiry into the place of women in the Church, the effort invariably leads to the most fundamental questions about the meaning of the incarnation and redemption of Jesus Christ, about the nature and function of the Church in carrying out his mission. This paper reveals a sufficient number of inconsistencies in formal Church teaching to show the critical need for: a new anthropology, based upon conclusions from contemporary studies, as a foundation for a reconsidered theology of incarnation in which all Christians, men and women, would be seen as participating fully in the redemption and saving mission of Jesus Christ; a candid opening of the question of the meaning of authority in the Church and how it is exercised in relation to the promulgation of teaching that is dependent upon highly specialized disciplines, such as philosophy, the human sciences, Scripture and the various areas of theology; serious attention to the ways in which the Church as a people of God can be fully formed, organized and actualized to participate in mission according to the gifts that belong to individual Christians; the need to address the perplexing question of ministry, what it is, how it is structured, who is responsible for it and how.

NOTES

1. "The Role of Women in Contemporary Society," *The Pope Speaks*, XIX (December 8, 1974), 314.

2. Synod of Bishops, *The Ministerial Priesthood and Justice in the World* (Washington: National Conference of Catholic Bishops, 1971), p. 44.

3. "The Role of Women in Contemporary Society," p. 316.

4. *Ibid.*, p. 315.

5. *Ibid.*

6. "To Women," Closing Messages of the Council, *The Documents of Vatican II*, ed. by Walter M. Abbott and Joseph Gallagher (New York: Guild Press, 1966), p. 733.

7. "The Right to Be Born." *The Pope Speaks*, XVII (No. 4, 1973), 335.

8. *Origins*, IV (May 1, 1975) 718.

9. *Origins*, V (February 19, 1976), 552.

10. *Ibid.*

11. *Origins*, IV (May 1, 1975), 719.

12. *The Documents of Vatican II*, p. 734.

13. *Origins*, IV (December 26, 1974), 431.

14. *Origins*, IV (May 1, 1975), 719.

15. *Origins*, V (April 22, 1976), 703-704.

16. In his address of December 8, 1974, to the Italian Catholic Jurists, Pope Paul repeated an assessment of woman which he had originally included in an address to the Italian Society of Obstetricians and Gynecologists on October 29, 1966: "As We see her, Woman is a reflection of transcendent beauty, a symbol of limitless goodness, a mirror of the ideal human being as God conceived it is in his own image and likeness. As We see her, Woman is a vision of virginal purity that revitalizes the highest affective and moral sentiments of the human heart. As We see her, she is, for man in his loneliness, the companion whose life is one of unreserved loving dedication, resourceful collaboration and help, courageous fidelity and toil, and habitual heroic sacrifice. As We see her, she is the Mother—let us bow in reverence before her!—the mysterious wellspring of life, through whom nature still receives the breath of God, creator of the immortal soul. . . . As We see her, she symbolizes mankind itself."

17. *Justice in the World, op. cit.*, p. 42.

18. "The Church and Human Rights," *Origins*, IV (September 4, 1975), 163.

19. *Ibid.*, p. 168.

20. *Origins*, V (April 22, 1976), 702.

21. *Ibid.*

22. *Ibid.*

23. *Ibid.*, p. 704.

24. *Ibid.*, p. 705.

25. *Ibid.*

26. *Ibid.*

27. *Origins*, V (February 19, 1976), 551.

28. *Ibid.*, p. 552.

29. *Ibid.*

30. "The Ministries of Lector and Acolyte," *The Pope Speaks*, XVII (Autumn, 1972), pp. 257-261.

31. "Woman as Possibility," *Woman and the Word. Toward a Whole Theology* (Berkeley, California: Office of Women's Affairs, 1972), pp. 8-10.

32. Edwin C. Lewis, *Developing Women's Potential* (Ames, Iowa: Iowa State University Press, 1968), p. 3.

33. Pope Paul, in his statement to the Italian Catholic Jurists, after recalling that his ministry required a theological and spiritual viewpoint, immediately referred to Mary. "We call attention to that creature whom Christ, her Son, frequently addressed as 'Woman,' for she can serve as a point of departure in the attempt to answer many questions even of the temporal order, the family and society. We wish to encourage the woman of today, in her quest for authentic development as a woman, to look to Mary as a model, for Mary is radiant with genuine beauty and spotless holiness . . ." *Origins*, "The Role of Women in Contemporary Society" (December 8, 1975), p. 315.

34. Harriet Holter, "Sex Roles and Social Change," *Toward a Sociology of Women*, ed. by Constantina Safilios-Rothschild (Lexington, Mass.: Xerox College Publishing, 1972). p. 331.

35. Ashley Montagu points out that throughout more than nine-tenths of the long history of humankind, its economy was characterized by food-gathering and hunting. He derives from this fact a basis for a long cultural conditioning of women and men which, precisely because of its beginnings in prehistory, can and has been mistaken for biological determination. Cf. *The Natural Superiority of Women*, New Revised Edition (New York: Collier Books, 1974), pp. 12-16.

36. Rhona Rapaport and Robert N. Rapaport, "The Dual-Career Family: A Variant Pattern and Social Change," *Toward a Sociology of Women*, pp. 236-237.

37. "The Role of Women in Contemporary Society," *Origins* (December 8, 1975), p. 318.

38. *Biblical Reflections on Crises Facing the Church* (New York: Paulist Press, 1975), p. 51.

39. "Can Women Be Priests?" Report of the Pontifical Biblical Commission, *Origins*, VI (July 1, 1976) pp. 92-96.

40. *Ibid.*, p. 92.

41. *Ibid.*, Part II, p. 94.

42. Samuel Terrien, "Toward a Biblical Theology of Womanhood," *Religion and Life* (Autumn, 1973), p. 333.

43. Letty M. Russell, "Theological Aspects of Women and Men in

Christian Communities," *Bulletin International. Femmes et Hommes dans L'Eglise,* No. 17 (Avril, 1976), p. 7.

44. *Ibid.,* p. 6.
45. *Ibid.*
46. *Ibid.,* p. 7.
47. *Ibid.*

Full Participation of Women in the Life of the Catholic Church

EDWARD J. KILMARTIN, S.J.

This essay is concerned with the question of the future possibilities of women for full participation in the life of the Roman Catholic Church and the foreseeable impact which changes in the legal structure would have on other churches, notably Anglican and Orthodox-Oriental Churches. Since the future is both proximate and remote, this theme will be treated in two parts. First the current official position of the Catholic Church is discussed together with some important changes in discipline which are seen as possible within this framework. This is followed by an evaluation of the impact which projected changes in discipline may have on other Christian churches.

The second part of this essay deals with an evaluation of the official doctrinal position of the Catholic Church on the key issue of ordination of women to the pastoral office and the theological significance of the pastoral responsibility currently awarded to women in the Catholic Church. These considerations provide partial grounds for judging whether full participation of women in the life of the Catholic Church is a remote possibility.

I

1. OFFICIAL POSITION AND PROJECTED CHANGES IN DISCIPLINE

Within the last six years the Roman Catholic Church has been in the process of developing an official position with regard to the question of participation of women in the life of the church. Within the scope of this theme the Roman Magisterium has been obliged to formulate a response to the problem of ordination of women to the episcopacy and presbyterate (= pastoral office).

An important step in this direction was taken by the Canadian delegation at the III Synod of Bishops, 1971. The spokesman for this group, Bishop Flahiff, raised the question of the possibilities for women in the ministries of the church and requested the formation of a mixed commission to study the problem.[1] A related statement and a recommendation were incorporated into the synod's document on *Justice in the World.* Here it is affirmed that women "should have their own share of responsibility and participation in the community life of society and likewise of the church." The further suggestion is made that "this matter be subjected to serious study employing adequate means." Among the adequate means is mentioned the formation of "a mixed commission of men and women, religious and lay people, of differing situations and competence."[2]

One year later the *Motu Proprio, Ministeria Quaedam,* did address the question of participation of women in the liturgy. On a relatively minor point, and running contrary to practice already widely established, Norm VII excludes women from admission to the ministries of lectorate and acolyte.[3] However this negative reaction to the participation of women in the liturgical ministries of the church was followed by the announcement, May 3, 1973, of the creation of the Vatican Study Commission on Women in Society and in the Church.[4]

Among the limitations of the commission's competence was the exclusion of the investigation of the question of ordination of women. At the press conference it was said that this pertained to the International Theological Commission.[5] However a more significant limitation came to light with the unauthorized publication of the secret memorandum on the mandate and competence of the commission which was leaked to the press three days later.[6]

This memorandum indicates that the commission is to take for granted that man and woman have "specifically different" and "yet complementary roles." The commission is asked to investigate the role of woman and related functions in society and church. Nevertheless the memorandum does not develop the scientific basis of the presupposed "specifically feminine." No indication is given of the extent to which the role determines woman's functions, nor, indeed, is function defined.

The memorandum states that the specific character of woman is lost if she extends her role. In the concrete it is affirmed that priesthood lies outside woman's role. On the other hand this document foresees the possibility of women actively participating in leadership of Catholic organizations or pastoral institutions of the church, membership or consultorship in curial organs of the universal church. The possibility of some more active share in the liturgy is also granted. To qualify women for certain tasks the suggestion is made that a "special rite" could be instituted "which would have a sacramental value."

At the IV Synod of Bishops, 1974, the study commission made a progress report. It refers briefly to the inconclusive contribution of the human sciences to its study. On the other hand it stresses the need for a theological investigation of the mystery of man and woman in their share in the mystery of the Trinity and which entails a deepening of ecclesiology and mariology.[7] The commission judged this study to be of the highest importance for clarifying the tradition of the church in the matter of accession of women to the ministries and for orientating current research on the new ways of participation of women in ecclesial responsibilities.

The next document originating from the study commission is the *Study Kit* provided on the occasion of the International Women's Year 1975.[8] It includes practical suggestions, a questionnaire on participation of women in the life of the ecclesial community, recommendations made to the synod of bishops, the *UN Declaration on the Elimination of Discrimination against Women* and a similar address of Paul VI. The theological content of the *Study Kit* conforms to the general direction of the commission's work. No attention is paid to the contribution of the human sciences. The first of two biblical studies emphasizes the nuptual symbol and mariology; the second treats of the novelty of the Gospel outlook on women. In the latter essay the following statement is inserted abruptly and without further explanation: "The women do not receive an official call to follow Christ, as do the men, they follow him spontaneously; but they are given a special mission in the apostolic community."[9]

This statement is unexpected in a document of a commission which is not *ex professo* concerned with the question of ordination of women to the ministerial priesthood. It implicitly bases the exclusion of women from the pastoral office on the practice of Jesus. The same thing is stated in an unequivocal manner by Paul VI on April 18, 1975, in his address to the Committee for the International Women's Year. In what appears to be a paraphrase of the aforementioned statement, he says that "women did not receive the call of the apostolate of the Twelve and therefore to the ordained ministry."[10]

The study commission met for the last time on January 26—31, 1976, to discuss its final report. In February, 1976, Bishop Bartoletti, president of the commission and the one who was to have edited the report, died. While the full report is not available, the recommendations formulated during the final session have been published.[11] They reflect an advance over the recommendations made to the IV Synod of Bishops. In the latter case the commission called for placing women "in positions of recognized and effective responsibility" in local communities, ecclesiastical organizations, temporary commissions of bishops or the Holy See, departments of the Holy See (as consultors, members, officials).[12] In the new recommendations, two are particularly significant.

In no. 3 the suggestion is made that "competent bodies" should make a thorough study of the following questions: 1) accession of women to non-ordained ministries of the church; 2) participation of women in the liturgy: considered in the light of II Vatican's Constitution on the Liturgy, the norms established by the Congregation of the Sacraments and Divine Worship and the current practice in various churches; 3) participation of "non-ordained persons in jurisdiction (in the wide sense) within the church." No. 4 asks that adequate provision be made in the revision of the Code of Canon Law for the responsible participation of women in the life and mission of the church.

The foregoing documents show considerable openness to participation of women in the ministries of the church. Still they exclude the possibility of ordination of women to the pastoral office. What, then, might one reasonably expect from a serious study of the question of ordination of women undertaken by Roman commissions? At least one answer was given by Bishop Bartoletti in an interview on November 24, 1975. He stated that the study commission on women was persuaded that a profound study on the ordination of women was necessary. However he judged that such a study would result in no recommendation for a change in practice. It would only provide a more adequate presentation of the grounds for excluding women from the ministerial priesthood.[13]

The decision to employ the Pontifical Theological Commission and the Pontifical Biblical Commission for such a study was made by the Vatican in 1975. The results of the work of the former commission are not available. The report of the Pontifical Biblical Commission, however, was recently obtained from unofficial sources by the press.[14]

A key sentence of this report, unanimously accepted by the members of the Biblical Commission which began its work on April 8, 1975, affirms: "It does not seem that the New Testament by itself alone will permit us to settle in a clear way and once for all the problem of the possible accession of women to the presbyterate."[15] This carefully qualified statement can be interpreted in several ways as is clear from the fact that the members of the commission could vote 12 to 5 in favor of this proposal: "Scriptural grounds alone are not enough to exclude the possibility of ordaining women."[16]

The reports of the two commissions were made to the Doctrinal Commission which is presumably preparing a paper on the question of ordination of women. As yet that document has not been published. In the meantime, however, as the work of the commissions was going on, no moratorium was declared on the issue. On July 9, 1975, the Archbishop of Canterbury wrote to inform the Pope about the growing consensus in the Anglican Communion "that there are no fundamental objections in principle to the ordination of women to the priesthood."[17] In response to his request for "ecumenical counsel," Paul VI wrote on November 30, 1975, that the Catholic Church "holds that it is not admissible to ordain women to the priesthood for very fundamental reasons." He then lists the arguments which he deems decisive in the matter: 1) the example of Christ choosing apostles only from among men; 2) the constant practice of the church; 3) the constant teaching of the magisterium that women are excluded from the priesthood "in accord with God's plan for His church."[18]

In this summary of Vatican documents relating to the question of ministry of women, one other must be mentioned. It is a study issuing from the Pastoral Commission of the Sacred Congregation for the Evangelization of Peoples. It was made public in March, 1976 and is entitled: "The Role of Women in Evangelization."[19]

This document deals with the "specific role of women in evangelization." This exclusive concentration on women is justified on the presupposition that the biological differentiation of the sexes and the complementarity in the physical procreation of life is intended by God to be extended to "every human enterprise, including therefore evangelization." To support this view an appeal is made to the Book of Genesis which "indicates briefly but clearly the complementary nature of the two sexes." Evidence is given for the active cooperation of women in the political and religious spheres in the Old Covenant. Mary, the Mother of Jesus, is seen as prototype of this role of women both through her cooperation in the Incarnation and in the time of the church as "Queen of the Apostles." Reference is made to the women who followed Jesus, who were associates of the apostles, and the modern missionary efforts of Christian women. All of this shows that in the course of history women have exercised a significant role in the work of evangelization.

Continuing on this historical perspective the document notes that current developments in the progress of emancipation of women call for a new study of the extent of the possibilities of women's participation in the work of evangelization. As a contribution to this study some reflections are offered on the "specifically feminine qualities" which must be considered in order that the responsibilities, functions and ministries of women be consistent with the "true nature of their charism."

What these specifically feminine qualities are can be gleaned from observations of women at work. They are grounded in the fact that women are "givers of life and consecrated by nature to its service." Thus in keeping with the intimate association which women have in the process of "germination of persons, according to nature and grace," women are more sensitive to the conditions required for the development of the human person and develop in themselves peculiar traits which foster their role as 'fashioners of life.' "

In the concrete, women, as opposed to men, are awarded a greater capacity for intimate personal relations: "A woman is better suited to all that relates to life rather than to structures. She is better equipped for acting in the areas of personal relations." This theme is amplified by stating that women have a "great capacity for loving," for self sacrifice, sensitivity toward the individual person and practical initiative based on the intuitive grasp of the proper response to be made to the aspirations of mankind. Man, on the other hand, is viewed as a "being of ideas," and is more suited to what relates to structures: leadership role in formulation of ideology and administration at the highest levels.

The document distinguishes between various activities in which women may legitimately engage in the life of the church. Along with the "indirect apostolate" traditionally exercised by missionary Sisters in hospitals, schools and welfare services, various modes of proclamation of the Gospel are enumerated. They extend from "apostolic home visiting" to teaching of theology. On the level of parish activities two situations are distinguished.

In the first case women can be placed at the service of a resident pastor and given responsibilities in administrative and directly pastoral activities. In the latter instance, however, the activities do not constitute "ministries in the strict sense." In the second case a situation is envisaged in which "Sisters" are "permanently in charge of parishes, with the authorization of the bishop." Here they can do everything which is not of its "nature sacerdotal and so may be made the object of 'diakonia' or service on the part of women." It is recommended that the commissioning for such responsibility "be left to the local bishop, once the conditions to be fulfilled have been determined by the highest competent authorities." It could be based on "a juridical type of mandate or on an appropriate blessing or on some other mode of commission to be determined." In any case the only women considered for such a ministry are women who belong to religious communities.

From the foregoing Vatican documents we can conclude that the current official Roman Catholic position on women excludes them only from pastoral functions which are "sacerdotal." While a list of such functions is not given, the celebration of the Eucharist, Confirmation and Penance are certainly included in the activities reserved to ordained ministers.

It is unlikely that the more open way taken by the National Conference of Catholic Bishops (NCCB) in their study of the question of ordination of women will be followed in the near future in any Vatican paper on the subject. This report of the NCCB lists seven arguments against the ordination of women to the ministerial priesthood.[20] While the first four are seen as inconclusive, the fifth argument: concerning the necessity of correspondence between Christ the male and those who act officially *in persona Christi*, and the sixth argument: derived from the practice of Jesus in selecting males as apostles, are judged to need further study. The seventh argument is based on the practice of the church and the traditional interpretation of it as "of divine law." This is considered to be of "ponderous theological import." Still the possibility of "contrary theological development" is not absolutely excluded. The report concludes that the main problem is this: Has the magisterium "already given a definite and final answer?"[21]

2. ECUMENICAL IMPACT

The ecumenical impact of the official Catholic position and projected changes regarding woman's participation in the life of the church can be discussed under three headings: (1) The Major Reformation Churches; (2) The Anglican Communion; (3) The Orthodox and Oriental Churches.

(1) *The Reformation Churches*

All major denominations have already gone beyond the official Catholic position in theory and practice. In general they do not foster a dualistic view of human nature which attributes precise roles to man and woman. Supported by their traditional theology of pastoral office, they consider the role of woman in the ministry to be a matter of church discipline subject to change under different historical conditions.[22] However any concrete change within the Catholic Church favorable to women may be expected to influence the attitude toward women ministers of those churches which still give them a position of "professional marginality."[23] Yet the refusal to ordain women by the Catholic Church will only serve to support theologians and others in these churches who are convinced that the practice of ordaining women is contrary to New Testament order and take for granted that a truly Christian anthropology excludes women from the pastoral office.[24]

(2) *Anglican Communion*

What has been said about the major Reformation Churches is partially applicable to the Anglican Communion. Practical changes in the Catholic Church will serve to support the present position of women in consultative and decision making positions within the Anglican Communion. But the official position of the Catholic Church on ordination of women will help to foster the present debate on the matter in Anglican circles. Furthermore this stand of the Catholic Church will cause a good measure of hesitancy among Anglicans who favor ordination of women only with the consent of the whole church.

However it seems unlikely that the present Catholic position will have any decisive effect on the future Anglican policy. While the Anglican Communion as a whole does not yet accept the practice of ordaining women to the office of presbyter and bishop, there has been a steady growth in this direction over the last fifty years.[25] The number of those opposed to such ordinations in principle seems to be waning.[26] The recent action of the General Convention of the Episcopal Church in the U.S.A. reflects this. The House of Bishops voted 95 to 61 to permit ordination of women to the priesthood and episcopacy on September 15, 1976. On the following day the House of Deputies approved this decision by slightly more than fifty percent, thus reversing its stand taken in 1970 and 1973. The immediate effect of this decision on the whole Anglican Communion is not yet known. Still it seems likely that this step as well as a similar one taken by the Episcopal Church of Canada will be imitated elsewhere.

The major difficulty for some Anglican leaders and theologians appears to be their desire for approval of the Catholic and Eastern Churches before any innovation takes place. The letter of Archbishop Coggan to Paul VI, which occasioned the letter of the Pope mentioned earlier, indicates this. He refers to the "slow but steady growth of a consensus of opinion within the Anglican Communion that there are no fundamental objections in principle to the ordination of women to the priesthood."[27] On the other hand, by informing the Pope in a formal way, he manifests his concern to act in the matter within a collegial context. Indeed, he goes on to say: "Thus in view of our concern, both for the truth as it is understood within the Anglican tradition, and for ecumenical counsel, we are already in correspondence with his Eminence Cardinal Jan Willebrands . . ."[28]

This communication shows sensitivity toward two types of argumentation which present a problem for the Anglican Communion: (1) the capacity of women for the ordained ministry; (2) the possibility of one "branch of the church" acting against the received tradition of the other branches of the church without their consent.[29] Archbishop Coggan would prefer to have the approval of other churches for any positive action of the Anglican Communion. Still his letter seems to imply that the Anglican Communion will act in accord with the truth as it understands it if arguments to the contrary are found untenable.

A decision of the Anglican Communion as a whole to ordain women will, of course, somewhat complicate the relationships being developed with the Catholic Church. One more difficulty will be raised for the Catholic Church in the matter of recognition of Anglican Orders. But it is unlikely that the recent decisions of the Episcopal Church in the U.S.A., or a similar general decision of the Anglican Communion, will have a decisively negative effect on Anglican-Catholic relations as a whole.[30]

(3) *Orthodox and Oriental Churches*

The official position of the Catholic Church falls in line with that of the Orthodox and Oriental Churches. These churches have made no official statements on the question of women. The mechanism for such an action is not readily at hand, especially for the Oriental Churches. The proposed Pan-Orthodox Synod would provide the occasion where such a statement might be made by the Orthodox Church as a whole. In the meantime we can only expect declarations of individual national churches. They will most certainly coincide with the official Catholic position. Orthodox theologians, in general, accept the duality of human nature, the essentially different roles of man and woman and so the impossibility of ordination of women to the priesthood.[31]

At the same time the Orthodox and Oriental Churches have no fixed stand against the involvement of women in decision making positions within the life of the church. The Greek Archdiocese of North and South America has women holding positions on Archdiocesan councils. In the matter of liturgy, of course, women are not given an active role as lector, homelist, etc.

Projected changes in Catholic Church discipline regarding women will probably cause some difficulty in two areas. Eastern churches will find problems with a decision to allow women a more active share in liturgical activity. They will have even greater difficulty with a decision to include women in a share in the power of jurisdiction traditionally given to those ordained to the priesthood or episcopacy. These churches already have difficulty with the Catholic Church's approach to the relationship between power of orders and power of jurisdiction. In practice the Orthodox and Oriental Churches do allow, at times, ordinations in which the candidate is not immediately given pastoral jurisdiction (e.g. auxiliary bishops in the Greek Archdiocese of North and South America). But they have no theology to justify this. Hence it remains an anomaly. In the Orthodox view ordination confers the power of being a priest (power of orders) and the right to actively function as such (power of jurisdiction). In other words it involves a pastoral installation into a community in some sense. Moreover this installation is always conditioned by an ordination. Hence any decision of the Catholic Church to grant power of jurisdiction traditionally related to ordination would be seen as a deviation from the recognized order. It would probably provoke the charge that the Catholic Church misunderstands the nature of the office of bishop and priest.

Certainly any movement of the Catholic Church in the direction of ordination of women would have a decisively negative effect on its relations with these churches. Individual Orthodox leaders and theologians take very seriously the arguments, also proposed in official Vatican circles, against the ordination of women: (1) the practice of Jesus;[32] (2) the traditional practice of the church;[33] (3) the order of creation as unfolded in Genesis in which the roles of man and woman are not interchangeable;[34] (4) symbolic correspondence between Christ the male, head of the church and the person who acts officially in the person of Christ.[35] Some Orthodox leaders have already indicated that a decision in favor of the ordination of women in the Anglican Communion would have a "decisively negative effect" on Anglican-Orthodox relations.[36]

II

Within the last six years the Vatican position on women has developed to the point where women are excluded in principle only from the ordained pastoral office. In certain circumstances not only may they be awarded a form of pastoral jurisdiction but also allowed to exercise leadership in various forms of liturgical worship, excluding perhaps only the celebration of the Eucharist, the Sacrament of Penance and the completion of the baptismal initiation: Confirmation. In brief women are seen as capable of exercising a ministry of word and sacrament. Only the ministry of the sacraments is limited in principle.

What is the theological explanation proposed to justify this latter limitation? Is the granting of pastoral jurisdiction compatible with this?

The exclusion of women from the full ministry of the sacraments is grounded in the theological arguments used to exclude women from the ordained ministry. But from the viewpoint of tradition ordination is the basis for the exercise of pastoral jurisdiction. In the course of history it is true that a *de facto* separation of the power of orders and power of jurisdiction obtained at times in both the East and West. Moreover this was justified theoretically in the West and so appears less of an anomaly than in the East. One can also point to the Western canonical theories of the late Middle Ages which required only tonsure as the basis for the power of jurisdiction. Still on the whole both traditions have required ordination at least as a *conditio sine qua non* for the exercise of the power of jurisdiction. Moreover in the Catholic Church today the pendulum is swinging back to the ancient view, witnessed in the authentic whole liturgical tradition, that the power of jurisdiction is rooted in the ordination rite and not in a *post factum* deputation to a concrete mission.

From the perspective of tradition the awarding of ordinary pastoral jurisdiction to women while refusing to ordain them appears to involve a failure of right order. However before discussing this question in some detail the arguments proposed in official Catholic circles against ordination of women will be analyzed.

1. EVALUATION OF THEOLOGICAL ARGUMENT
AGAINST ORDINATION OF WOMEN

These arguments are reducible to two types: (1) appeal to scriptural and traditional theological statements about the specific role of women vis-à-vis man and the practice of excluding woman from the pastoral office; (2) theological explanations of traditional doctrine and practice which attempt to fathom the divine plan reflected in the received doctrine and practice. The first argument is considered decisive; the second, since it offers an explanation of the reasonableness of the practice, is an attempt to support the conviction that the practice is "of divine origin." Hence one who grants the validity of the first argument accepts only the responsibility of showing the reasonableness of the church's practice. On the other hand, one who finds difficulty with the first argument will look on the theological explanation as crucial.

(1) *Argument from Traditional Practice and Doctrine*

Those who simply appeal to traditional practice and statements to exclude women from the pastoral office view the historical facts as directly reflecting the mind and will of God for us now. They presuppose that at least some statements and practices can be generalized and so considered independently of the situation in which they arose. They do not appear to accept the position that an adequate hermeneutic always demands that the interpreter discover an analogy between the historical situation and the practice and statement linked to it, on the one hand, and the present historical situation and question which is being asked, on the other hand.

The extreme form of this outlook ignores or denies the historicity of all human speech and conduct in those aspects of church life where a seemingly constant practice and consistent interpretation have been maintained. Consequently little attempt is made to distinguish between constant practices which express Catholic Faith from those which pertain to cultural conditions. The context of the message that is expressed: its purpose, its relation to local and temporal conditions, is not explored. Within this mind set one feels secure in simply transposing the message and practice across space and time and expects the Spirit to exercise only a basically conservative role, i.e., of not allowing the church to deviate from the established doctrine and practice.

In this understanding of historical reality, scripture, Jesus and the apostles are seen to have handed on a complete set of truths applicable to any historical situation. These truths are considered to be eternally valid, independent of the context in which they were first spoken and always known by the church. No problem is envisaged in the process of transmission of these truths from age to age or the need of anything but the negative assistance of the Spirit. The question of the emergence of truth out of a previous pre-cognitive state is not given serious attention.

Operating on this basis it is clear that a *non constat* will be written against proposed women priests. On the other hand, this view of reality is being seriously challenged under its various forms by Catholic and Western Christian theology in general. Modern Catholic theology and biblical exegesis works from the principle of the historicity of all human speech and conduct, including that of Jesus. Catholic scholars are conscious of the problem of the normative value of traditional practices and interpretation. They take for granted that truth emerges to some extent from pre-cognitive stages. They appeal to the concrete history of the church for the fittingness of awarding to the Spirit a creative role in guiding Christians in the formulation of doctrine and practice for new times and conditions.

This fundamental difference of perspective within the Catholic Church will have to be overcome before any general consensus can be attained—whether pro or con—on the question of ordination of women. To set a timetable for the resolution of the problem would be too daring. One can only point to the general trend of thinking, evidenced also in II Vatican, which inclines to take seriously the historical dimension of ecclesial practices and teaching. This movement affords the basis for judging that in the future more weight will be given to the theological arguments and the results of the work of the human sciences in settling the question of ordination of women.

In this connection one has but to reflect on the change of thinking regarding the significance of the term *jus divinum*. Traditionally it was used in Catholic circles to describe the value of certain historical concretizations of church structure. When used, the structures were understood to have been instituted by positive divine law, at least in most cases, and so to be absolutely immutable. In the Code of Canon Law the statement is made that the tripartite form of ministry in its present form is derived from divine institution.[37] However history tells a slightly different story and it is well known that II Vatican was sensitive to this history. Thus while the Council of Trent states: "If anyone says that in the Catholic Church there is not a hierarchy, instituted by divine ordination, which consists in bishops, presbyters and ministers, ans."[38], II Vatican is more cautious: "The divinely instituted ecclesial ministry is exercised in different degrees by those who from ancient times have been called bishops, priests and deacons."[39]

This example shows how important it is to relate ecclesiastical decisions to their historical context, to be sensitive to the many open questions concerning the dogmatic history of the sacrament of orders and to recognize the distinct possibility that many individual structures of pastoral office derive from human changeable right. In fact it is extremely difficult to escape the conclusion that while pastoral office concretizes certain data of revelation, the concretizations are always determined by historical factors and so not only are changeable but should be changed with varying circumstances lest they become irrelevant and ineffective.[40]

In view of the many difficulties associated with the assessment of the normative value of any traditional practices and interpretations, the simple appeal to the traditional exclusion of women from the ministerial priesthood and the sporadic attempts to link this to divine institution do not provide a solid basis for refusing ordination to women in principle. To move toward a solution of the question theological arguments which relate this problem to the whole economy of salvation are important. Perhaps they will prove even decisive in conjunction with the findings of the human sciences.

(2) *Theological Reflections on Traditional Practice*

The theological justification for the traditional practice of excluding women from the ministerial priesthood usually involves considerations of the order of creation, the mystery of the Trinity, christology and ecclesiology. While the argument is presented as a whole, the christological and ecclesiological groundings are considered crucial. We can begin with an outline of this argument. This will be followed by some comments on one central issue which it raises.

A. *Order of Creation.* Since God created male and female with complementary functions and gifts, they have different roles. Some functions and gifts are common to both realizations of human nature and so they are interchangeable. The fundamental roles are not. Man has the role of headship; women has the role of protectress and channel of life. Since these roles are intrinsic to man and woman, a change of roles leads to dehumanization.

B. *Trinitarian Considerations.* Gen 1:27 reveals partially why this order of creation was instituted: "God made man to his image and likeness; in the divine image he created him: male and female he created him." Here it is implied that the division of humanity into male and female is one of God's ways of revealing His mystery. The male reveals God as one who continually presides over His handiwork; the female serves as transparency for God as source of life and harmony in family and society.

With the explicit revelation of the Trinity through Jesus Christ one comes to know God more fully: God the Father, as primordial source of all life; God the Son, as creative source of the world; God the Spirit, as the perfective cause of the world. Consequently one recognizes that the male is to witness to its prototype, the Father and the female to its prototype, the Spirit. Where both use their gifts to build up the family and community, they reflect the mystery of the Son: creative cause of the world.

C. *Christological Considerations.* The Incarnation of the Second Person of the Trinity as male has deep symbolic significance. Because he is Lord of the Church, he comes as male in accord with the order of creation in which the male has headship and represents the Father: primordial source of all blessings.

D. *Ecclesiological Considerations.* Christ is the head of the Church composed of males and females. Hence all believers are called to represent Christ to the world as mediator of salvation. They do this through the charisms of the Spirit which they possess and which allow them to serve as transparency for Christ's active presence in the world in a variety of ways. Among the charisms which believers possess are included either malehood or femalehood. This particular charism fits the person for different roles and functions.

In the matter of pastoral office the charism of maleness is required. To this must also be added the special charism given by the Spirit which qualifies the person to serve as representative of Christ, the Lord of the Church. This special charism is not given to females and not given to all males. It is a relational entity which enables the chosen male to directly represent Christ in the task of leadership of the Christian community. This charism is bestowed through ordination within the community. This act enables the community to recognize the gift of the Spirit which is bestowed and so enables the person to exercise his pastoral office. Thus the pastor directly represents Christ the head of the church before the community through the charism of the Spirit which makes him an icon of Christ and so enabled to build up the church. Of course the pastor also represents the church, as confessing believer, in his official acts.

In this interpretation of the economy of salvation, women are excluded from the pastoral office in principle. In the order of creation the role of headship is given to male. This order is followed in the New Covenant where the headship of the church is given to Christ the male. In the order of creation the role of protectress and channel of life is given to the female. This order is followed in the New Covenant where the role of protectress and channel of life is given to Mary. The role of Mary, type of all women, has its prototype in the Spirit; the role of Christ the man, type of all men, has its prototype in the Father who presides over all life.

Women can share in many functions of men in the church because they are interchangeable. But the role of woman cannot be exchanged for that of man. Hence they cannot be ordained to pastoral office: leadership of the church. In principle all men have an essential charism required for pastoral office but more is necessary since the church is hierarchically structured. Only some males receive the additional call and charism of the Spirit to fulfill the task of pastoral office.

Argued abstractly this view of the economy of salvation can appear very consistent. The trouble comes when it is confronted with the concrete situation where women exercise with success leadership functions together with males in secular society and in Christian communities without any apparent "dehumanization." The proponents of this argument are thus forced into the position of affirming the unique situation of the pastoral office vis-à-vis secular office. The pastor has the function of representing Christ the head of the church. Hence the appeal is made to the necessity of the church preserving the "ideal" order of creation in order to witness to the mystery of the Trinity and to the fact that Christ the male is Lord of the church. Only male pastors can fulfill this role.

A detailed criticism of this argument cannot be presented here. Only one basic affirmation will be analyzed in some detail because it is so basic to the whole structure of the reasoning that its weakness is indicative of the value of the whole argument and the faulty methodology employed.

Some modern papal encyclicals and documents of II Vatican speak of the priest as representative of Christ.[41] Although in these same writings the precise theological explanation of the relationship of the priest to Christ is not developed, some modern Catholic theologians, taking their cue from these official statements, have insisted on this theme as the key to the theology of ministerial priesthood.[42]

Much of the recent literature which follows this line of thought is open to criticism from two directions. First of all the typical mistake of traditional scholastic theology is made: failure to use the liturgy as a true source of theology.[43] Secondly the assumption is made that the representative role of the priest in relation to Christ can be explained apart from the priest's role to represent the church.

An adequate answer to the question of the relationship of the priest to Christ and the church requires a systematic consideration of the various modes of presence of Christ in the church and their relationship to the faith of the church. When all this is taken into consideration one is drawn to the conclusion, in harmony with the authentic whole tradition of the liturgy of ordination and the Eucharist, that the pastoral office directly represents the faith of the church and so represents Christ who is the sharing source of this faith along with the Holy Spirit.[44]

Because the office bearer represents the church united in faith and love in his role as leader, he represents Christ the head of the church. Of course this conclusion does not imply that the pastoral office arises from a simple delegation of the community. From the christological point of view, it is grounded in Christ who is present as active source of the faith of the church. Consequently the office bearer acts in the name of but not simply by the commission of the local church.

In this interpretation the peculiarity of pastoral office consists in the official caring for the common matter of all believers: the mission of Christ. But the fulfillment of the mission of Christ is only possible through the active presence of the "Spirit of truth" whom Christ promised (Jn 16:7-14) and who, with the development of Trinitarian theology, is identified as the Third Person of the Trinity: the principle of sanctification in the time of the church. Therefore an adequate theology of pastoral office must take into account its function to represent the Holy Spirit who is present as sharing source of the faith of the church. This pneumatological dimension sheds light on the essential relationship of the ministerial priest-hood to the church. It guards against the temptation to define the priest only in relation to Christ and so to forget the essentially social character of the ministerial priesthood.

The christomonism underlying the scholastic theology of priesthood is not adequate to express the theology of pastoral office expressed in the ordination rites of the East and West, which stress participation in the Holy Spirit. Sufficient attention is not paid to the *and* in the theological statement that the priest represents Christ *and* the church. This *and* signifies a relationship of interdependence of one representative role on the other. Only by attending to this is one able to develop an adequate theology of ministerial priesthood which is sensitive to the principle of intelligibility in all theology: the relationship of each aspect of the economy of salvation to all the others.

Certainly the ministerial office, an essential aspect of the sacramental reality of the church, represents Christ. But the priesthood of all believers grounds another form of representation of Christ. Both representative functions derive from the sacramental nature of the church in which Christ is present together with the Holy Spirit as sharing source of the faith. Consequently the peculiarity of ordained ministry cannot be explained by an unqualified appeal to the concept of representation of Christ or even by making a distinction between the general mission of the baptized to represent the mystery of Christ in the world and the role of the ordained ministry to represent Christ as head of the church. The context of the ordination rites offers a more ample perspective which must be taken into account. Celebrated in the framework of the prayer of invocation of the entire community, the ordained is seen as inserted in a special way into the Spirit-filled church.

The unilateral view of the priest as representative of Christ inevitably leads to stress on the individual character of the grace of ordination. In this theology it is difficult to explain the inner connection between ministry and community. Thus scholastic theology, which takes this point of departure, was constrained to develop the theory that insertion of the priest into ecclesiastical responsibility is not included in ordination but rather depends on a *post factum* concrete assignment.

This christological perspective is intimately linked, possibly in a reciprocal cause-effect relationship, with the medieval scholastic theory of "absolute ordination" wherein ordinations were recognized when carried out by a bishop without jurisdiction and involving candidates who had no title of mission.[45] It rests on a serious misunderstanding of the relation between law and sacrament. Another result of this faulty outlook is the conception of the relationship of the priest to the universal church and local church. It tends to see the priest in immediate relationship to the universal church and only secondarily to the local church and bishop.[46]

By failing to articulate the pneumatological and ecclesiological aspects of ordination, the christomonistic view of ministerial priesthood is incapable of explaining the relationship between law and sacrament, local church and universal church, specific responsibilities of ministers and responsibilities of all Christians in the mission of Christ. It lacks a Trinitarian perspective which gives due consideration to the role of the Spirit.

Recent studies on the ordination rite of bishop and presbyter have underlined the fact that the authentic whole tradition of the East and West understands that the bishop receives the threefold office of pastor, priest and teacher and that the priest is given a share in this threefold office.[47] This research serves to support recent attempts to rethink the doctrine of "priestly character" in terms of a permanent relation of the subject to a gift of the Holy Spirit, a collegial charism, received at ordination in view of a pastoral ministry. Within this theology of *character*, the ordained minister is understood to be committed without reservation to a leadership role and to be representative of the Spirit in an eminent way: the Spirit of the priestly church, the source of all sanctification in the time of the church.[48]

The relevance of this more ample christological, pneumatological and ecclesiological theology of ministerial priesthood for the question of ordination of women seems obvious. Here the priest emerges as directly representing the church united in faith and love and so representing Christ and the Holy Spirit, sources of unity and faith of the church. Consequently the argument based on the presupposition that the priest directly represents Christ is difficult to use against the proposal to ordain women. Logically an appeal to the representative function of the priest would seem to support the view that women should be ordained. For the priest must be seen as representing the one church composed of males and females and so the Lord of the church and the Spirit who ground the unity of faith and love. But this seems to demand, in the proper cultural context, both male and female office bearers. Moreover if one is inclined to follow through the argument from symbolic correspondence to its logical conclusion, it would seem to end with a preference for females, given the traditional role awarded to the Holy Spirit in the liturgical tradition of the ordination rites. But there is another reason why the question of ordination of women represents a true theological problem. It has to do with the concrete structure of pastoral office being realized in the modern Catholic Church.

(3) Theological Significance of Pastoral Responsibility Currently Awarded to Women

The Vatican document on the role of women in evangelization refers to the current practice of placing Sisters "permanently in charge of parishes, with the authorization of the bishop." This is only one aspect of the recent move within the Catholic Church to award an increased share in ecclesiastical tasks to women as well as to married men.

These persons are being given assignments formerly exercised exclusively by the ordained. While they are unable to receive ordination because of marital status or sex, they do perform works for which the power of jurisdiction, linked to the power of orders, was formerly necessary. Even today these works can only be undertaken by special ecclesiastical mandate. Consequently in functioning as leader of the liturgy of the word, preaching at gatherings of Christians, giving religious instructions at all levels of parish life, these persons must be recognized as acting in the name of the church.

Circumstances are forcing the sharing of women and married men in regular pastoral tasks. This development is initiating a situation in which the ordained are being replaced by others in the sphere of the ministry of the word. Because of their dwindling number, priests are being forced to concentrate more on the particular ministry of the sacraments. Thus the genuine interlacing between the ministry of sacraments and word is increasingly loosened.

Moreover the commissioning of laity to act in the name of the church goes against the ancient tradition in which ordination and commission to a ministry came together. Even in the Middle Ages and up to the recent present the understanding of pastoral office involved an essential relation between ordination and official commission to act in the name of the church. Therefore the practice of appointing laity to pastoral ministry raises the question concerning the identity of ecclesiastical office: the essential Catholic unity of the ministry of word and sacrament, of rationality and grace.

At present we are in a situation in which, on the grounds of the traditional practice of not ordaining females and married men and considerations such as the maleness of Christ, church authorities are content to loosen the unity of the ministry of word and sacrament and the connection between sacramental ordination and juridical commission for a particular pastoral service.

In a recent article J. Neumann points out that these considerations show why the question of ordination of women is an essentially theological one and an important one. He does not view the developments which have taken place as healthy and foresees a situation in which the priest will be more of a "magician" who goes about celebrating certain sacraments without exercising a true ministry of the word.[49] He advises that the Catholic Church should reflect on the fact that it lives in history and in its historicity is bearer of God's truth and fidelity. Church leaders should ask whether they are acting in conformity with the comprehensive will of God when they exclude at least half of the members of the church from full participation in pastoral office on the grounds of sex or marital status. In his judgment the tradition of almost two thousand years should not provide an obstacle to ordaining women if serious attention is paid to the dependence of religious structures on historical circumstances. Preference should be given to the creative role of the Spirit in the life of the church rather than to a Latin-Stoic tradition. He concludes with this remark: "The exclusion of women and married men from spiritual office does violence not only to the spiritual 'right' of all baptized, but clashes with the freedom of the Spirit."[50]

The situation we have been discussing is concerned with the woman who is commissioned to act as pastor. It would be incorrect to qualify her as a "church employee," as though she was acting without a juridical mandate and so without true authority. In this connection the Study Commission on the Role of Women in Society and in the Church speaks of "participation of nonbaptized in jurisdiction (in the wide sense) within the church." In this instance a separation of the power of orders from jurisdiction is difficult to justify theologically. And, in any case, those who would justify this separation in the case of women who exercise a true pastoral office seem to be open to the charge of inconsistency. At least this question can be raised: Can they logically maintain the historicity of this church structure and at the same time appeal merely to the constant tradition of the church to exclude women from ministerial priesthood?

Conclusion

The current theological arguments raised against the ordination of women to the ministerial priesthood in official Catholic circles are rather weak. Moreover the practice of awarding permanent pastoral assignments to women in certain parts of the Catholic Church does not harmonize well with the exclusion of women from the ordained pastoral office. In this situation a definitive decision to rule out ordination of women would clash the "majesty of the facts." One might even say that the *onus probandi* is shifting from those who advocate change to those who support the *status quo*.

It is difficult to avoid the impression that an adequate explanation of the official Catholic Church position on ordination of women must go beyond the theological arguments proposed. A number of pastoral concerns and at least one important ecumenical consideration are involved. Among the pastoral concerns can be enumerated the following: 1) the lack of readiness of many local churches to accept women priests coupled with the administrative inability of the Catholic Church to allow local decisions in such matters; 2) the shocking effect which such ordinations would have on the self-understanding of many priests; 3) the desire to upgrade the self-image of priests through stressing in every way possible the essential distinction between ministerial priesthood and the common priesthood of all believers; 4) the fear of what this change in church discipline would have on the relatively stable administrative life of the Catholic Church.

Beyond these concerns which pertain to the inner life of the Catholic Church, there is an important ecumenical one. The Catholic Church will be able to live with the decision of the Anglican Communion to ordain women and this decision, when it comes on the international level, cannot be expected to greatly influence Catholic Church practice. Churches look to their past for their identity. The Catholic Church is always able to say to the Anglican Communion: We are your past; you are not our past. The situation, however, is different in the case of the churches of the East.

There is discernible in the Catholic Church a genuine longing for reunion with the churches of the East. This is evident in the spectacular declaration of II Vatican about the reverence for Eastern Churches and the openness of the Catholic Church to "worship in common."[51] In this regard one can also point to the Vatican's current ecumenical efforts directed especially toward the Eastern Churches. Coupled with this is the anxiety not to fall under the judgment of these churches which never cease to repeat: We represent your past; you do not represent our past.

It is perhaps the fear of the effects of change within the Catholic Church and the guilt feeling which the Eastern Churches instill through their criticism of the Western Church's "lack of fidelity to the past" which may prove for the proximate future to be the real grounds for excluding women from full participation in the life of the church.

NOTES

1. A request which received considerable support. Cf. M. T. van Lunen-Chenu, "La Commission pontificale de la femme: une occasion manquée," *Études* 34 (1976) 880.

2. Third Synod of Bishops (1971). *The Ministerial Priesthood and Justice in the World* (Washington: USCC, 1972) 44.

3. August 15, 1972. Cf. J. O'Connor, ed., *Canon Law Digest* 7 (New York: Bruce Publ. Co., 1973) 694. Also: *Ministries in the Church.* Bishops' Committee on the Liturgy, Study Text 3 (Washington: USCC, 1974) 7.

4. On the occasion of this announcement it was stated that this action was inspired by a discourse of Pius XII and the address of Paul VI to the women of the world given at the close of II Vatican. Cf. L.-Chenu, *op. cit.*, 884.

5. L.-Chenu, *op. cit.*, 884.

6. *Ibid.*, 884-889.

7. *Ibid.*, 889.

8. *International Women's Year 1975: Study Kit* (Washington: USCC, 1975).

9. *Ibid.*, 20.

10. *Origins* 4 (1975) 719.

11. "Recommendations on Women in Church and Society," *Crux Special* (September 20, 1976). Also: *L'Osservatore Romano* (English ed.) August 12, 1976, 4-5.

12. *Study Kit*, 28-29.

13. L.-Chenu, *op. cit.*, 886, n. 29.

14. "Biblical Commission Report: Can Women be Priests?" *Origins* 6 (1976) 92-96.

15. *Ibid.*, 96.

16. *Ibid.*, 92.

17. "Letters Exchanged by Pope and Anglican Leader," *Origins* 6 (1976) 129.

18. *Ibid.*, 131.

19. *Crux Special* (October 4, 1976).

20. "Theological Reflections on the Ordination of Women," *Journal of Ecumenical Studies* 10 (1973) 695-699.

21. *Ibid.*, 699. In his statement on behalf of the Administrative Committee of the NCCB, October 7, 1975, Archbishop Bernardin draws on this document. While noting the importance of the seventh argument, he maintains a cautious openness toward further development (*Origins* 5 (1975) 257-260).

22. J. E. Lynch, "The Ordination of Women: Protestant Experience in Ecumenical Perspective," *Journal of Ecumenical Studies* 12 (1975) 194.

23. *Ibid.*, 194-195.

24. *Ibid.*, 195.

25. *Ibid.*, 186-191, 194.

26. For reports of discussion groups on the possibility of Ordination of women at the April 1975 meeting of the Conference of Anglican Theologians (Seabury-Western Seminary, Evanston, Ill.), cf. W. T. Stevenson, "A Case for the Ordination of Women," *Nashotah Review* 15 (1975) 310-319; E. G. Wappler, "Theological Reasons Against the Ordination of Women to the Priesthood and Episcopate," *Ibid.*, 320-324.

27. *Origins, op. cit.*, 131.

28. *Ibid.*

29. This was a major concern of the commission on the ministry of women appointed by the Archbishops of Canterbury and York. Its report, published in 1935, affirms that one branch of the church cannot rightfully ordain women to the priesthood without the consent of the other branches (Cf. Lynch, *op. cit.*, 187).

30. For a discussion of the effect which such a change might have on the Anglican-Catholic Dialogue, cf. "Anglican-Roman Catholic Consultation: Statement on the Ordination of Women," *Origins* 5 (1975) 349-352. This document recognizes that some difficulties will be created and attempts to show why the move to ordain women in the Anglican Communion will not lead to ARC's "termination or the abandonment of its declared goal" (349).

31. There is no real evidence of a debate in Orthodox theological circles on this question. Cf. "Orthodox-Roman Catholic Consultation: Bishops and Presbyters," *Origins* 6 (1976) 142-143: The omission of any reference to an Orthodox discussion on the matter is due to the fact that the consultation knows of no published positions of Orthodox theologians which run contrary to the Orthodox tradition.

32. Archbishop Athenagorus, in a letter to his archdiocese, refers with approval to the statement of Paul VI made in his address to the Committee for the International Women's Year 1975 ("The Question of the Ordination of Women: A Letter to the Reverend Priests and People of the Archdiocese of Thyatiera and Great Britain, May 14, 1975," *L'Osservatore Romano*, July 3, 1975, 9-10.).

33. A. Schmemann, "Concerning Women's Ordination: A Letter to an Episcopal Friend," *St. Vladimir's Theological Quarterly* 17 (1973) 239-244; J. Meyendorff, "The Orthodox Churches," *The Ordination of Women: Pro and Con*, ed. M. P. Hamilton and N. S. Montgomery (New York: Morehaus-Barlow, 1975) 129-130.

34. "Joint Orthodox-Episcopal Statement: A Reaction to a Proposed Ordination of Women from the Orthodox-Anglican Consultation," issued June 25, 1973 (Text obtained from the Orthodox Secretary, V. Rev. P.W.S. Schnierla). In its separate statement the Orthodox approve the concept of the duality of human nature and the different roles which exclude women from ordination.

35. "Orthodox-Roman Catholic Consultation: Bishops and Presbyters," *op. cit.*, 143.

36. Letter of Archbishop Athenagorus, *op. cit.*; Joint Orthodox-Episcopal Statement, *op. cit.*

37. Canon 108.

38. Sess. XXIII. *Decr. de sacramento ordinis*, canon 6 (DS 1776).

39. *Lumen gentium* 28 (A. Flannery, *Vatican Council II:* The Conciliar and Post-Conciliar Documents (Collegeville: Liturgical Press, 1975) 384.

40. P. Huizing, "Divine Law and Church Structures, *Theology Digest* 18 (1970) 144-150.

41. The expression is used in Mediator Dei to affirm that ministerial authority "is not a delegation from the people" (Encyclical Letter of Pope Pius XII on the Sacred Liturgy "Mediator Dei" [St. Paul Editions: Boston, Mass., 1948] no. 40, p. 20). II Vatican's *Lumen gentium* (21, 37) applies "*in persona ejus*" to bishops who share in the triple office of Christ. The concept is used in recent encyclicals especially to distinguish the role of the priest from the laity in the eucharistic celebration (*Mediator Dei* [AAS 39 (1947) 556]; Pius XII, *Mystici corporis* [AAS 35 (1943) 232-233]; Paul VI, *Mysterium fidei* [AAS 57 (1965) 761-763]). II Vatican's *Lumen gentium* 10 paraphrases the text of Mediator Dei (*Ibid.*). For other references to this role of the priest in the eucharistic celebration, cf. *Lumen gentium* 28; *Sacrosanctum concilium* 7; *Presbyterium ordinis* 2, 13.

Some difficulties arise from II Vatican's presentation of the theology of ordained ministry: 1) the conceptual fluctuation between the view of the representation of Christ *in the minister* or *in the exercise of the ministry* (For example, *Presbyterium ordinis* 12 points in the former direction); 2) the stress on the relation of the ministerial priesthood to Christ which is not balanced with the pneumatological perspective of the ordination prayers of the Roman Rite; 3) the use of the concept priesthood to express the different "essence" of the role of the laity and pastoral office in the church (*Lumen gentium* 10) and the different degrees of hierarchy in the ordained ministry (*Presbyterium ordinis* 7) which results in a conceptual impasse.

In regard to no. 3, modern Catholic theology takes a different point of departure to explain the differences between laity and ordained ministry. It bases itself on an ecclesiology which situates the ministry in a twofold representative role (Christ and the Church) and which gives place to the Holy Spirit. In this perspective the church is a fraternity constituted by different charisms of which no one is superior or inferior to the other but necessary in their differences. The starting point for the theology of priesthood is not *powers* but the community and functions which build it up and order it. Presbyter is different from laity and bishop from presbyter because each has a different role in the ordering of the church (Cf. D. N. Power, *Ministers of Christ and His Church:* The Theology of Priesthood (London: Geoffrey Chapman, 1969) 141-162).

42. L. Scheffczyk, "Das kirchliche Amt im Verständnis der katholischen Theologie," *Amt im Widerstreit*, ed. K. Schuh (Berlin: Morus, 1973) 17-25; Idem, "Die Christusreprasentation als Wesensmoment des Priesteramtes," *Catholica* 27(1973) 293-311; H. Muhlin, "Das mögliche Zentrum der Amtsfrage," *Catholica* 27 (1973) 329-358; W. H. Dodd, "Toward a Theology of Priesthood," *Theological Studies* 28 (1967) 683-705.

43. Despite the wealth of literature on this subject during the last twenty years this theme has only recently received the attention it deserves in Catholic theology. For a good brief discussion of the importance and use of the liturgy as source of theology, cf. G. Lukken, "La liturgie comme lieu théologique irremplaçable," Questions Liturgiques 56 (1975) 97-112. Also: E. J. Kilmartin, "Liturgical Theology II," *Worship* 50 (1976) 312-315.

44. E. J. Kilmartin, "Apostolic Office: Sacrament of Christ," *Theological Studies* 36 (1975) 243-264; Idem, "The Orthodox-Roman Catholic Dialogue on the Eucharist," *Journal of Ecumenical Studies* 13 (1976) 218-219.

45. This theory is foreign to the East even now and to the West up to the tenth century. Cf. C. Vogel, "Titre d'ordination et lien du presbytre a la communauté locale dans l'église ancienne," *La Maison Dieu* 115 (1973) 70-85; Idem, "Chirotonie et chirothésie," Irenikon 45 (1972) 7-21; 207-238. In these articles the author points out the earlier understanding of the importance of the ecclesial context for the bestowal of pastoral office.

46. II Vatican's *Presbyterium ordinis* 7 relates the priest immediately to the universal church and secondarily to his bishop: "All priests share with the bishops the one identical priesthood and ministry of Christ. Consequently the very unity of their consecration and mission requires their hierarchical union with the order of bishops. Bishops, therefore . . . . . will regard them as their indispensable helpers. . . ." (Flannery, *op. cit.*, 875).—This presentation conflicts with recent Catholic theological investigation of the relationship between the local and universal church which tends to favor the patristic and Eastern theological outlook. In this view the universal church exists in and from particular churches: primarily episcopal churches; secondarily communities dependent on them; thirdly gatherings of particular churches. While the unity belonging to the essence of the church is essentially transcendent: unity of faith and love, it is expressed sacramentally in local churches and among local churches through the Eucharist and hierarchically organized offices in which the local bishop is focal point in his church and the bishop of Rome serves the same function for all particular churches. The communion structure of the

church must be described primarily in terms of love since it is grounded on the Spirit. The relationships within this communion can also be described juridically because love needs order. But a delicate balance must be achieved lest in the conception of the ecclesial community merely juridical or political categories prevail. Where the pneumatological dimension is not given first consideration excessive centralization or congregational federation inevitably results and a juridical concept of ministerial authority based on the power of delegation in the hands of the highest authorities or in the concrete community as a whole.

47. D. Power, *op. cit.*; H.-J. Schulz, "Das liturgisch-sakramental übertragene Hirtenamt in seiner eucharistischen Selbstverwirk-lung nach dem Zeugnis der liturgischen Uberlieferung, *Amt und Eucharistie*, ed. P. Bläser (Paderborn: Bonifacius, 1973) 208-255; Idem, "Die Grundstructur der kirchlichen Amtes im Spiegel der Eucharistiefeier und der Ordinationsliturgie des römischen und des byzantinischen Ritus," *Catholica* 29 (1975) 325-340; D. Eissing, "Ordination und Amt des Presbyters: zur Interpretation der römischen Priesterweihegebetes," *Zeitschrift für katholische Theologie* 98 (1976) 35-51.

48. H.-J. Legrand, "The 'Indelible Character' and the Theology of Ministry," *The Plurality of Ministries*, ed. H. Kung and W. Kasper, *Concilium* 74 (1972) 54-62; J. Macquarrie, "Priestly Character," *To Be a Priest:* Perspectives on Vocation and Ordination, ed. R. E. Terwilliger and U. T. Holmes (New York: Seabury, 1976) 147-156; Idem, "The Church and the Ministry I: Ministerial Functions," *Expository Times* 87 (1976) 113-118; "II: Ministerial Character," *Ibid.*, 147-151.

49. "Wort und Sakrament nicht spalten," *Orientierung* 40 (1976) 86. This article offers a development of the third part of a longer article: "Die Stellung der Frau in der Sicht der katholischen Kirche heute," *Theologische Quartalschrift* 156 (1976) 111-128. In a book soon to be published the author treats the same theme from the viewpoint of basic Christian right (*Menschenrechte auch in der Kirche?* [Benziger, 1976]).

50. *Ibid.*, 87.

51. *Unitatis reintegratio* 15 (Flannery, *op. cit.*, 465).

Postscript

In January 1977 the Sacred Congregation for the Doctrine of the Faith published a document dealing with the current official teaching of the Roman Catholic Church on the subject of the ordination of women to the priesthood: *A Declaration on the Question of the Admission of Women to the Ministerial Priesthood.* It was approved and ordered published by Pope Paul VI on October 15, 1976.

As the official position of the Magisterium of the Roman Catholic Church, Catholics are expected to give it serious attention. However in accord with the nature of this document, it is not intended to put an end to the study of the question. Catholic theologians will recognize their duty to communicate their difficulties with this study to the Sacred Congregation.

This document reflects the position which Pope Paul has taken over the past two years. It affirms that the basis for the exclusion of women from the ordained priesthood is the *constant practice of the churches of the East and West* understood by the Magisterium to be grounded in the will of Christ. Scriptural evidence is introduced to show the reasonableness of the position of the Catholic Church. Some texts of the patristic period and of mediaeval theologians are adduced which show that at times the question of ordination of women was explicitly considered and rejected. Furthermore this teaching is clarified by the *analogy of faith.* An appeal is made to another teaching of the Catholic Church to show the "fittingness" of the practice of excluding women from the priesthood. A summary of this argument follows.

According to the teaching of the Catholic Church the priest acts in the person of Christ in the exercise of his ministry. To illustrate this teaching the traditional Catholic theology of the role of the priest in the eucharistic celebration is introduced. According to this view when the priest reads the words of institution he acts in the person of Christ "to the point of being his very image." Therefore since he is a sacramental sign, and all such signs represent what they signify by natural resemblance (according to St. Thomas), the priest must be a man: "For Christ himself was and remains a man." To explain how the priest can also represent the church, "act in the person of the church," this way is taken: "It is true that the priest represents the church. . . . . But if he does so, it is precisely because he first represents Christ himself, who is the Head and Shepherd of the church."

From the viewpoint of this writer the clarification by the analogy of faith labors under two disadvantages. First of all it has recourse to a scholastic theology of moment of consecration of the Eucharist which is almost unanimously recognized by Catholic scholars as inadequate. In its concern to underline the intervention of Christ present to his church in the person of the celebrant, this theology neglects to take into account the epicletic character of all liturgies: the function of the invocation (explicit or implicit) of the Spirit made by the community with a view to the accomplishment of the mysteries signified by the liturgical celebrations of the church. Secondly it presents a view of sacramental signification which bypasses the problem of levels of signification of liturgical celebrations of the church. It ignores the fact that all sacramental celebrations, by their very nature, signify first of all a human and social reality which, in turn, signifies for the eyes of faith a mystery dimension: the presence and activity of Christ and the Holy Spirit. From this perspective the priest directly represents the faith of the church and so Christ and the Holy Spirit who are sharing sources of the exercise of the faith in the celebration of the liturgy.

Edward J. Kilmartin
University of Notre Dame
Department of Theology
Notre Dame, Ind. 46556

An Agenda for Dialogue between Catholic Feminists and Church Authorities

JOHN T. FINNEGAN

The issue of women in the Church does not need another book.[1] There is in fact a surfeit of literature, and one cannot assimilate it all. There are many aspects of the matter that make it a particularly painful topic for the Roman Catholic Church in the United States. First, the American Catholic Church has been identified to the larger community through apostolates and enterprises chiefly staffed by women: the parochial schools, hospitals, orphanages, and other caritative agencies. Catholicism in the United States has given women opportunities to serve and leave a mark upon the institutions that shape Catholic values.[2] There is then a reserve of "women power" and a history of dedication and service that is seeking a new outlet of expression. Hardly a decision maker in the American Catholic Church—be he bishop, pastor or priest—has been untouched here, and in a very human way seek outlets to express esteem and gratitude. Another aspect of the issue on the role of women in the Church is the public nature of the question. In other areas of dissent between Catholic laity and the official teachers of the Church an informed conscientious decision can possibly be achieved which in the practical order would defuse the situation, at least personally. Not so, here. In James Carroll's book, *Madonna Red*,[3] Cardinal O'Brien listens to Sr. Dolores deny she ever attempted to celebrate Mass, and then the shrewd prelate produces an affidavit . . . the sworn testimony to the contrary. The external, public nature of this issue keeps pressure on Church authorities, and is reason to believe it will not go away.

The character of the discussion on women in the Church has taken the following form to date:

1. Authoritative statements which equivalently exclude the possibility of ordaining women. This approach distances itself from a genuine dialogue and seems to rest on the premise that a repetition of these statements will eventually suffice.[4]

2. A plethora of authoritative statements by the Church magisterium urging the full equality of women in the Catholic Church, and demanding women's inclusion in the decision making process of ecclesial life (excluding ordination, of course).[5] A delightful combination of events has led to the ignoring of these directives: women are going for the ultimate—ordination to the diaconate and the priesthood—and have not politicized around these other goals.[6] In addition, Church decision makers are content to see the question escalated to the ordination question because that is an affair over which they have no immediate authority, and it relieves them from changing the status quo. "Keep the issue focused on the unattainable, and we won't have to confront the vexing features of the attainable" . . . seems to be the latent, but real attitude.

3. The "Ordination Now" approach, and in the meantime, "act as if you are ordained." This posture recommends that women allow themselves to be chosen as community leaders and then preside at the eucharist, reconcile the sinner to the Church, etc.[7] Being sensitive to the pain women experience when they are in ministry and find themselves unable to perform tasks associated with Holy Orders is essential. However, disregard of the Catholic theology and practice of the selection and training and ordaining of priests, as well as Catholic sacramentology, can only have negative results. The fact that such a posture is being urged in some quarters should encourage Catholic leaders to insure competent theological training for women in ministry, and to involve women in the life of the Church to the limit of present ecclesiastical discipline.

4. The "Ordination Never" approach[8] is the posture of conservative theological weeklies and journals, and much of the national Catholic diocesan press. This position sees the women's movement as a cause and sign of the disruption of Catholic life and associates it with the breakdown of family values, the movement towards the acceptance of ERA, and the popularization of the abortion mentality. Whatever distortion is present here the women's movement has not taken such criticism seriously to its own detriment in Catholic circles. As the Bicentennial Catholic consultation in preparation for the Detroit Conference, October 21-23, 1976, proves, American Catholics are very much concerned with, and principally so, family values.[9] The American Catholic Church at the grass-roots is preoccupied with the protection and building up of family life. To the extent that feminist expectations appear to challenge these values, to that extent will "Ordination Never" flourish.[10] The irony of this attitude is that it faces-off with its companion, "Ordination Now," and peaks the argument at a level that intensifies discouragement and resentment. It may well be that the recent decision of the Episcopal Church of the United States to ordain women will for a time perpetuate this anxiety.

The following agenda item is being proposed to the Detroit Conference, "A Call to Action," previously referred to:

That the National Conference of Catholic Bishops working with the appropriate organizations of scholars, lay women, and religious women, and in consultation with women who feel called to the priesthood, sponsor an interpretive study of recent papal and episcopal statements on the subject of the ordination of women, and on the basis of that study and in the light of the needs of the American Church, offer clear leadership to the Catholic community by specifying their policies and plans on the subject of the ordination of women.[11]

The question arises: if the above proposal is accepted, what issues will be involved in this interpretive study? What arguments are used by the papal and episcopal documents, and can these arguments be stated in a way and manner that engages the other side? The magisterium is quite able to affirm that the issue is beyond study, and this seemed to be the approach of the Vatican Study Commission on Women and Society and in the Church. Having learned the lesson of the opinion shifts that can develop when issues are placed under study, the papal magisterium was always attentive to state the ordination of women was no part of the research of the Vatican Study Commission. It is unlikely then that either the Vatican or the Conference of Bishops will undertake a study that will create the opinion or impression of a present theological dubium. Since "current discussion of the issue has shown that traditional reasons for refusing the ordination of women are not universally acceptable,"[12] and since the Pontifical Biblical Commission states:

It does not seem that the New Testament by itself alone will permit us to settle in a clear way once and for all the problem of the possible accession of women to the presbyterate.[13]

then it would seem appropriate for the magisterium to state its reasons in a more convincing manner. All the more so since the "Theological Reflections on the Ordination of Women"[14] published by the Bishops Committee on Pastoral Practice in 1972 outlines the traditional arguments and concludes by urging further study.

It seems evident that the magisterium will not be the sponsoring agent for the research into the possible ordination of women,[15] nor should it be. If what Avery Dulles states is true, that "magisterial statements . . . should ordinarily express what is already widely accepted in the

Church. . . ."[16] then the role of the magisterium is to explain its own position and to encourage theological reflection.

It is my opinion that prolonged discussion on the women's ordination question is at the present time counterproductive and fruitless. The "Catholic typology"[17] is so different from Anglicanism, and the American Episcopal Church, that it cannot model itself on strategies peculiar to those churches. If that be the case, what is the agenda of the American Catholic community as it addresses itself to the issue of the role of women in the Church?

Issues in Dialogue with the Magisterium

The first issue is practical. How do we as Church go about the implementation of expressed magisterial goals regarding women in the Church? This includes equality before the law,[18] full participation in decision making functions of Church life with a view to modifying the present canonical understanding of "ecclesiastical office" and "jurisdiction,"[19] and the opening up of professional theological and pastoral education to qualified women. There have been some notable developments in this latter area during the past five years. One cannot help but be impressed by laywomen who undertake theological education without the financial, spiritual and emotional supports of seminarians, or even religious women. Seminaries that enroll women are shifting from a self-understanding and concept of a traditional seminary or theological school to that of a Center for Ministerial Training, some of whose students will move on to the ordained ministry. This is frequently a painful realization and process for such schools. The Detroit Conference, "A Call to Action," previously referred to, proposes:

> That affirmative action be taken by the NCCB and local Ordinaries to bring about participation of women in leadership and decision making at all levels, assure an equal status to women in Church agencies and provide professional theological and pastoral training for women in seminaries and other educational programs available for those involved in the work of the Church.[20]

Realistically and politically this is the first order of business. It is interesting to note that under the issue of "Justice in the Church," the forthcoming Detroit Conference calls for:

> the Church (to) honor the right of the faithful to competent pastoral care by providing professional seminary training in light of current pastoral priorities and needs. For example, professional training

should be provided for those lay, clerical and religious, who are to be assigned to special ministries required by diocesan pastoral plans; seminary training should be available to women preparing for the active ministry. . . .[21]

The gradualism that is already underway in the implementation of the above proposal will eventuate in the American Church having feminine models of pastoral care. Hence any future possibilities for ordination to the diaconate and priesthood will be enhanced by these new models for ministry. Certainly the almost exclusive male model for the ordained ministry has to be changed. The very sight of the irregularly ordained women priests of the Episcopal Church in roman collars is itself an indication that these new models for ministry have not been developed. This then is a task of Roman Catholicism, and in the meantime men and women working together in teams have opportunities to create an atmosphere of acceptance and trust.[22] It has been suggested that a variety of ministries should be developed for women, and that in some instances these be identified and authenticated and liturgically celebrated.[23] One wonders whether the role-free behavior evaluation of male and female life styles—so much in vogue today—would permit such a development.

A second agenda item for the American Catholic Church is the liturgy. Our Catholic liturgy is male-centered and offends Catholic men and women sensitive to the change of language current in American life . . . especially in newspapers, books and media. If Barbara Walters is the new anchor*person* in the ABC nightly news, then surely statements like "Christ died for all *man*kind" will need some modification. As "homoousion" and "hypostasis" attest, words are important. The link between "lex orandi" and "lex credendi" is so essential that it is imperative that language changes be carefully chosen and theologically accurate.[24] Since such changes touch our basic understanding of God, Christ, Redemption . . . it may well be that we are building up momentum for a future ecumenical council, dogmatic in nature, that will try to strike a Trinitarian and Christological balance as did the Council of Nicea (325), and the Council of Chalcedon (451).[25]

Protestant churches, unaccustomed to solving theological issues such as the ordination of women by the declarations of a centralized teaching office, or to being restrained by the weight of Tradition, have given the Catholic community some excellent contemporary literature on symbolism, sexual differentiation, the gender of Christ, suggested rules for the formation of new liturgical language, etc. The Scriptures are apt to be more of a problem for some Protestant traditions (e.g., Lutheran, Evangelical) than they would be for Catholics. Respect for the Word of God in

Scripture sometimes prevents Protestants from changing simple terms like "men" to "men and women," or "brothers" to "brothers and sisters." Although this would not be true in all cases, the Catholic priest would most likely be uncomfortable in changing the consecratory formula from, "It will be shed for you and for all men" to "It will be shed for you and for all men and women."

At the Faith and Order Commission meeting in Ghana, July 23— August 5, 1974, it was decided to establish sixteen regional sub-committees in various areas of the world. These committees were to research such issues as: the Christian concept of God, symbols involving gender, the authority of Scripture with reference to cultural backgrounds of biblical writings, to their theological meaning, and to comparisons with present day cultural situations, the fullness of diakonia, the ministry of the whole People of God as it affects the relationship of men and women, language, imagery symbols of Scripture and the living traditions of the Church as they influence man-woman relations. These studies were made in preparation for the Fifth General Assembly of The World Council of Churches in Nairobi, November 1975. This research is available to Catholic scholars. Catholics do not have to "invent the wheel" on the revision of liturgical language and symbols, however, there will be the task of translating this learning to the practical problems that will be generated by Catholic attitudes and experience. As a member of one of the Faith and Order regional sub-committees (1974-1975), and at the same time participant in studies and research going on in Roman Catholic circles, I was amazed at the methodological differences and the differing agendas.[26] The Catholic approach researches the tradition,[27] focuses on the teachings of Vatican II, analyzes the current cultural and sociological situations, and then holds the official magisterium accountable in responding constructively to the pastoral needs of the present moment.[28] I would describe this as a methodology quite responsive to and compatible with the "Catholic typology." From the research of the WCC we have some excellent papers on bible translations[29] and biblical language as well as considerable experimentation with the liturgy of which a trend toward Marian liturgies played a significant part. The growing acceptance in literature and the media of the "McGraw-Hill Book Company Guidelines for the Equal Treatment of the Sexes"[30] will demand changes in our liturgical books and devotional habits.[31] The suggestion of the Conference, "A Call to Action" that

> official Church documents, catechisms and liturgical books and rites be reviewed with sensitivity to language that could be offensive to persons,[32]

will, if approved, be the beginning of a long journey. This issue of revision of language and symbol should receive immediate attention, and if we are to take our cues from other Christian churches, it will be painful. The very nature of the manner and style necessary to reform liturgical books for Roman Catholics . . . with approval from Rome . . . adds a difficulty factor that will be vexing, perhaps even irritating. However, it should begin in earnest, and it should be made public that it is underway.

Finally, there must be some way of treating the ordination question in stages; first, ordination to the diaconate, secondly, ordination to the priesthood and episcopacy. The diaconate for women may well be realizable in the near future. Research is being done on the role of women in the early Church when the deaconess was an integral part of Church life.[33] It may well be that we have today something very close to the early Church deaconesses in the woman who is an "extraordinary minister" of the eucharist, and who prays with, guides, directs and teaches a portion of the faithful. Insufficient attention has been given to the 1973 decree, "Immensae Caritatis"[34] which permits women to distribute the eucharist even within the liturgical ceremony of the Mass.[35] A convincing argument can be made that a contemporary woman can pastorally do all that her sister deaconesses could do in the early Church. It is the *missio canonica*, the dimension of being sent officially in the name of the Church, as well as the liturgical ordination ceremony, that is missing. It is my contention that the Catholic Church already has some sort of "deaconess" present and active in ministry. What is now awaited is the authentication of this by the official Church, a canonical mission in the name of the Church, and an ordination ceremony. Some research has yet to be done to compare the duties and responsibilities of today's deacon with the deacons and deaconesses of the early Church. A redevelopment of the deaconess today may make her a sister of her early Church antecedents, however, it would not necessarily prove from the historical argument that she could perform the same duties as todays deacon.

In regard to the ordination of women to the priesthood, I suggest a moratorium on certain types of writing—all good in themselves—but essentially counter-productive. A type of theological and historical evaluation of the present Catholic position that makes it appear discredited and backward is not helpful.[36] The Catholic treatment of the issue at present has to be "de-Westernized." Why is it that the Bilateral Consultations between Roman Catholic and Protestant Churches of the West declare the issue an open question, or even, "the ordination of women must come to be a part of the Church's life,"[37] and yet when dealing with Eastern Orthodoxy, the Bilateral Consultations reaffirm a negative position? It would be unwise of the Pope to take a stand in such a climate. Even the

World Council of Churches has had to always preface its arguments regarding women's ordination to priesthood with: "those member Churches who agree in principle to the ordination of women to the priesthood."[38] The Association of Theological Schools uses similar language when dealing with its constituency. There are serious scholars and segments of the Church who maintain that there are valid theological issues involved in the ordination of women. These theological questions cannot be dismissed.[39] The theological issues have been identified[40] by recent papal statements and those of the President of the National Conference of Catholic Bishops as:

1. "If women did not receive the call to the Apostolate of the Twelve, and therefore to the ordained ministry; nevertheless, they are called to follow Christ as disciples and co-workers . . . We cannot change the behavior of the Lord . . ." Pope Paul VI, April 18, 1975.[41]

2. The points that surfaced in the exchange of letters between Pope Paul VI and the Archbishop of Canterbury:

   a. Letter of Pope Paul VI—Nov. 30, 1975

      —the example recorded in Scripture of Christ choosing His Apostles from men

      —the constant practice of the Church which has imitated Christ in choosing only men

      —the living teaching authority which has consistently held that the exclusion of women from the priesthood is in accord with God's plan for His Church

   b. Letter of Archbishop Coggan—Feb. 10, 1976

      —sometimes what seems to one tradition to be a genuine expression of . . . diversity in unity will appear to another tradition to go beyond the bounds of legitimacy.[42]

3. "It is not correct to say that no serious theological obstacle stands in the way of ordaining women to the priesthood."
   Statement of Archbishop Bernardin, Oct. 7, 1975.[43]

4. "The constant tradition and practice of the Catholic Church against the ordination of women . . . is of divine law . . . constitutes a clear teaching of the ordinary magisterium . . . this is Catholic doctrine."
   Statement of Archbishop Bernardin, Oct. 7, 1975.[44]

5. Whether canon 968 of the present Code of Canon Law requiring a baptized male as necessary for the validity of Orders is a doctrinal or disciplinary canon is disputed. It is clear that the official statements of the magisterium indicate that it is a juridicized doctrine of the Church.[45]

The ecclesiastical polity of the Roman Catholic Church does not permit an issue of such magnitude to be settled at the local or national level. This means that each area of the universal Church must treat aspects of the issue that it would ordinarily for cultural and historical reasons overlook, put to one side, or consider insignificant and irrelevant. For the American Catholic Church this means we cannot pass over or dismiss arguments as readily, for example, as the Episcopal Church.[46]

Summary

The American Catholic Church has to be pragmatic and practical. This is not difficult because it corresponds to national character. As this feature of our American culture applies itself to the issue of ordination of women, it will mean:

A much greater effort to seek after what is attainable and to stop using the ordination issue as a means of raising the consciousness of American women. The irony is that what is suggested, even required, in official Church documents is allowed to be disregarded because of the ordination question. A de-escalation on the ordination question and a focus on the prior pastoral-canonical changes will serve as a basis for future theological developments in regard to the ordination of women.

A serious effort should be made to re-establish the office of deaconess.

Liturgical and catechetical language changes should be made which will permit our teaching and prayer life to speak to people in words and symbols that touch the human heart and experience.

The theological discussion should be de-westernized and a serious effort made by Roman Catholic scholarship to mediate the differences in its own Bilateral Consultations with Protestants and Orthodox.

In conclusion, advocates for change on this issue concerning the ordination of women have to be ready for a lengthy struggle. They must have the spiritual resources for a long, yet fruitful, interim period of slow change characterized by dialogue, courage and patience. On the journey we might just purify ourselves and the Church of Christ.

NOTES

1. Cf. Appendix B— "A Selected Bibliography (1965-1975)" in *Women and Catholic Priesthood: An Expanded Vision*, ed. by Anne Marie Gardiner, S.S.N.D. (New York: Paulist Press, 1976), pp. 199-208. Also, "Women and Religion: A Survey of Significant Literature (1965-1974)", Anne E. Patrick, *Theological Studies*, Dec. 1975 (vol. 36 no. 4), pp. 737-765.

2. Langdon Gilkey, *Catholicism Faces Modernity* (New York: Seabury Press, 1975). This work is excellent in identifying the distinctive features of the Roman Catholic tradition. A shorter version of Gilkey's thesis is in, *Proceedings of the Catholic Theological Society of America*—29th Annual Convention, vol. 29, pp. 323-330.

3. James Carroll, *Madonna Red* (Boston: Little, Brown and Co., 1976).

4. Pope Paul VI, Statement of April 18, 1975 to the Committee Studying the Church's response to the International Women's Year. Cf., *Origins*, May 1, 1975, pp. 718-719; Correspondence of Pope Paul VI with Archbishop Coggan of Canterbury—reprinted in *Origins*, Aug. 12, 1976, pp. 129-132; Statement of Archbishop Bernardin of October 7, 1975, pp. 257-260. This is also published in, *Women and Catholic Priesthood* . . . , *op. cit.*, pp. 193-198.

5. For a short summary of these statements, cf., "Le Feminisme, Les Femmes et L'Avenir de L'Eglise," *Pro Mundi Vita*, 56/1975, p. 18; *Vatican Study Commission on Women in Society and in the Church*— Study Kit—(1975), U. S. C. C. Publications Office; "We must . . . address ourselves seriously to the question of women in the Church"— Archbishop Bernardin Statement, *op. cit.;* Report of NCCB Committee on Women and Society and the Church, printed in *Origins*, June 24, 1976, pp. 69-74; Committee Report to NCCB by Bishop McAuliffe's Special Study Group, *Origins*, Dec. 11, 1975, pp. 396-400; A frequent theme in all the papal and episcopal statements is the full integration of women in society and the Church.

6. An oversight in the publication of, *Women and Catholic Priesthood, op. cit.*, Proceedings of the Detroit Ordination Conference, Nov. 28-30, 1975, was the exclusion of Majorie Tuite's, O.P. talk on strategy and goals. An eminently sensible moment in the Detroit Ordination Conference was not included in the record.

7. Cf., Rosemary R. Ruether, "Ordination: What is the Problem?" in *Women and Catholic Priesthood, op. cit.*, pp. 30-34. Some sample opinions of the author are; "Any Christian community gathering together with the intention of being the Church of Christ has the power to celebrate the Lord's Supper as an expression of their common life; that community

has the power to designate particular persons to represent it in sacramental actions of the Church to itself, and to pastor the community." Also, "when a brother or sister confesses to us, we already have the power to forgive. When two or three gather together in Christ's name, we already have the fullness of the eucharist."

The distance of these opinions from the traditional Catholic doctrine of priesthood and sacraments is obvious. R. P. McBrien in the same work is critical of the Catholic women's movement for the failure to monitor its own ranks concerning its more extreme positions—cf., "Women's Ordination: Effective Symbol of the Church's Struggle," pp. 89-93.

8. A sample of these negative opinions is; Vincent P. Miceli, "Women and the Priesthood," *Homiletic and Pastoral Review*, Aug.-Sept., 1976, pp. 28-32.

9. Cf. Agenda document, "Family" in the U.S. Bishops' Conference, "A Call to Action," which will meet in Detroit, Oct. 21-23, 1976. A sample section of this document reads:

> One of the areas of concern noted most frequently in the Bicentennial Consultations was family life; one of the actions most often suggested was that the Church should support family life. (Page 6)

10. The Bicentennial Consultations in preparation for the U.S. Bishops' Conference meeting, "A Call to Action," in Detroit, Oct. 21-23, 1976, was instructive on this point. Recommendations to the Detroit meeting had to be based on data surfaced in the nation-wide consultation. While the position of the feminists was ably presented, the grass-roots reaction was hesitant and cautious on the ordination issue. For this reason the recommendations, while politically sound, will not please some because the issue of women's ordination is not advocated. The report calls for further study. Cf., Document on "Church," p. 20, Recommendation II, 2.

11. *Ibid.*

12. Symposium of Roman Catholic-Anglican theologians, June 22-25, 1975, Cincinnati, Ohio. Cf., *Origins*, July 17, 1975, p. 100 for complete statement.

13. *Origins*, July 1, 1976, pp. 92-96.

14. Pamphlet published by U.S.C.C. Publications Office, 1312 Mass. Ave., N.W., Washington, D.C. 20005.

15. I would interpret the proposal of the forthcoming Detroit Conference as *not* suggesting the NCCB sponsor research into the pro-con of the women's ordination question, but rather an engaging and understandable explanation of magisterial statements already made. To the extent that St. Augustine's dictum is true; "God speaks to people in the way people speak to themselves," then these papal-episcopal statements are inadequate and unsettling.

16. "What is Magisterium?", Catholic Theological Society Presiden-

tial Address, by Avery Dulles, S.J., June 12, 1976—reprinted in *Origins*, July 1, 1976, pp. 81-88.

17. For reflections on "Catholic Typology," cf. talk by Jan Cardinal Willebrands at Cambridge University, England, January 18, 1970—An excerpt quoted in, "Papal Primacy and the Universal Church"—Lutheran-Catholic Dialogue V (Minneapolis: Augsburg Press, 1974), pp. 215-218. For view into what might be called the "Protestant Typology," cf., John E. Lynch, C.S.P., "The Ordination of Women: Protestant Experience in Ecumenical Perspective," *Journal of Ecumenical Studies* 12 (1974), pp. 173-195.

18. Lucy Vasquez, O.P., "The Position of Women According to the Code," *The Jurist* 34 9 (1974), pp. 128-142: Clara Henning, "Canon Law and the Battle of the Sexes," in *Religion and Sexism*—ed. by Rosemary R. Ruether (New York: Simon and Shuster, 1974), pp. 267-291. Also, cf., Joan Range, "Legal Exclusion of Women from Church Office," *The Jurist* 34 (1974), pp. 112-127.

19. "Women in Canon Law"—CLSA Report—cf., *Origins*, October 16, 1975, pp. 260-264. The issue here is the revision of canons 108-110; 145; 196-210. The present Code permits ordinary jurisdiction and ecclesiastical office only to male clerics. For some further reflection here, cf., Haye van der Meer, S.J., *Women Priests in the Catholic Church?* (Philadelphia: Temple University Press, 1973), Chapter V, "Theological Speculations—The Power of Jurisdiction," pp. 106-127; "Canonical Reflections on Priestly Life and Ministry," *American Ecclesiastical Review*, June 1972, pp. 363-392; James A. Coriden, "Ministries for the Future," *Studia Caonica* (vol. 8 no. 2), 1974, pp. 255-276.

20. Proposed Statement on the "Church," Recommendation II, 3, page 20.

21. Proposed Statement on "Church," Recommendation I, 5, page 18.

22. A glimpse of what this would involve is suggested in, "Women's Liberation/Men's Liberation," Margaret Brennan, I.H.M., *Origins*, July 17, 1975, pp. 97-105.

23. Originally proposed by the Colloquium on Women in Ministry, Siena Heights College, Adrian, Michigan, July 30-August 3, 1973, in a Report submitted to the NCCB. (unpublished) Also, suggested in the Bicentennial Conference, "A Call to Action," October 21-23, 1976, proposed statement on the "Church"; "That ministries presently being performed by women in the Church be identified, and where appropriate, formally authenticated, and that the ministries be reviewed to insure that women involved have the opportunities for training and the authority and responsibility they need to perform this work effectively." Cf., Recommendation II, 5, page 21.

24. Stanley Marrow, S.J., "God the Father in the New Testament (unpublished manuscript), March 1975. The author, whose paper was sub-

mitted to a sub-committee preparing for the World Council of Churches meeting, Nairobi, Kenya, November 1975, takes a strong position on the validity of the word, "Father," as pertaining to God.

25. Cf., John R. Sheets, S.J., "The Ordination of Women," *Communio*, Spring 1976, pp. 3-15. The author suggests that the ordination of women question cannot be resolved without a dogmatic statement by the Church.

26. For the report of the Fifth Assembly of the World Council of Churches, November 1975, cf., *Breaking Barriers*—the official Assembly Report, Nov. 23-Dec. 10, 1975—ed. by David M. Paton (London/New York: SPCK/Erdmans, 1976). Cf. p. 114 where it states, "those member Churches which do ordain women and those which do not continue dialogue with each other and with non-member Churches about the full participation of women in the full life of the Church including ordained ministries, according to the measure of their gifts. Faith and Order's reflections are contained in the pamphlet, *One Baptism One Eucharist and a Mutually Recognized Ministry* (Geneva: World Council of Churches, 1975), "The Ministry," pp. 29-57.

27. George H. Tavard, *Women in Christian Tradition* (Notre Dame: University of Notre Dame Press, 1973). For some negative reactions to the tradition, cf., *Des Femmes Accusent L'Eglise*—Les Cahiers du Grif—#8 (September 1975), *passim*. Also, "Sex and Anti-Sex in the Early Church Fathers," Donald F. Winslow—and—"Male and Female in the Christian Tradition: Was There a Reformation in the Sixteenth Century?", Eleanor L. McLaughlin in *Male and Female*, ed. by Ruth Tiffany Barnhouse and Urban T. Holmes, III (New York: Seabury Press, 1976), pp. 28-38; 39-52.

28. The writings of Elizabeth Carroll, R.S.M. are typical of this approach. Cf. her study, "Women and Ministry," *Theological Studies*, Dec. 1975 (vol. 36 no. 4), pp. 660-687.

29. In the sub-committee which convened in the Boston area scholarly papers were presented by Dieter Georgi and Gordon Kaufman and Paul Hanson of the Harvard Divinity School. For a light and pleasant description of the problem, cf., "Games Bible Translators Play," private paper by Ruth Hoppin, 15 Portola Ave., Daly City, California. 94015.

30. Available at the McGraw-Hill Book Co., 1221 Avenue of the Americas, New York, N.Y. 10020. Also, from the Task Force on Women in the Church and Society, United Church of Christ, 297 Park Avenue South, New York, N.Y. 10010.

31. Cf. *Liturgy for All the People*, Box 592, Hyattsville, Md., 20782 (Price: $1.00). This booklet is published by the Baltimore Task Force on the Status of Women in the Church and modifies the Catholic Mass rite—including the four canons—in a manner that is judged sensitive to Catholic feminists. This work indicates the International Committee for English in the Liturgy (ICEL) will have a new agenda. Much could be learned from the recent efforts of the Episcopal Church to revise the Book of Common Prayer.

32. From, "A Call to Action"—U.S. Bishops Conference—Detroit meeting, October 21-23, 1976. Cf. Statement on "Church," Recommendation II, 4, page 20-21.

33. E.g., Agnes Cunningham, "The Role of Women in Ecclesial Ministry: Biblical and Patristic Foundations" (U.S.C.C. Publications, 1976).

34. "Immensae Caritatis," Congregation for the Discipline of the Sacraments, January 29, 1973. Cf. *Study Text #1—Holy Communion—* Bishops Committee on the Liturgy—(U.S.C.C. Publications, 1973).

35. Jean Laporte, "Women's Ministry in the Early Church"—unpublished—Presented at the Colloquium on Women in Ministry, Siena Heights College, Adrian, Michigan, July 30-August 3, 1973.

36. A suggested example of the "counter-productive" method is, Hans Kung, "Feminism: A New Reformation—A Dissident Catholic Nails his Theses for the Liberation of Women to the Church Door," *New York Times* (Magazine Section), May 23, 1976.

37. *Proceedings of the Catholic Theological Society of America—* 27th Annual Convention, September 1972, p. 204.

38. *Breaking Barriers*—Nairobi 1975—*op. cit., passim;* and especially pp. 98, 113-115, 309-311.

39. Cf. Joseph A. Komonchak, in "Theological Questions on the Ordination of Women," *Women and Catholic Priesthood . . . , op. cit.,* Appendix E, pp. 241-259. This is a fine article and wrestles responsibly with the argument, however, it may well be a case of "he who proves too much proves nothing." Those who believe there is a theological argument against the ordination of women should be haunted by his words: "the defenders of the tradition . . . must defend it; it is not enough to repeat it, nor is it reasonable to require an unthinking deference to it." p. 257.

40. Some other descriptions of the theological issues involved are; Rt. Rev. Arthur A. Vogel, "The Ordination of Women: Issues in the Debate," *Ecumenical Trends*, September 1976, pp. 113-119; Cunningham, "The Role of Women in Ecclesial Ministry . . .", *op. cit.*, pp. 21-22; Sheets, "The Ordination of Women," *op. cit.*; "Theological Reflections on the Ordination of Women," NCCB, 1972.

41. *Origins*, May 1, 1975, p. 719.

42. *Origins*. August 12, 1976, p. 131.

43. *Origins*, October 16, 1975, p. 257, 259-260.

44. *Ibid.* In a news conference, Archbishop Bernardin said the issue remains open for discussion and research. Cf., *Women in Catholic Priesthood . . . , op. cit.*, pp. 197-198.

45. "Theological Reflections on the Ordination of Women," NCCB (1972) implies that canon 968 is doctrinal.

46. As Vogel does in, "The Ordination of Women: Issues in the Debate," *op. cit.*

Consensus Statement from the Symposium on Women and Church Law

God has provided the Church founded by His Son, Jesus Christ, with the means necessary to respond not only to the needs of the time, but also with the desire to read the signs of the times. From this reading the Church can learn, in order to provide for the future. Through the action of the Spirit, inspiring Christians to seek a better world wherein all are called to the same holiness, to promote justice and to pursue the search for a better understanding of God's plan for humanity, we are guided to discern with God's help what is best for the People of God and what corresponds to the divine plan for universal salvation in Jesus Christ.

Responsive to this call, the Canon Law Society of America, basing itself upon the teachings of the Second Vatican Council and of Pope Paul VI, addressed itself to one of those signs of the times which the Spirit is instilling in the hearts and minds of humanity today: the necessity of recognizing the God-given right of Christian women to equality in the Church of Christ, an equality based on the common dignity of all the baptized, in whom "there is neither Jew nor Greek; there is neither slave nor freeman; there is neither male nor female" (Gal. 3:28; cf. *Lumen Gentium*, 32).

Gathered at Rosemont College, Pennsylvania on October 9-11, 1976, some twenty-four men and women—theologians, canonists and scholars from other fields—have studied the juridical significance of this prompting of the Spirit. We have discerned a number of areas that must be taken into consideration if the equality of all the baptized is to be recognized and respected. Likewise, the participants in this Symposium, one of many organized by the C.L.S.A., have prepared recommendations for future action by the C.L.S.A. and by the Church at large. These points constitute the object of the present Consensus Statement.

I. AREAS FOR CONSIDERATION

In studying the general situation of women in ecclesial law, it has become evident that a number of basic themes are exerting an influence on contemporary thinking in the Church. We have also found, regretfully, numerous instances of discrimination in Church law. The same discriminatory attitude is also evident in some Church persons, perhaps unconsciously. We shall attend to these points in the following paragraphs.

A. Basic Themes

1. *Christian Anthropology*

Christian revelation presents a view of humanity that affirms the primacy of the person and the preeminence of mutuality between human persons. A modern western anthropology emphasizing the relational nature of all reality implies a society which is inherently dynamic, living out a process of structural change that enables it continually to adapt itself to needs. The Christian understanding of personhood, moreover, corresponds to human experience in history. For example, the roles of persons within the varied forms of government and institutions in civil society have changed and developed through the course of history.

Underlying some perspectives on the question of women in Church law, however, is an anthropology which retains a conventional understanding of dichotomies (e.g., spirit/matter, soul/body, masculine/feminine) which is incompatible with the findings of the modern human sciences. The obstacles to the contemporary mission of the Church created by bifurcations of reality are too obvious and numerous to be recounted. But the most serious indictment against these divisions is that they work grave injustice by preventing access to mutual sharing in the religious dimension of life.

2. *Historical-Theological Considerations*

Historically, the Church had ministries before it had a theory of ministry; it had laws before it had a theory of law. Theories that eventually developed were attempts at describing, understanding and ordering the previous practice. When such theory began to be expressed in classicist terms, it became itself a factor of immense practical significance in the life of the Church by determining, often on non-historical assumptions, what the actual practice could or could not become.

The classical notion of *jus divinum* and its relation to specific legislation and institutions in Church law has been seriously called into question by historical investigations. These have shown that much of what was later considered to be *jus divinum* was, in fact, the result of historical developments of the post-apostolic Church; e.g., "monarchical" episcopate. Likewise, recent studies point out that there is a great variety to the meanings and applications of the phrase.

3. *Ministry in the Church*

Certain theological axioms and presuppositions regarding ministry and its relationship to the Church have characterized the ecclesiology and law of the past several centuries. These must be reexamined to see if they truly respond to the economy of salvation.

For instance, it is often stated that no individual has a right to ordination to priesthood by virtue of baptism. Yet, in what sense can this be said to be true? What ecclesiology underlies this statement? Can it provide an adequate theology of charism which would recognize God-given calls and obligations?

Likewise, it is often repeated that by virtue of the specific form of its divine and apostolic constitution, the Church in history has no right to alter its major forms of ministry. Yet, to what extent is this compatible with the historical facts of change and the sound theological position that the Holy Spirit exercises a creative function in guiding Christians in the formation of doctrine and practice for new times and new conditions?

A final example may be given. It is often affirmed that women are excluded from the Church's ordained ministry both by the constant practice of the Church and by theological necessity. What theology of history underlies this statement? How is this to be reconciled with a theology of the freedom of all persons in Christ, and how is this to be related to the creative guidance that the Holy Spirit seems to be exercising today in the signs of the times?

These basic considerations lead us to recognize the fact that we do not yet have the answers to such serious questions. We believe that further historical and theological effort is necessary for a finer discernment of the divine will in these matters.

Any doctrinal clarification may have to be accompanied by a change in practice. At the present time, our practice is discriminatory against women in many areas. We will now examine some of these instances.

B. DISCRIMINATION IN CHURCH LAW

With new anthropological, historical and behavioral concerns being expressed throughout the world for the progression of peoples and the recognition and protection of basic human rights, it becomes necessary to examine the legislation within the Church that makes such aspirations and needs become a reality. In the question immediately before us, we have asked ourselves whether our present law properly recognizes the rights of women, and whether there are encouraging signs on the horizon enabling us to believe that any discrimination which now exists will be overcome.

1. *The State of the Law Regarding the Rights of Women*

The thinking of men and women on vital and significant issues is eventually reflected in the legislation governing their behavior. The laws of society usually ascertain new trends which, once they have proven their worth, are enshrined and embodied in legal principles and juridical expressions.

The necessity of acknowledging and implementing women's rights in the Church has led many canonists to realize the inadequacies of our present legislation. As emphasis shifts from institutions to persons, all persons must be recognized for their qualifications and aptitudes. Recognition must not be based on any particular sex, but on the qualities of all the baptized in the Church.

The laws of the Church are often couched in terms—and practices— that reveal a subordination of women to men. This subordination may at times be protective, at other times paternalistic in approach. For example, in Privilege of the Faith cases (cf. canon 1125), a man may in certain specified circumstances choose upon baptism to live with one of many wives he had been united to either simultaneously or successively. No such provision exists for women. Jurisprudence on questions of impotency and consummation (cf. canons 1068, 1119) is presented almost exclusively in terms of the male, with the woman having only a passive role in the entire coitional process. Norms for burial are preferential to the husband (canon 1229). In post-conciliar legislation, we find other examples, such as the requirement of papal cloister for contemplative orders of women, which is not required for contemplative orders of men (cf. Motu Proprio *Venite Seorsim*).

There are other instances relative to the life and ministry of priests. Out of a desire to protect the chastity of the priest, legislation has been written which gives the impression of suspicion of women rather than promotion of priestly virtue. Norms on housekeepers (canon 133), women's confessions (canon 910), and admission to the Cloister (canon 597) are but three examples of this situation.

In addition, the canonical legislation excludes women from administrative and judicial offices (canon 1574, and cf. Motu Proprio *Causas Matrimoniales*), from self-determination in many areas through exclusion of participation, and from full participation in the cultic and public life of the Church. Not only are women excluded from the Sacrament of Orders (canon 968); they are also excluded from reception of certain ministries (Motu Proprio *Ministeria Quaedam*). Since lay men are admitted to many of these functions, it is evident that the discrimination is based exclusively on sexual differences, at least in those areas which at present do not require the power of Orders.

Another area of discrimination concerns the juridical status of persons in the Church. A person presently acquires status in virtue of the following juridical facts: legitimacy of birth, baptism, age, place of origin, domicile, marital state, exercise of rights, proper bishop, consanguinity, affinity, and rite (canons 87-98). Many of these elements are specifically referred to the male: place of origin, domicile, legitimacy of birth, rite. A woman's juridical status is directly related to that of her husband, if she is married; or, in many instances, to her father if she is a minor child. A single adult woman enjoys status in law, but the married woman loses her status to acquire another based on necessary factors. No status is assigned directly by reason of sex, yet maleness and femaleness really determine a person's juridical standing.

2. *Emerging Trends in Law*

The principles of Vatican II regarding the dignity of persons (e.g., *Gaudium et Spes*, 13-15), non-discrimination (*Lumen Gentium*, 32), and the universal call to holiness (*Lumen Gentium*, 39), give rise in the new canonical documentation to positive trends in the recognition of women's rights. The proposed new marriage legislation, following upon the teachings of *Gaudium et Spes*, recognizes complete mutuality in the marriage partnership. Consummation of marriage must be a human act, and not simply a biological function (cf. proposed new canon 245). In mixed marriage, the consciences of both husband and wife are to be respected. The statements of the Synod of Bishops avoid anything referring to a special "role" for women, and base their teachings on the very mission of the Church. New organisms established to provide for consultation make no difference between men and women. There are bases for hope.

Yet, there are also serious inadequacies. Women are consistently barred from ordination and some ministries; they are still excluded from administrative positions; they are still spoken of in terms of "proper nature" or "role." These points will have to be considered carefully.

C. Discrimination in Attitudes of Church People

We recognize that discrimination is often based not on law, but on personal and social attitudes.

There has been an apparent assumption that women constitute a group with a "special" role, function, nature, and thus "special" status. Because of this supposed "special status," there is an existing protectiveness toward women which views them as quasi-adolescents and prohibits their assuming a full and responsible participation in the life of the Church.

The polarity of inequity can be cast in terms of the paradigm male/female, to which clergy/laity corresponds. Women seem to experience this discrimination in the Church within an atmosphere of fear and mutual uncomfortableness. Discrimination against women can result in apathy and alienation, frustration and anger, and often a commensurate clerical defensiveness.

A new status of women, still primarily identified with functions or roles, is being legitimized by a theology of non-discrimination, a theology of personhood, and a practice that meets growing acceptance. Barriers are falling and law must provide for juridical recognition of rights.

We regret that many people today do not wish to avail themselves of the opportunities provided in law and practice to promote the equality of women in all areas where it is possible. Fidelity to the promptings of the Holy Spirit calls for revision of attitudes in this regard.

* * *

With this basis, we turn to recommendations to help redress a situation that calls for a serious examination of conscience. Listening to the promptings of the Spirit, we feel invited to urge adoption of the following measures which will make the Church a more authentic witness to its own teaching.

II. RECOMMENDATIONS SUBMITTED TO THE CANON LAW SOCIETY OF AMERICA

A. JURIDICAL PERSONALITY

The participants in the Symposium on Women and Church Law find great potential for recognition of women's rights in a better understanding and utilization of the concept of a "single" juridical personality.

Although no provision of the *Codex* per se states that sex is a juridic fact, men are treated as the normative subjects of the law and women are frequently assigned a special "status." This results in conditional juridical personality in various instances. The declaration of a single juridical personality, common to both men and women before the law, would clarify the basis for equality in rights of all the baptized.

Canonists are urged to utilize this important clarification in their various endeavors.

B. ANALYSIS OF JURIDICAL DOCUMENTS

We recommend that the C.L.S.A. assign a permanent committee to analyze all new legislation, as well as drafts of proposed legislation, from the perspective of women's juridical status.

It is important that all new laws, decrees, etc., be examined as to their fidelity to the conciliar principles of non-discrimination and the dignity of the person, and as to their application of the concept of a single juridical personality.

C. IMPLICATIONS OF CURRENT PRACTICE

We discern in the current practice of the Church regarding women the basis for future legislative trends. We urge full development of the potential open in the following areas.

1. *The Teaching Mission of the Church*

Women are active in the teaching mission of the Church as educators in schools and religious education, in teacher training and academic pursuits. Women on occasion have been authorized to teach the Word of God in the liturgy. This exercise of the teaching mission should now be proposed in more positive and coherent terms officially.

2. *The Sanctifying Mission of the Church*

In recent times, women have been authorized to celebrate baptism solemnly, to be ministers of the Eucharist, to lead communal prayer, and to participate in more active liturgical roles including, for example, witnessing marriages (cf. October 19, 1975 Statement on "The Role of Women in Evangelization" from the Congregation for the Evangelization of Peoples). The implications of full involvement in the sanctifying mission of the Church should be carefully studied and promoted.

3. *The Mission of Service in the Church*

While women have been excluded from traditional functions of government, we have noted the beginnings of active participation in consultative bodies and their more direct role at all levels of the Church from the Roman Curia to parish councils. The new concept of "Team Ministry" is opening the way for many women to take a more active role in the pastoral service of the community. These developments deserve to be promoted and fostered.

D. MORE IMMEDIATE ACTION TO BE TAKEN

Since all the faithful have the right to participate in promoting the well-being of the Church, and in receiving quality pastoral care, we recommend that steps be taken to implement these rights.

A first series of actions lies in utilizing all the faculties now granted by law.

The *lay* ministries of lector and acolyte are restricted currently to *male lay* persons by Norm 7 of the Motu Proprio *Ministeria Quaedam*. We find this inconsistent with the principles stated earlier in the same Motu Proprio concerning the rights and responsibilities of all the faithful. These ministries should be open to men and women.

Women should be given equal access to serve as extraordinary ministers of the Eucharist.

The development of pastoral teams, comprising faithful of both sexes, should be promoted.

In addition, unified efforts should be made to bring about changes in four specific areas of Church law:

1. Qualified lay women and men should be commissioned to preach the Word of God.
2. Women should be given the same access to Tribunal functions as has been given to lay men.
3. All administrative positions in the Church not requiring the power of Orders should be open to lay women and men.
4. Other instances of discrimination against women should be corrected, such as the question of Papal Cloister imposed on contemplative communities of women and other examples cited above.

E. Studies To Be Carried Out

1. *Jus Divinum*

We recommend that the CLSA undertake or sponsor a study of *jus divinum* in the light of recent historical findings. Particular attention should be given to the methodological parallels with the hermeneutics employed in contemporary biblical and historical studies. Attention should also be given to applying these in the following questions:

a. Does *jus divinum* exist in a "pure form"? This question has also surfaced in examining the proposed *Lex Ecclesiae Fundamentalis*.
b. What is the relationship between "divine authority" and the laws and institutions which are thought to realize it?
c. What is the relationship between "divine authority" and the supposed immutability of that to which it is related?

2. *Theory—Practice*

We recommend that the CLSA undertake or sponsor an investigation into the history of the relation between theory and practice with regard to law and ministries in the Church. Likewise, we recommend that the CLSA investigate the possibility of developing an historically conscious theory of ministries and law which would clarify the relation between practice and theory, and lead to further developments.

3. *Charisms*

We recommend that the CLSA undertake or sponsor a study of the juridical effects of charisms among the baptized. Such a study would include investigation of:

a. The juridical development of the notion of charism as a gift from God for the building up of the community.
b. The criteria and process for the recognition of charisms.
c. Conditions for the exercise of charisms.
d. A system to evaluate and up-date the above criteria and process.

The "charismatic Church" and the "institutional Church" are one. The juridical consequences of charisms are such that they will probably lead us to an entirely new understanding of ministry in the Church.

4. *Orders and Jurisdiction*

There are two contradictory developments in the Church on the relationship of Orders and Jurisdiction. Vatican II reinforced the theoretical tie of jurisdiction and orders. Yet the pastoral practice of granting jurisdiction to the non-ordained has been officially sanctioned (cf. Motu Proprio *Causas Matrimoniales*). We recommend a thorough study of this phenomenon, leading to recommendations for resolving the contradiction.

* * * * *

In addition to the above recommendations addressed to the C.L.S.A., we have the following recommendations to the Church at large. These form the third part of our Statement.

III. RECOMMENDATIONS TO THE CHURCH AT LARGE

Our studies indicate much can be done at the present time to improve the juridical recognition of the status of women in the Church. We strongly urge that the following points be carefully considered and applied.

A. RECOMMENDATIONS TO THE CATHOLIC BISHOPS OF THE U.S.A.

1. *Implications of Current Church Practices*

The current practice of the Church, as noted above concerning women actively engaged in the mission and ministry of the Church, deserves formal recognition within our juridical system rather than being treated as exceptional or by means of dispensation. We urge the N.C.C.B. to develop particular legislation to regularize the present situation and to promote the active involvement of all Catholic people in the Church's mission and ministry.

2. *Sexist Language*

We ask that the N.C.C.B., in conjunction with other Episcopal Conferences, work to replace sexist language in liturgical texts. We ask that such language be replaced in Conference statements, in existing Church legislation, and carefully avoided in any future statements and legislation.

3. *Implementing Stated Goals*

Since the Bishops of the Church, both in the Second Vatican Council and in their particular pronouncements, have stated the necessity of promoting the active participation of women in the decision-making processes of the Church, we ask them to see that these statements and resolutions are implemented.

Areas of special concern are pastoral councils and consultation on new legislation even prior to distribution of new legal texts for comment.

4. *Theological Preparation of Women*

We urge the bishops, to the extent that it is their responsibility, to see that women have full access to theological training and the obtaining of professional academic degrees in the field of pastoral ministry. We likewise urge that their professional talents be fully recognized and utilized.

5. *Due Process Procedures*

We ask that dioceses and communities apply the approved Due Process Procedures to resolve instances of discriminatory action against women.

B. Recommendations to the Clergy

We urge all priests to work toward affirmative action in filling positions in the Church. Women should not be excluded because of their sex, but should be afforded the same opportunities as others with equal qualifications.

We urge all priests and deacons to participate in continuing education programs, especially in regard to such matters as sexuality and relationships with women.

We ask them to include both lay and religious women in all liturgical roles already permitted to them.

C. Recommendations for All Catholic Men and Women

We urge all the faithful to support women as they strive to assume decision-making positions in the ministerial Church.

We are calling for affirmative action on parochial, diocesan and national levels in urging that all appropriate means be employed to promote the juridical equality of women.

Conclusion

The participants in the C.L.S.A. Symposium on Women and Church Law are grateful for the opportunity afforded us to study the important issues considered above.

We are trying to be responsive, as are all Church people, to the promptings of the Holy Spirit who urges us, in many ways, to strive for the betterment of humanity and the respect of God-given rights.

We have come to a better understanding of the mutuality of men and women. We have seen during our studies that distinctions must not be made on the basis of a so-called "special nature" or "special role" of women. We have seen how the concept of single juridical personality, with its ensuing rights and obligations, holds great potential for the furthering of a correct understanding of the juridical status of women.

We thank the Lord for this gift. We hope now that it may be shared with all other men and women of good will who are seeking for the perfection of charity and for the perfection of the Church of Christ, which has been established as a light and guide for all nations.

October 11, 1976
Rosemont College

PARTICIPANTS IN THE SYMPOSIUM

Sr. Judy Barnhiser, O.S.U.
Diocese of Toledo, Ohio

Dr. James Biechler
Dept. of Theology
LaSalle College, Philadelphia

Dr. Emily Binns
Dean, Rosemont College

Dr. Francine Cardman
Wesley Theological Seminary
Washington, D.C.

Sr. Elizabeth Carroll, R.S.M.
Center for Concern
Washington, D.C.

Rev. James Coriden
Washington Theological Coalition
Silver Spring, Maryland

Sr. Ann Durst, S.H.C.J.
President, Rosemont College

Sr. Catherine Edgar, S.H.C.J.
Provincial House
Drexel Hill, Pennsylvania

Rev. John Finnegan
Pope John XXIII Seminary
Weston, Massachusetts

Sr. Nadine Foley, O.P.
Dominican Mother House
Adrian, Michigan

Sr. Doris Gottemoeller, R.S.M.
Sisters of Mercy Generalate
Potomac, Maryland

Rev. Paul Golden, C.M.
Kenrick Seminary, St. Louis

Rev. Bertram F. Griffin
President, C.L.S.A.
Portland, Oregon

Dr. Margaret Healy
Assistant to President
Bryn Mawr College

Dr. Hamilton Hess
Department of Theology
University of San Francisco

Sr. Patricia Cook
St. Joseph's College
West Hartford, Connecticut

Mrs. Grace Kennedy
Legal Staff, Sun Company
Philadelphia

Rev. Edward Kilmartin, S.J.
Department of Theology
University of Notre Dame

Rev. Joseph Komonchak
St. Joseph's Seminary
Yonkers, New York

Sr. Katherine Meagher, S.C.
Chancellor
Diocese of Nelson (B.C.)

Rev. Francis Morrisey, O.M.I.
Dean, School of Canon Law
St. Paul's University, Ottawa

Rev. James Provost
Chancellor
Diocese of Helena (Montana)

Ms. Arlene Swidler
Associate Editor
Journal of Ecumenical Studies

Sr. Lucy Vazquez, O.P.
Family Life Office
Diocese of Orlando (Florida)

Appendix I
Biblical Commission Report
Can Women Be Priests?

The following report was originally printed in Origins, NC News Service, *July 1, 1976, Vol. 6: No. 6, Copyright © 1976 by NC News Service. The text of the report was translated from the original French by* Origins. *Used by permission.*

The Pontifical Biblical Commission was asked to study the role of women in the Bible in the course of research being carried out to determine the place that can be given to women today in the church.

The question for which an answer is especially sought is whether or not women can be ordained to the priestly ministry (especially as ministers of the eucharist and as leaders of the Christian community). In making this biblical inquiry, one must keep in mind the limits of such a study.

1. In general the role of women does not constitute the principal subject of biblical texts. One has to rely often on information given here and there. The situation of women in the biblical era was probably more or less favorable judging from the limited data that we have at our disposal.

2. The question asked touches on the priesthood, the celebrant of the eucharist and the leader of the local community. This is a way of looking at things which is somewhat foreign to the Bible.

A) Surely the New Testament speaks of the Christian people as a priestly people (I Peter 2, 5.9; Apoc. 1,6; 5,10). It describes that certain members of this people accomplish a priestly and sacrificial ministry (I Peter 2, 5.12; Rom 12, 1; 15, 16; Phil 2, 17). However it never uses the technical term *hiereus* for the Christian ministry. *A fortiori* it never places *hiereus* in relationship with the eucharist.

B) The New Testament says very little on the subject of the ministry of the eucharist, Luke 22, 19 orders the apostles to celebrate the eucharist in memory of Jesus (cf. I Cor 11, 24). Acts 20, 11 shows also that Paul broke the bread (see also Acts 27, 35).

C) The pastoral epistles which give us the most detailed picture of the leaders of the local community (episkopos and prebyteroi), never attribute to them a eucharistic function.

3. Beyond these difficulties resulting from a study of the biblical data from the perspective of a later conception of the eucharistic priesthood, it is necessary to keep in mind that this conception itself is now placed in question as one can see in the more recent declarations of the magisterium which broaden the concept of priesthood beyond that of eucharistic ministry.

PART I

WOMAN'S PLACE IN THE FAMILY

(1) "In the Beginning."

In Genesis, the "beginning" serves less to present the beginning of history than the fundamental plan of God for mankind. In Genesis 1, man and woman are called together to be the image of God (Gen. 1, 26f) on equal terms and in a community of life. It is in common that they receive rule over the world. Their vocation gives a new meaning to the sexuality that man possesses as the animals do.

In Gen. 2, man and woman are placed on equal terms: woman is for man a "helper who is his partner" (2, 18), and by community in love they become "the two of them one body" (2, 24). This union includes the vocation of the couple to fruitfulness but it is not reduced to that.

Between this ideal and the historical reality of the human race, sin has introduced a considerable gap. The couple's existence is wounded in its very foundations: love is degraded by covetousness and domination (3, 16). The woman endures pains in her condition as mother which nevertheless put her closely in contact with the mystery of life. The social degradation of her condition is also related to this wound, manifested by polygamy (cf. Gen. 4), divorce, slavery, etc. She is nevertheless the depository of a promise of salvation made to her descendants.

It is noteworthy that the ideal of Gen. 1 and 2 remained present in the thought of Israel like a horizon of hope: it is found again explicitly in the book of Tobias.

(2) The Symbolism of the Sexes in the Old Testament

The Old Testament excluded the sexual symbolism used in Eastern mythologies, in relation to the fertility cults: there is no sexuality in the God of Israel. But very early, the biblical tradition borrowed traits from the family structure to trace pictures of God the Father. Then also it had recourse to the image of the spouse to work out a very lofty concept of the God of the covenant.

In correlation with these two fundamental images, the prophets gave value to the dignity of women by representing the people of God with the help of feminine symbols of the wife (in relation to God) and of the mother (in relation to the human partners of the covenant, men and women). These symbols were used particularly to evoke in advance the eschatological covenant in which God is to realize his plan in its fullness.

(3) The Teachings of Jesus

Considering the social and cultural milieu in which Jesus lived, his teaching and behavior with regard to women are striking in their newness. We leave aside here his behavior (cf. the following reports). Questioned about divorce by the Pharisees (Mk. 10, 1-12), Jesus moves away from the rabbinic casuistry that, on the basis of Deut. 24, 1, discriminated between the respective rights of men and women.

Reminding the Pharisees of the original plan of God (Gen. 1, 27 and 2, 24), he shows his intention of establishing here below a state of things that realizes the plan fully: the reign of God, inaugurated by his preaching and his presence, brings with it a full restoration of feminine dignity. But it brings also a surpassing of the ancient juridical structures in which repudiation showed the failure of marriage "by reason of the hardness of hearts." It is in this perspective that the practice of celibacy "for the sake of the kingdom of God" (Matt. 19, 12), for himself and for those "to whom it is given" (19, 11) is understood. His attitude toward women should be examined from that point of departure.

Thus Jesus inaugurates in the framework of the present world the order of things that constitutes the final horizon of the kingdom of God: that order will result, in "a new heaven and a new earth," in a state in which the risen will no longer need to exercise their sexuality (Matt. 21, 31). Consequently, to represent the joy of the kingdom of heaven, Jesus can properly use the image of the virgins called to the wedding feast of the bridegroom (Matt. 25, 1-10).

(4) From the Mother of Jesus to the Church

Considering the historical existence of Jesus, son of God sent into the world (Gal. 4, 4 etc.), one might take a look at his beginnings.

The evangelists, Matthew and especially Luke, have made clear the irreplaceable role of his mother Mary. The value proper to femininity that the Old Testament presented are recapitulated in her, so that she accomplishes her unique role in the plan of God. But in the very accomplishment of this maternal role, she anticipates the reality of the new covenant of which her son will be the mediator. In fact she is the first one called to a faith that concerns her son (Luke 1, 42) and to an obedience in which she "listens to the word of God and puts it into practice" (Luke 11, 28, cf. 1, 38).

Moreover, the Spirit who brings about in her the conception of Jesus (Luke 1, 35, Matt. 1, 18) will make a new people spring up in history on the day of Pentecost (Acts 2). Her historic role is therefore linked to a resumption of the feminine symbolism used to evoke the new people: from then on, the church is "our mother" (Gal. 4, 20). At the end of time, it will be the "spouse of the Lamb" (Apoc. 21). It is by reason of this relationship between Mary, concrete woman, and the church, symbolic woman, that in Apoc. 12 the new humanity rescued from the power of sin and death can be presented as giving birth to Christ, her first born (Apoc. 12, 4-15), expecting to have as posterity "those who keep the word of God and have the testimony of Jesus."

(5) Woman in the Church

Nuptial symbolism is specifically taken up again by St. Paul to evoke the mystery of Christ and his church (Eph. 5, 22-33). But it is first of all the relationship between Christ and the church, his body, which casts light on the reality forming the basis for Paul's approach.

Despite an institutional framework which implies the submission of women to their husbands (cf. Eph. 5, 22; Col. 3, 18; I Pt. 3, 1), Paul reverses the perspective to emphasize their mutual submission (Eph. 5, 21) and love (5, 25.33) for which Christ's love is the source and model: charity (cf. I Cor. 13) becomes the measure of conjugal love. It is through it that the "original perfection" (that is to say the fullness of the plan of God for the human couple) can be attained (cf. Eph. 5, 31 citing Gen. 2, 24). That supposes between man and woman not only an equality of rights and duties explicitly affirmed (I Cor. 7, 3-4), but also an equality in adoptive sonship (Gal. 3, 28, II Cor. 6, 18) and in the reception of the Spirit who brings about participation in the life of the church (cf. Acts 2, 17-18).

Marriage, having thus received its full meaning, thanks to its symbolic relationship with the mystery of Christ and the church (Eph. 5, 32), can regain also its indissoluble solidity (I Cor. 7, 10-12; cf. Luke 16, 18).

At the heart of a sinful world, maternity has a saving value (I Tim. 2, 15). Outside conjugal life, the church grants a place of honor to consecrated widowhood (I Tim. 5, 3) and it recognizes in virginity the possible meaning of eschatological witness (I Cor. 7, 25-26) and of a more complete freedom to consecrate oneself to "the business of the Lord" (I Cor. 7, 32ff.). Such is the background against which theological reflection on the place and function of women in society and in the church takes place.

PART II

THE SOCIAL CONDITION OF WOMAN ACCORDING TO BIBLICAL REVELATION

I. The Bible, especially the New Testament, teaches very clearly the equality of man and woman in the spiritual domain (relationships with God) and in the moral area (relationships with other human beings). But the problem of the social condition of woman is a sociological problem that must be treated as such:

1. In terms of the laws of sociology: physical and psychosomatic data of feminine behavior in an earthly society;

2. In terms of the history of the societies in which the people of God lived during and after the composition of the Bible;

3. In terms of the laws of the church of Christ, his body, whose members live an ecclesial life under the direction of a magisterium instituted by Christ, while belonging to other societies and states.

II. The biblical experience shows that the social condition of woman has varied, but not in a linear manner as if there were continual progress. Ancient Egypt experienced a real flourishing of woman before the existence of Israel. The Israelite woman experienced a certain flourishing under the monarchy, then her condition became subordinate once more. In the time of Christ the status of woman appears, in Jewish society, inferior to what it is in Greco-Roman society where their lack of legal status is in the process of disappearing and in which "women handle their business themselves" (Gaius).

In relation to his contemporaries, Christ has a very original attitude with regard to woman which gives renewed value to her situation.

III. Christian society is established on a basis other than that of Jewish society. It is founded on the cornerstone of the risen Christ and is built upon Peter in collegiality with the twelve. According to the witness of the New Testament, especially the Pauline epistles, women are associated with the different charismatic ministries (*diaconies*) of the church (I Cor. 12, 4; I Tim. 3, 11, cf. 8): prophecy, service, probably even apostolate . . . without, nevertheless, being of the twelve. They have a place in the liturgy at least as prophetesses (I Cor. 11, 4). But according to the Pauline corpus (I Cor. 14, 33-35; cf. I Tim. 2, 6-15) an apostle such as Paul can withdraw the word from them.

This Christian society lives not only on the government of the twelve who are called apostles in Luke and elsewhere in the New Testament, but also on the liturgical sacramental life in which Christ communicates his spirit as high priest no longer according to Aaron but according to Melchisedech, king and priest (Heb. 8; cf. Ps. 110).

Sociologically speaking, in Jewish society, therefore for Christians until the break, the consecrated priesthood of Aaron (Lev. 9) assured an authentic liturgical and sacrificial life in the temple of stone. But Christ is the true high priest and the true temple (John 2, 21). He was consecrated and sent (*hagiazein, apostellein*) by the Father (Jn. 10, 26), and he consecrates himself in order to consecrate the apostles in the truth that he himself is (Jn. 17, 17.19). It is a fundamental characteristic of the society that is the church in the midst of other societies, that it dispenses eternal life through its own liturgy.

IV. The problem is to know whether in Christian society ruled by the apostles—the twelve, Paul, Titus, Timothy—and by their successors (bishops, presbyters, *higoumenes*) women can be called to participate in this liturgical ministry and in the direction of local communities, as the queens of the Old Testament, especially widows, were called to participate in the royal functions of anointed kings. In fact in the New Testament no text formally supports this hypothesis, even though one may note the role of widows in the pastoral epistles (I Tim. 5) and what Luke says of Anna in the Temple (*latreuein*). This study is no longer a matter of sociology, but of the labors of our third section (condition of woman in cult).

PART III

ECCLESIAL CONDITION OF WOMAN

Old Testament

In the Old Testament, the Yahwist religion was not reserved to men alone, as is said elsewhere. Women as well as men could have sacrifices offered, participate in worship. Nevertheless, contrary to the customs of the contemporary pagan peoples, the worship of the second temple was exclusively reserved to men of the tribe of Levi (not only the function of priests, but also that of cantor, porter, etc.).

Moreover, there are women who bore the name of prophetess (Maria, Deborah, Huldam, Noiada), while not playing the role of the great prophets. Other women exercised an important function for the salvation of the people of God at critical moments of this people's history (for example, Judith, Esther) (cf. section 2).

(Amendment of Father Wanbacq:) "In the Old Testament, the Yahwist religion was not a religion in which women were excluded, as is sometimes held. Women as well as men could participate in worship. Contrary to the usages of the contemporary pagan peoples, the official exercise of the temple worship was reserved to men, in the second temple to those of the tribe of Levi."

THE GOSPELS

In striking contrast to the contemporary usages of the Jewish world, we see Jesus surrounding himself with women who follow him and serve him (Luke 8, 2-3). Mary of Bethany is even described as the examplary disciple "listening to the word" (Luke 10, 38-42). It is the women who are charged with announcing the resurrection "to the apostles and to Peter." (Mark 16, 7).

The fourth gospel stresses this role of witness attributed to women: the Samaritan woman, whose mere conversation with Jesus had astonished the apostles, goes carrying her witness to Jesus to her fellow citizens. After the resurrection, the evangelist emphasizes the role of Mary Magdalene whom tradition will call "the apostle of the apostles."

ACTS AND PAUL

As Christianity spread, women took a notable part. That again distinguished the new religion sharply from contemporary Judaism.

Some women collaborated in the properly apostolic work. This is shown at numerous points in the Acts and the epistles. We shall limit ourselves to a few of them.

In the establishment of local communities, they are not content with offering their houses for meetings, as Lydia (Acts 16, 14-15), the mother of Mark (Acts 12, 12), Prisca (Rom. 16, 5), but, according to Phil. 4, 2, for example, Evodia and Syntyche are explicitly associated with "Clement and the other collaborators of Paul" in the community. Of the 27 persons thanked or greeted by Paul in the last chapter of the Epistle to the Romans, nine or perhaps 10 are women. In the case of several of them, Paul insists on specifying that they have tired themselves for the community, using a Greek verb (kopian) most often used for the work of evangelization properly so called.

The case of Prisca and her husband Quila whom Paul calls "his collaborators in Christ" and of whom he says that "to them are indebted not only himself but all the churches of the Gentiles" (Rom. 16, 3-4), shows us concretely an example of this "collaboration": their role in the story of Appollo is well known (Acts 18, 24-28).

Paul mentions explicitly a woman as "deacon" (*diaconos*) of the church of Cenchrees, who "was also," he says, "for many Christians and for himself, a protectress" (Rom. 16, 1-2). In the pastoral epistles, the women indicated after the bishops and the deacons probably had a status of *diaconos* (1 Tim. 3, 11). Also notable is the case of Junias or Junio, placed in the rank of the apostles (Rom. 16, 7), with regard to whom one or another raises the question of whether it is a man.

PART IV

REPLY TO THE QUESTION ABOUT THE EVENTUAL ORDINATION OF WOMEN TO THE PRIESTHOOD

(1) The Ministry of Leadership According to Jesus and the Apostolic Church

In establishing the kingdom of God, Jesus, during his ministry, chose a group of 12 men who, after the fashion of the 12 patriarchs of the Old Testament, would be the leaders of the renewed people of God (Mk. 3:14-19) these men whom he destined to "sit upon twelve thrones judging the twelve tribes of Israel" (Mt. 19:28) were first sent to "proclaim that the kingdom of heaven is at hand." (Mt. 10:7)

After his death and resurrection, Christ confided to his apostles the mission of evangelizing all nations (Mt. 28:19, Mk 16:5). These men would become his witnesses, beginning at Jerusalem and reaching to the ends of the earth (Acts 1:8, Lk. 24:47). "As my Father sent me," he told them, "I also send you." (Jn. 20:21).

Upon leaving the earth to return to his Father, he also delegated to a group of men whom he had chosen the responsibility to develop the kingdom of God and the authority to govern the church. The apostolic group thus established by the Lord appeared thus, by the testimony of the New Testament, as the basis of a community which has continued the work of Christ, charged to communicate to humanity the fruits of his salvation.

As a matter of fact, we see in the Acts of the Apostles and the epistles that the first communities were always directed by men exercising the apostolic power.

The Acts of the Apostles show that the first Christian community of Jerusalem knew only one ministry of leadership, which was that of the apostles: this was the *urministerioum* from which all the others derived. It seems that, very early, the Greek community received its own structure, presided over by the college of seven (Acts 6:5). A little later there was a question for the Jewish group about a college of presbyters (ibid. 11:30). The church at Antioch was presided over by a group of "five prophets and teachers" (ibid. 13:1). At the end of their first missionary journey, Paul and Barnabas installed presbyters in the newly founded churches (ibid. 14:23).

There were also presbyters at Ephesus (ibid., 20:17), to whom were given the name of bishop (ibid. 20:28).

The epistles confirm the same picture: There are *proistamenoi* in I Thess. 5:12 (cf. I Tim. 5:17 *"hoi kalos proetotes presbyteroi"*), of Christian *presbyteroi* (I Tim. 5:1, 2, 17, 19; Titus 1, 5; James 5, 4; I Pet. 5:1, 5), of *episkopoi*, of *hegoumenoi* (Heb. 13:7, 13, 24. cf. Lk. 22:26).

I Cor. 16:16 recommends "submission" to Christians regarding those of the "house of Stephanas" who were sent for the service of the saints.

Whatever this last designation may be, (verse 17 speaks of Stephanas, Fortunatus and Achaikos), all that we can know of those who held a role of leadership in the communities leads to the conclusion that this role was always held by men (in conformity with the Jewish custom). (N.B. The *"presbytides"* mentioned in Titus 2:3 were elderly women, and not priestesses.)

The masculine character of the hierarchical order which has structured the church since its beginning thus seems attested to by scripture in an undeniable way. Must we conclude that this rule must be valid forever in the church?

We must however recall that according to the gospels, the Acts and St. Paul, certain women made a positive collaboration in service to the Christian communities.

Yet one question must still always be asked: What is the normative value which should be accorded to the practice of the Christian communities of the first centuries?

(2) The Ministry of Leadership and the Sacramental Economy

One of the essential elements of the church's life is the sacramental economy which gives the life of Christ to the faithful. The administration of this economy has been entrusted to the church for which the hierarchy is responsible.

Thus the question is raised about the relationship between the sacramental economy and the hierarchy.

In the New Testament the primordial role of the leaders of the communities seems always to lie in the field of preaching and teaching. These are the people who have the responsibility of keeping the communities in line with the faith of the apostles.

No text defines their charge in terms of a special power permitting them to carry out the eucharistic rite or to reconcile sinners.

But given the relationship between the sacramental economy and the hierarchy, the administration of the sacraments should not be exercised independently of this hierarchy. It is therefore within the duties of the leadership of the community that we must consider the issue of eucharistic and penitential ministry.

In fact there is no proof that these ministries were entrusted to women at the time of the New Testament. Two texts (I Cor. 14:33-35 and I Tim. 2:11-15) forbid women to speak and to teach in assemblies. However, without mentioning doubts raised by some about their Pauline authenticity, it is possible that they refer only to certain concrete situations and abuses. It is possible that certain other situations call on the church to assign to women the role of teaching which these two passages deny them and which constitute a function belonging to the leadership.

Is it possible that certain circumstances can come about which call on the church to entrust in the same way to certain women some sacramental ministries?

This has been the case with baptism which, though entrusted to the apostles (Mt. 28:19 and Mk. 16:15f.) can be administered by others as well. We know that at least later, it will be entrusted also to women.

Is it possible that we will come to this even with the ministry of eucharist and reconciliation which manifest eminently the service of the priesthood of Christ carried out by the leaders of the community?

It does not seem that the New Testament by itself alone will permit us to settle in a clear way and once and for all the problem of the possible accession of women to the presbyterate.

However, some think that in the scriptures there are sufficient indications to exclude this possibility, considering that the sacraments of eucharist and reconciliation have a special link with the person of Christ and therefore with the male hierarchy, as borne out by the New Testament.

Others, on the contrary, wonder if the church hierarchy, entrusted with the sacramental economy, would be able to entrust the ministries of eucharist and reconciliation to women in light of circumstances, without going against Christ's original intentions.

Appendix II
Declaration on the Question of the Admission of Women to the Ministerial Priesthood

INTRODUCTION

THE ROLE OF WOMEN IN MODERN SOCIETY AND THE CHURCH

Among the characteristics that mark our present age, Pope John XXIII indicated, in his Encyclical *Pacem in Terris* of 11 April 1963, "the part that women are now taking in public life . . . This is a development that is perhaps of swifter growth among Christian nations, but it is also happening extensively, if more slowly, among nations that are heirs to different traditions and imbued with a different culture."[1] Along the same lines, the Second Vatican Council, enumerating in its Pastoral Constitution *Gaudium et Spes* the forms of discrimination touching upon the basic rights of the person which must be overcome and eliminated as being contrary to God's plan, gives first place to discrimination based upon sex.[2] The resulting equality will secure the building up of a world that is not levelled out and uniform but harmonious and unified, if men and women contribute to it their own resources and dynamism, as Pope Paul VI recently stated.[3]

In the life of the Church herself, as history shows us, women have played a decisive role and accomplished tasks of outstanding value. One has only to think of the foundresses of the great religious families, such as Saint Clare and Saint Teresa of Avila. The latter, moreover, and Saint Catherine of Siena, have left writings so rich in spiritual doctrine that Pope Paul VI has included them among the Doctors of the Church. Nor could one forget the great number of women who have consecrated themselves to the Lord for the exercise of charity or for the missions, and the Christian wives who have had a profound influence on their families, particularly for the passing on of the faith to their children.

But our age gives rise to increased demands: "Since in our time women have an ever more active share in the whole life of society, it is very important that they participate more widely also in the various sectors of the Church's apostolate."[4] This charge of the Second Vatican Council has already set in motion the whole process of change now taking place: these various experiences of course need to come to maturity. But as Pope Paul VI also remarked,[5] a very large number of Christian communities are already benefitting from the apostolic commitment of women. Some of these women are called to take part in councils set up for pastoral reflection, at the diocesan or parish level; and the Apostolic See has brought women into some of its working bodies.

For some years now various Christian communities stemming from the sixteenth-century Reformation or of later origin have been admitting women to the pastoral office on a par with men. This initiative has led to petitions and writings by members of these communities and similar groups, directed towards making this admission a general thing; it has also led to contrary reactions. This therefore constitutes an ecumenical problem, and the Catholic Church must make her thinking known on it, all the more because in various sectors of opinion the question has been asked whether she too could not modify her discipline and admit women to priestly ordination. A number of Catholic theologians have even posed this question publicly, evoking studies not only in the sphere of exegesis, patrology and Church history but also in the field of the history of institutions and customs, of sociology and of psychology. The various arguments capable of clarifying this important problem have been submitted to a critical examination. As we are dealing with a debate which classical theology scarcely touched upon, the current argumentation runs the risk of neglecting essential elements.

For these reasons, in execution of a mandate received from the Holy Father and echoing the declaration which he himself made in his letter of 30 November 1975,[6] the Sacred Congregation for the Doctrine of the Faith judges it necessary to recall that the Church, in fidelity to the example of the Lord, does not consider herself authorized to admit women to priestly ordination. The Sacred Congregation deems it opportune at the present juncture to explain this position of the Church. It is a position which will perhaps cause pain but whose positive value will become apparent in the long run, since it can be of help in deepening understanding of the respective roles of men and of women.

I. THE CHURCH'S CONSTANT TRADITION

The Catholic Church has never felt that priestly or episcopal ordination can be validly conferred on women. A few heretical sects in the first centuries, especially Gnostic ones, entrusted the exercise of the priestly ministry to women: this innovation was immediately noted and condemned by the Fathers, who considered it as unacceptable in the Church.[7] It is true that in the writings of the Fathers one will find the undeniable influence of prejudices unfavourable to women, but nevertheless, it should be noted that these prejudices had hardly any influence on their pastoral activity, and still less on their spiritual direction. But over and above considerations inspired by the spirit of the times, one finds expressed—especially in the canonical documents of the Antiochian and Egyptian traditions—this essential reason, namely, that by calling only men to the priestly Order and ministry in its true sense, the Church intends to remain faithful to the type of ordained ministry willed by the Lord Jesus Christ and carefully maintained by the Apostles.[8]

The same conviction animates mediaeval theology,[9] even if the Scholastic doctors, in their desire to clarify by reason the data of faith, often present arguments on this point that modern thought would have difficulty in admitting or would even rightly reject. Since that period and up to our own time, it can be said that the question has not been raised again, for the practice has enjoyed peaceful and universal acceptance.

The Church's tradition in the matter has thus been so firm in the course of the centuries that the Magisterium has not felt the need to intervene in order to formulate a principle which was not attacked, or to defend a law which was not challenged. But each time that this tradition had the occasion to manifest itself, it witnessed to the Church's desire to conform to the model left to her by the Lord.

The same tradition has been faithfully safeguarded by the Churches of the East. Their unanimity on this point is all the more remarkable since in many other questions their discipline admits of a great diversity. At the present time these same Churches refuse to associate themselves with requests directed towards securing the accession of women to priestly ordination.

II. THE ATTITUDE OF CHRIST

Jesus Christ did not call any woman to become part of the Twelve. If he acted in this way, it was not in order to conform to the customs of his time, for his attitude towards women was quite different from that of his milieu, and he deliberately and courageously broke with it.

For example, to the great astonishment of his own disciples Jesus converses publicly with the Samaritan woman (cf. Jn 4:27); he takes no notice of the state of legal impurity of the woman who had suffered from haemorrhages (cf. Mt 9:20-22), he allows a sinful woman to approach him in the house of Simon the Pharisee (cf. Lk 7:37ff.); and by pardoning the woman taken in adultery, he means to show that one must not be more severe towards the fault of a woman than towards that of a man (cf. Jn 8:11). He does not hesitate to depart from the Mosaic Law in order to affirm the equality of the rights and duties of men and women with regard to the marriage bond (cf. Mk 10:2-11; Mt 19:3-9).

In his itinerant ministry Jesus was accompanied not only by the Twelve but also by a group of women: "Mary, surnamed the Magdalene, from whom seven demons had gone out, Joanna the wife of Herod's steward Chuza, Susanna, and several others who provided for them out of their own resources" (Lk 8:2-3). Contrary to the Jewish mentality, which did not accord great value to the testimony of women, as Jewish law attests, it was nevertheless women who were the first to have the privilege of seeing the risen Lord, and it was they who were charged by Jesus to take the first paschal message to the Apostles themselves (cf. Mt 28:7-10; Lk 24:9-10; Jn 20:11-18), in order to prepare the latter to become the official witnesses to the Resurrection.

It is true that these facts do not make the matter immediately obvious. This is no surprise, for the questions that the Word of God brings before us go beyond the obvious. In order to reach the ultimate meaning of the mission of Jesus and the ultimate meaning of Scripture, a purely historical exegesis of the texts cannot suffice. But it must be recognized that we have here a number of convergent indications that make all the more remarkable the fact that Jesus did not entrust the apostolic charge[10] to women. Even his Mother, who was so closely associated with the mystery of her Son, and whose incomparable role is emphasized by the Gospels of Luke and John, was not invested with the apostolic ministry. This fact was to lead the Fathers to present her as the example of Christ's will in this domain; as Pope Innocent III repeated later, at the beginning of the thirteenth century, "Although the Blessed Virgin Mary surpassed in dignity and in excellence all the Apostles, nevertheless it was not to her but to them that the Lord entrusted the keys of the Kingdom of Heaven."[11]

III. THE PRACTICE OF THE APOSTLES

The apostolic community remained faithful to the attitude of Jesus towards women. Although Mary occupied a privileged place in the little circle of those gathered in the Upper Room after the Lord's Ascension (cf. Acts 1:14), it was not she who was called to enter the College of the Twelve at the time of the election that resulted in the choice of Matthias:

those who were put forward were two disciples whom the Gospels do not even mention.

On the day of Pentecost, the Holy Spirit filled them all, men and women (cf. Acts 2:1; 1:14), yet the proclamation of the fulfilment of the prophecies in Jesus was made only by "Peter and the Eleven" (Acts 2:14).

When they and Paul went beyond the confines of the Jewish world, the preaching of the Gospel and the Christian life in the Greco-Roman civilization impelled them to break with Mosaic practices, sometimes regretfully. They could therefore have envisaged conferring ordination on women, if they had not been convinced of their duty of fidelity to the Lord on this point. In the Hellenistic world, the cult of a number of pagan divinities was entrusted to priestesses. In fact the Greeks did not share the ideas of the Jews: although their philosophers taught the inferiority of women, historians nevertheless emphasize the existence of a certain movement for the advancement of women during the Imperial period. In fact we know from the book of the Acts and from the Letters of Saint Paul that certain women worked with the Apostle for the Gospel (cf. Rom 16:3-12; Phil 4:3). Saint Paul lists their names with gratitude in the final salutations of the Letters. Some of them often exercised an important influence on conversions: Priscilla, Lydia and others; especially Priscilla, who took it on herself to complete the instruction of Apollos (cf. Acts 18:26); Phoebe, in the service of the Church of Cenchreae (cf. Rom. 16:1). All these facts manifest within the Apostolic Church a considerable evolution vis-à-vis the customs of Judaism. Nevertheless at no time was there a question of conferring ordination on these women.

In the Pauline Letters, exegetes of authority have noted a difference between two formulas used by the Apostle: he writes indiscriminately "my fellow workers" (Rom 16:3; Phil 4:2-3) when referring to men and women helping him in his apostolate in one way or another; but he reserves the title "God's fellow workers" (1 Cor 3:9; cf. 1 Thess 3:2) to Apollos, Timothy and himself, thus designated because they are directly set apart for the apostolic ministry and the preaching of the Word of God. In spite of the so important role played by women on the day of the Resurrection, their collaboration was not extended by Saint Paul to the official and public proclamation of the message, since this proclamation belongs exclusively to the apostolic mission.

IV. PERMANENT VALUE OF THE ATTITUDE OF JESUS AND THE APOSTLES

Could the Church today depart from this attitude of Jesus and the Apostles, which has been considered as normative by the whole of tradition up to our own day? Various arguments have been put forward in favour of a positive reply to this question, and these must now be examined.

It has been claimed in particular that the attitude of Jesus and the Apostles is explained by the influence of their milieu and their times. It is said that, if Jesus did not entrust to women and not even to his Mother a ministry assimilating them to the Twelve, this was because historical circumstances did not permit him to do so. No one however has ever proved —and it is clearly impossible to prove—that this attitude is inspired only by social and cultural reasons. As we have seen, an examination of the Gospels shows on the contrary that Jesus broke with the prejudices of his time, by widely contravening the discriminations practised with regard to women. One therefore cannot maintain that, by not calling women to enter the group of the Apostles, Jesus was simply letting himself be guided by reasons of expediency. For all the more reason, social and cultural conditioning did not hold back the Apostles working in the Greek milieu, where the same forms of discrimination did not exist.

Another objection is based upon the transitory character that one claims to see today in some of the prescriptions of Saint Paul concerning women, and upon the difficulties that some aspects of his teaching raise in this regard. But it must be noted that these ordinances, probably inspired by the customs of the period, concern scarcely more than disciplinary practices of minor importance, such as the obligation imposed upon women to wear a veil on the head (1 Cor 11:2-16); such requirements no longer have a normative value. However, the Apostle's forbidding of women "to speak" in the assemblies (cf. 1 Cor 14:34-35; 1 Tim 2:12) is of a different nature, and exegetes define its meaning in this way: Paul in no way opposes the right, which he elsewhere recognizes as possessed by women, to prophesy in the assembly (cf. 1 Cor 11:5); the prohibition solely concerns the official function of teaching in the Christian assembly. For Saint Paul this prescription is bound up with the divine plan of creation (cf. 1 Cor 11:7; Gen 2:18-24): it would be difficult to see in it the expression of a cultural fact. Nor should it be forgotten that we owe to Saint Paul one of the most vigorous texts in the New Testament on the fundamental equality of men and women, as children of God in Christ (cf. Gal 3:28). Therefore there is no reason for accusing him of prejudices against women, when we note the trust that he shows towards them and the collaboration that he asks of them in his apostolate.

But over and above these objections taken from the history of apostolic times, those who support the legitimacy of change in the matter turn to the Church's practice in her sacramental discipline. It has been noted, in our day especially, to what extent the Church is conscious of possessing a certain power over the sacraments, even though they were instituted by Christ. She has used this power down the centuries in order to determine their signs and the conditions of their administration: recent decisions of Popes Pius XII and Paul VI are proof of this.[12] However, it must be emphasized that this power, which is a real one, has definite limits. As Pope Pius XII recalled: "The Church has no power over the substance of the sacraments, that is to say, over what Christ the Lord, as the sources of Revelation bear witness, determined should be maintained in the sacramental sign."[13] This was already the teaching of the Council of Trent, which declared: "In the Church there has always existed this power, that in the administration of the sacraments, provided that their substance remains unaltered, she can lay down or modify what she considers more fitting either for the benefit of those who receive them or for respect towards those same sacraments, according to varying circumstances, times or places."[14]

Moreover, it must not be forgotten that the sacramental signs are not conventional ones. Not only is it true that, in many respects, they are natural signs because they respond to the deep symbolism of actions and things, but they are more than this: they are principally meant to link the person of every period to the supreme Event of the history of salvation, in order to enable that person to understand, through all the Bible's wealth of pedagogy and symbolism, what grace they signify and produce. For example, the sacrament of the Eucharist is not only a fraternal meal, but at the same time the memorial which makes present and actual Christ's sacrifice and his offering by the Church. Again, the priestly ministry is not just a pastoral service; it ensures the continuity of the functions entrusted by Christ to the Apostles and the continuity of the powers related to those functions. Adaptation to civilizations and times therefore cannot abolish, on essential points, the sacramental reference to constitutive events of Christianity and to Christ himself.

In the final analysis it is the Church, through the voice of her Magisterium, that, in these various domains, decides what can change and what must remain immutable. When she judges that she cannot accept certain changes, it is because she knows that she is bound by Christ's manner of acting. Her attitude, despite appearances, is therefore not one of archaism but of fidelity: it can be truly understood only in this light. The Church makes pronouncements in virtue of the Lord's promise and the presence of the Holy Spirit, in order to proclaim better the mystery of Christ and to safeguard and manifest the whole of its rich content.

This practice of the Church therefore has a normative character: in the fact of conferring priestly ordination only on men, it is a question of an unbroken tradition throughout the history of the Church, universal in the East and in the West, and alert to repress abuses immediately. This norm, based on Christ's example, has been and is still observed because it is considered to conform to God's plan for his Church.

V. THE MINISTRIAL PRIESTHOOD IN THE LIGHT OF THE MYSTERY OF CHRIST

Having recalled the Church's norm and the basis thereof, it seems useful and opportune to illustrate this norm by showing the profound fittingness that theological reflection discovers between the proper nature of the sacrament of Order, with its specific reference to the mystery of Christ, and the fact that only men have been called to receive priestly ordination. It is not a question here of bringing forward a demonstrative argument, but of clarifying this teaching by the analogy of faith.

The Church's constant teaching, repeated and clarified by the Second Vatican Council and again recalled by the 1971 Synod of Bishops and by the Sacred Congregation for the Doctrine of the Faith in its Declaration of 24 June 1973, declares that the bishop or the priest, in the exercise of his ministry, does not act in his own name, *in persona propria*: he represents Christ, who acts through him: "the priest truly acts in the place of Christ," as Saint Cyprian already wrote in the third century.[15] It is this ability to represent Christ that Saint Paul considered as characteristic of his apostolic function (cf. 2 Cor 5:20; Gal 4:14). The supreme expression of this representation is found in the altogether special form it assumes in the celebration of the Eucharist, which is the source and centre of the Church's unity, the sacrificial meal in which the People of God are associated in the sacrifice of Christ: the priest, who alone has the power to perform it, then acts not only through the effective power conferred on him by Christ, but *in persona Christi*,[16] taking the role of Christ, to the point of being his very image, when he pronounces the words of consecration.[17]

The Christian priesthood is therefore of a sacramental nature: the priest is a sign, the supernatural effectiveness of which comes from the ordination received, but a sign that must be perceptible[18] and which the faithful must be able to recognize with ease. The whole sacramental economy is in fact based upon natural signs, on symbols imprinted upon the human psychology: "Sacramental signs," says Saint Thomas, "represent what they signify by natural resemblance."[19] The same natural resemblance is required for persons as for things: when Christ's role in the Eucharist is to be expressed sacramentally, there would not be this "natural resemblance" which must exist between Christ and his minister if the role of Christ were not taken by a man: in such a case it would be difficult to see in the minister the image of Christ. For Christ himself was and remains a man.

Christ is of course the firstborn of all humanity, of women as well as men: the unity which he re-established after sin is such that there are no more distinctions between Jew and Greek, slave and free, male and female, but all are one in Christ Jesus (cf. Gal 3:28). Nevertheless, the Incarnation of the Word took place according to the male sex: this is indeed a question of fact, and this fact, while not implying an alleged natural superiority of man over woman, cannot be disassociated from the economy of salvation: it is, indeed, in harmony with the entirety of God's plan as God himself has revealed it, and of which the mystery of the Covenant is the nucleus.

For the salvation offered by God to men and women, the union with him to which they are called—in short, the Covenant—took on, from the Old Testament Prophets onwards, the privileged form of a nuptial mystery: for God the Chosen People is seen as his ardently loved spouse. Both Jewish and Christian tradition has discovered the depth of this intimacy of love by reading and rereading the Song of Songs; the divine Bridegroom will remain faithful even when the Bride betrays his love, when Israel is unfaithful to God (cf. Hos 1-3; Jer 2). When the "fullness of time" (Gal. 4:4) comes, the Word, the Son of God, takes on flesh in order to establish and seal the new and eternal Covenant in his blood, which will be shed for many so that sins may be forgiven. His death will gather together again the scattered children of God; from his pierced side will be born the Church, as Eve was born from Adam's side. At that time there is fully and eternally accomplished the nuptial mystery proclaimed and hymned in the Old Testament: Christ is the Bridegroom; the Church is his bride, whom he loves because he has gained her by his blood and made her glorious, holy and without blemish, and henceforth he is inseparable from her. This nuptial theme, which is developed from the Letters of Saint Paul onwards (cf. 2 Cor 11:2; Eph 5:22-23) to the writings of Saint John (cf. especially Jn 3:29; Rev 19:7, 9), is present also in the Synoptic Gospels: the Bridegroom's friends must not fast as long as he is with them (cf. Mk 2:19); the Kingdom of Heaven is like a king who gave a feast for his son's wedding (cf. Mt 22:1-14). It is through this Scriptural language, all interwoven with symbols, and which expresses and affects man and woman in their profound identity, that there is revealed to us the mystery of God and Christ, a mystery which of itself is unfathomable.

That is why we can never ignore the fact that Christ is a man. And therefore, unless one is to disregard the importance of this symbolism for the economy of Revelation, it must be admitted that, in actions which demand the character of ordination and in which Christ himself, the author of the Covenant, the Bridegroom and Head of the Church, is represented, exercising his ministry of salvation—which is in the highest degree the case of the Eucharist—his role (this is the original sense of the word *persona*) must be taken by a man. This does not stem from any personal superiority of the latter in the order of values, but only from a difference of fact on the level of functions and service.

Could one say that, since Christ is now in the heavenly condition, from now on it is a matter of indifference whether he be represented by a man or by a woman, since "at the resurrection men and women do not marry" (Mt 22:30)? But this text does not mean that the distinction between man and woman, insofar as it determines the identity proper to the person, is suppressed in the glorified state; what holds for us holds also for Christ. It is indeed evident that in human beings the difference of sex exercises an important influence, much deeper than, for example, ethnic differences: the latter do not affect the human person as intimately as the difference of sex, which is directly ordained both for the communion of persons and for the generation of human beings. In Biblical Revelation this difference is the effect of God's will from the beginning: "male and female he created them" (Gen 1:27).

However, it will perhaps be further objected that the priest, especially when he presides at the liturgical and sacramental functions, equally represents the Church: he acts in her name with "the intention of doing what she does." In this sense, the theologians of the Middle Ages said that the minister also acts *in persona Ecclesiae*, that is to say, in the name of the whole Church and in order to represent her. And in fact, leaving aside the question of the participation of the faithful in a liturgical action, it is indeed in the name of the whole Church that the action is celebrated by the priest: he prays in the name of all, and in the Mass he offers the sacrifice of the whole Church. In the new Passover, the Church, under visible signs, immolates Christ through the ministry of the priest.[20] And so, it is asserted, since the priest also represents the Church, would it not be possible to think that this representation could be carried out by a woman, according to the symbolism already explained? It is true that the priest represents the Church, which is the Body of Christ. But if he does so, it is precisely because he first represents Christ himself, who is the Head and Shepherd of the Church. The Second Vatican Council[21] used this phrase to make more precise and to complete the expression *in persona Christi*. It is in this quality that the priest presides over the Christian assembly and celebrates the Eucharistic sacrifice "in which the whole Church offers and is herself wholly offered."[22]

If one does justice to these reflections, one will better understand how well-founded is the basis of the Church's practice; and one will conclude that the controversies raised in our days over the ordination of women are for all Christians a pressing invitation to meditate on the mystery of the Church, to study in greater detail the meaning of the episcopate and the priesthood, and to rediscover the real and pre-eminent place of the priest in the community of the baptized, of which he indeed forms part but from which he is distinguished because, in the actions that call for the character of ordination, for the community he is—with all the effectiveness proper to the sacraments—the image and symbol of Christ himself who calls, forgives, and accomplishes the sacrifice of the Covenant.

VI. THE MINISTERIAL PRIESTHOOD ILLUSTRATED BY THE MYSTERY OF THE CHURCH

It is opportune to recall that problems of sacramental theology, especially when they concern the ministerial priesthood, as is the case here, cannot be solved except in the light of Revelation. The human sciences, however valuable their contribution in their own domain, cannot suffice here, for they cannot grasp the realities of faith: the properly supernatural content of these realities is beyond their competence.

Thus one must note the extent to which the Church is a society different from other societies, original in her nature and in her structures. The pastoral charge in the Church is normally linked to the sacrament of Order: it is not a simple government, comparable to the modes of authority found in States. It is not granted by people's spontaneous choice: even when it involves designation through election, it is the laying on of hands and the prayer of the successors of the Apostles which guarantee God's choice; and it is the Holy Spirit, given by ordination, who grants participation in the ruling power of the Supreme Pastor, Christ (cf. Acts 20:28). It is a charge of service and love: "If you love me, feed my sheep" (cf. Jn 21:15-17).

For this reason one cannot see how it is possible to propose the admission of women to the priesthood in virtue of the equality of rights of the human person, an equality which holds good also for Christians. To this end use is sometimes made of the text quoted above, from the Letter to the Galatians (3:28), which says that in Christ there is no longer any distinction between men and women. But this passage does not concern ministries: it only affirms the universal calling to divine filiation, which is the same for all. Moreover, and above all, to consider the ministerial priesthood as a human right would be to misjudge its nature completely:

baptism does not confer any personal title to public ministry in the Church. The priesthood is not conferred for the honour or advantage of the recipient, but for the service of God and the Church; it is the object of a specific and totally gratuitous vocation: "You did not choose me, no, I chose you; and I commissioned you . . ." (Jn 15:16; cf. Heb 5:4).

It is sometimes said and written in books and periodicals that some women feel that they have a vocation to the priesthood. Such an attraction, however noble and understandable, still does not suffice for a genuine vocation. In fact, a vocation cannot be reduced to a mere personal attraction, which can remain purely subjective. Since the priesthood is a particular ministry of which the Church has received the charge and the control, authentication by the Church is indispensable here and is a constitutive part of the vocation: Christ chose "those he wanted" (Mk 3:13). On the other hand, there is a universal vocation of all the baptized to the exercise of the royal priesthood by offering their lives to God and by giving witness for his praise.

Women who express a desire for the ministerial priesthood are doubtless motivated by the desire to serve Christ and the Church. And it is not surprising that, at a time when they are becoming more aware of the discriminations to which they have been subject, they should desire the ministerial priesthood itself. But it must not be forgotten that the priesthood does not form part of the rights of the individual, but stems from the economy of the mystery of Christ and the Church. The priestly office cannot become the goal of social advancement; no merely human progress of society or of the individual can of itself give access to it: it is of another order.

It therefore remains for us to meditate more deeply on the nature of the real equality of the baptized which is one of the great affirmations of Christianity: equality is in no way identity, for the Church is a differentiated body, in which each individual has his or her role. The roles are distinct, and must not be confused; they do not favour the superiority of some vis-à-vis the others, nor do they provide an excuse for jealousy; the only better gift, which can and must be desired, is love (cf. 1 Cor 12-13). The greatest in the Kingdom of Heaven are not the ministers but the saints.

The Church desires that Christian women should become fully aware of the greatness of their mission: today their role is of capital importance, both for the renewal and humanization of society and for the rediscovery by believers of the true face of the Church.

His Holiness Pope Paul VI, during the audience granted to the undersigned Prefect of the Sacred Congregation on 15 October 1976, approved this Declaration, confirmed it and ordered its publication.

Given in Rome, at the Sacred Congregation for the Doctrine of the Faith, on 15 October 1976, the feast of Saint Teresa of Avila.

Franjo Cardinal Šeper
Prefect

✠ Fr. Jérôme Hamer, O.P.
Titular Archbishop of Lorium
Secretary

NOTES

1. *Acta Apostolicae Sedis* 55 (1963), pp. 267-268.

2. Cf. Second Vatican Council, Pastoral Constitution *Gaudium et Spes*, 29 (7 December 1965): *AAS* 58 (1966), pp. 1048-1049.

3. Cf. Pope Paul VI, Address to the members of the Study Commission on the Role of Women in Society and in the Church and to the members of the Committee for International Women's Year, 18 April 1975: *AAS* 67 (1975), p. 265.

4. Second Vatican Council, Decree *Apostolicam Actuositatem*, 9 (18 November 1965): *AAS* 58 (1966), p. 846.

5. Cf. Pope Paul VI, Address to the members of the Study Commission on the Role of Women in Society and in the Church and to the members of the Committee for International Women's Year, 18 April 1975: *AAS* 67 (1975), p. 266.

6. Cf. *AAS* 68 (1976), pp. 599-600; cf. *ibid.*, pp. 600-601.

7. Saint Irenaeus, *Adversus Haereses*, I, 13, 2: *PG* 7, 580-581; ed. Harvey, I, 114-122; Tertullian, *De Praescrip. Haeretic.* 41, 5: *CCL* 1, p. 221; Firmilian of Caesarea, in Saint Cyprian, *Epist.*, 75: *CSEL* 3, pp. 817-818; Origen, *Fragmentum in I Cor.* 74, in *Journal of Theological Studies* 10 (1909), pp. 41-42; Saint Epiphanius, *Panarion* 49, 2-3; 78, 23; 79, 2-4: vol. 2, *GCS* 31, pp. 243-244; vol. 3, *GCS* 37, pp. 473, 477-479.

8. *Didascalia Apostolorum*, ch. 15, ed. R. H. Connolly, pp. 133 and 142; *Constitutiones Apostolicae*, bk. 3, ch. 6, nos. 1-2; ch. 9, nos. 3-4: ed F. H. Funk, pp. 191, 201; Saint John Chrysostom, *De Sacerdotio* 2, 2: *PG* 48, 633.

9. Saint Bonaventure, *In IV Sent.*, Dist. 25, art. 2, q. 1, ed. Quaracchi, vol. 4, p. 649; Richard of Middleton, *In IV Sent.*, Dist. 25, art. 4, n. 1, ed. Venice, 1499, f⁰ 177ʳ; John Duns Scotus, *In IV Sent.*, Dist. 25: *Opus Oxoniense*, ed. Vives, vol. 19, p. 140; *Reportata Parisiensia*, vol. 24, pp. 369-371; Durandus of Saint-Pourçain, *In IV Sent.*, Dist. 25, q. 2, ed. Venice, 1571, f⁰ 374ᵛ.

10. Some have also wished to explain this fact by a symbolic inten-

tion of Jesus: the Twelve were to represent the ancestors of the twelve tribes of Israel (cf. *Mt* 19:28; *Lk* 22:30). But in these texts it is only a question of their participation in the eschatological judgment. The essential meaning of the choice of the Twelve should rather be sought in the totality of their mission (cf. *Mk* 3:14): they are to represent Jesus to the people and carry on his work.

11. Pope Innocent III, *Epist.* (11 December 1210) to the Bishops of Palencia and Burgos, included in *Corpus Iuris, Decret. Lib.* 5, tit. 38, *De Paenit.*, ch. 10 *Nova:* ed. A. Friedberg, vol. 2, col. 886-887; cf. *Glossa in Decretal. Lib. I*, tit. 33, ch. 12 *Dilecta*, v° *Iurisdictioni*. Cf. Saint Thomas, *Summa Theologiae,* III, q. 27, a. 5 ad 3; Pseudo-Albert the Great, *Mariale*, quaest. 42, ed. Borgnet 37, 81.

12. Pope Pius XII, Apostolic Constitution *Sacramentum Ordinis*, 30 November 1947: *AAS* 40 (1948), pp. 5-7; Pope Paul VI, Apostolic Constitution *Divinae Consortium Naturae*, 15 August 1971: *AAS* 63 (1971), pp. 657-664; Apostolic Constitution *Sacram Unctionem*, 30 November 1972: *AAS* 65 (1973), pp. 5-9.

13. Pope Pius XII, Apostolic Constitution *Sacramentum Ordinis: loc. cit.*, p. 5.

14. Session 21, chap. 2: Denzinger-Schönmetzer, *Enchiridion Symbolorum* 1728.

15. Saint Cyprian, *Epist.* 63, 14: *PL* 4, 397 B; ed. Hartel, vol. 3, p. 713.

16. Second Vatican Council, Constitution *Sacrosanctum Concilium*, 33 (4 December 1963): ". . . by the priest who presides over the assembly in the person of Christ . . ."; Dogmatic Constitution *Lumen Gentium*, 10 (21 November 1964): "The ministerial priest, by the sacred power he enjoys, moulds and rules the priestly people. Acting in the person of Christ, he brings about the Eucharistic Sacrifice, and offers it to God in the name of all the people . . ."; 28: "By the powers of the sacrament of Order, and in the image of Christ the eternal High Priest . . . they exercise this sacred function of Christ above all in the Eucharistic liturgy or synaxis. There, acting in the person of Christ . . ."; Decree *Presbyterorum Ordinis*, 2 (7 December 1965): ". . . priests, by the anointing of the Holy Spirit, are marked with a special character and are so configured to Christ the Priest that they can act in the person of Christ the Head"; 13: "As ministers of sacred realities, especially in the Sacrifice of the Mass, priests represent the person of Christ in a special way"; cf. 1971 Synod of Bishops, *De Sacerdotio Ministeriali* I, 4; Sacred Congregation for the Doctrine of the Faith, *Declaratio circa catholicam doctrinam de Ecclesia*, 6 (24 June 1973).

17. Saint Thomas, *Summa Theologiae*, III, q. 83, art. I, ad 3: "It is to be said that [just as the celebration of this sacrament is the representative image of Christ's Cross: *ibid.* ad 2], for the same reason the priest also enacts the image of Christ, in whose person and by whose power he pronounces the words of consecration".

18. "For since a sacrament is a sign, there is required in the things that are done in the sacraments not only the 'res' but the signification of the 'res'," recalls Saint Thomas, precisely in order to reject the ordination of women: *In IV Sent.*, dist. 25, q. 2, art. 1, quaestiuncula 1ª, corp.

19. Saint Thomas, *In IV Sent.*, dist. 25, q. 2, quaestiuncula 1ª ad 4ᵘᵐ.

20. Cf. Council of Trent, Session 22, chap. 1: *DS* 1741.

21. Second Vatican Council, Dogmatic Constitution *Lumen Gentium*, 28: "Exercising within the limits of their authority the function of Christ as Shepherd and Head"; Decree *Presbyterorum Ordinis*, 2: "that they can act in the person of Christ the Head"; 6: "the office of Christ the Head and the Shepherd." Cf. Pope Pius XII, Encyclical Letter *Mediator Dei:* "the minister of the altar represents the person of Christ as the Head, offering in the name of all his members": *AAS* 39 (1947), p. 556; 1971 Synod of Bishops, *De Sacerdotio Ministeriali*, I, 4: "[The priestly ministry] . . . makes Christ, the Head of the community, present . . .".

22. Pope Paul VI, Encyclical Letter *Mysterium Fidei*, 3 September 1965: *AAS* 57 (1965), p. 761.

Index

Notes on the Contributors

Francine Cardman is Assistant Professor of Church History at Wesley Theological Seminary in Washington, D.C. She received her Ph.D. in Historical Theology with a concentration in Patristics from Yale University in 1974. She is the author of a translation of Augustine's homily "Our Lord's Sermon on the Mount" published as *The Preaching of Augustine.*

James Coriden is the Academic Dean of the Washington Theological Coalition. His licentiate in Theology and doctorate in Canon Law are from the Gregorian University, and he holds a civil law degree from Catholic University. He has published several articles on matters of church discipline and ministry.

John T. Finnegan is on the faculty of Pope John XXIII Seminary in Weston, Massachusetts, and is Visiting Professor at the Weston School of Theology, Cambridge. He is the author of several articles in canon law, and is a past-president of the Canon Law Society of America.

Nadine Foley, O.P., is a member of the Adrian Dominican Congregation. She holds an M.S. in Biology and a Ph.D. in Philosophy from the Catholic University of America and an S.T.M. in Scripture from Union Theological Seminary, New York. She has had a wide range of teaching and ministerial experiences, and has contributed to publications on the issue of women's role in the church.

Hamilton Hess is on the theology faculty at the University of San Francisco. He received a Ph.D. in Patristics from Oxford, and wrote his doctoral dissertation on the *Canons of the Council of Sardica* (a. 343). He has written several articles on church order and authority in the early church.

Edward J. Kilmartin, S.J., is Professor of Liturgy in the Department of Theology at the University of Notre Dame. He received an S.T.D. from the Gregorian University, and wrote *The Eucharist in the Primitive Church* as well as several articles in sacramental theology. He is currently the Executive Director of the Bishops' Committee for Dialogue with the Orthodox and Other Eastern Churches.

Katherine Meagher, S.C. is a Sister of Charity of Halifax, Nova Scotia. She holds a Master of Commerce degree from Boston University and a doctorate in Canon Law from St. Paul University, Ottawa. She has served as a teacher, an administrator in her congregation, and a notary in the Matrimonial Tribunal of Toronto. She is currently Chancellor at the Diocese of Nelson, British Columbia.

Francis Morrisey, O.M.I., is the Dean of the Faculty of Canon Law at St. Paul University, Ottawa, and the Secretary-Treasurer and past-President of the Canadian Canon Law Society. He holds licentiate degrees in Philosophy and Theology as well as a doctorate in Canon Law. He is the editor of *Studia Canonica* and has contributed numerous articles on canonical matters to various publications.